RESEARCH
METHODOLOGY
FOR ECONOMISTS

RESEARCH METHODOLOGY FOR ECONOMISTS
Philosophy and Practice

Glenn L. Johnson
Michigan State University

MACMILLAN PUBLISHING COMPANY

New York

Collier Macmillan Publishers

London

Macmillan Publishing Company
866 Third Avenue, New York, NY 10022

Collier Macmillan Canada, Inc.

Printed in the United States of America

printing number
1   2   3   4   5   6   7   8   9   10   6   7   8   9   0   1   2   3   4   5

Library of Congress Cataloging-in-Publication Data

Johnson, Glenn Leroy, 1918–
    Research methodology for economists.

    Includes bibliographies and index.
    1. Economics—Research. 2. Economics—Methodology.
3. Economics—Philosophy. I. Title.
HB74.5.J65   1986   300'.72   85-24240
ISBN 0-02-949840-0

DEDICATED WITH LOVE
  to
SANDY

My wife and mother of our children.
Also my inspiration, teacher and
lifetime co-worker

Contents

The Variety and Extent of Research Efforts Involving
    Economists
What is Methodology?
Why Not a Book on Research Techniques and
    Methods?
Undergirding Philosophies
Sensitivities About Philosophic Orientations
Semantic Fears
This Book is for Economists, Not Philosophers

Foreword

This volume is an important service, not only to the economics profession, but to the whole scientific, scholarly, and research community. Just as biological evolution has been dominated by the steady increase in the "know-how" possessed by genetic structures, from the first "primeval atomic globule" to Pooh Bah, so the history of the human race has been dominated by what seems to be an almost irreversible increase in human knowledge, a rate of increase that also seems to have been accelerating. It begins with the folk knowledge of ordinary daily life, which becomes specialized in the course of the division of labor, and thereby increases faster. It then moves into scholarly knowledge, produced by specialists in the knowledge-increasing field. These are what Adam Smith calls the "philosophers or men of speculation, whose trade it is not to do anything, but to observe everything; and who, upon that account, are often capable of combining together the powers of the most distant and dissimilar objects." [Adam Smith, *The Wealth of Nations* (Cannon edition), p. 10.]

Adam Smith, with his usual wisdom, goes on to say, "In the progress of society, philosophy or speculation becomes, like every other employment, the principal or sole trade and occupation of a particular class of citizens. Like every other employment too, it is subdivided into a great number of different branches, each of which affords occupation to a peculiar tribe or class of philosophers; and this subdivision of employment in philosophy, as well as in every other business, improves dexterity and saves time. Each individual becomes more expert in his own peculiar branch, more work is done upon the whole, and the quantity of science is considerably increased by it." Each of these "branches," however, studies a different part of the real world about which we are trying to find knowledge, and this division of labor should result in specialized techniques of knowledge increase, a considerable part of which, though not all of it, is called "research."

This problem, unfortunately, has been neglected by the scholarly community. Instead of developing that "trade," or interchange of methods and ideas, which is the necessary outcome of specialization if specialization is to be fruitful, there has been too much hierarchical imposition of methods from particular disciplines and branches on others where these methods are not suitable. Particularly, we have seen the imposition of methods derived from the physical sciences on both the biological and the social sciences to their great detriment, simply because these other sciences are investigating systems with very different properties from the systems the physical sciences investigate.

Part of this imperial methodological domination results from the success of many of the physical sciences (especially celestial mechanics)—in investigating systems of extraordinary stability of parameters and relative simplicity or regularities, so that it becomes possible to make very accurate predictions. As soon as we move into systems with information as an essential characteristic, exactness becomes impossible and prediction is severely limited, simply because information has to be surprising or it is not information. Furthermore, as we move into the social sciences, we are studying systems whose parameters are under constant change—often unpredictable change.

This is true even in the biological sciences, where evolution is a process dominated by the time at which very improbable events happen. It is a highly indeterministic system. Life on earth could have evolved in an uncountable number of ways. Its past history is only one of innumerable possible histories. It is absurd to look for exactness when we study an inexact real world, or for prediction when we are studying the inherently unpredictable.

Professor Glenn Johnson's book is a very important corrective to what might be called the "epistemological superstition" that has dominated so much of the social sciences, especially economics. It also develops a very useful taxonomy of inquiry and knowledge increase, and demolishes the illusion that there is a single "holy" scientific method. Its distinction between disciplinary, subject-matter, and problem-solving research is very useful. The balance between positive and normative knowledge is very well maintained, and one of the most unfortunate results of logical positivism, the illusion that human valuations are not a proper subject for human inquiry, is effectively dispelled. This book should cheer a lot of people up who are undeservedly rather low on the totem pole of academia.

This book was originally designed as a textbook for graduate students, but it should be widely read by all those concerned with the increase in human knowledge. The principles it develops are very general and apply to virtually all subject-matter and problem-solving researches, which have to be inter-disciplinary. What Glenn Johnson has shown is that the interdisciplinary does not have to be the undisciplined, and while it may be true that the narrower the discipline, the easier it is to prevent it from becoming undisciplined, it is also true that the discipline that is involved in the subculture of those who study a narrow field can also become oppressive and lead to the strangling of new knowledge through the imposition of powerful orthodoxies. The very existence of Kuhnian revolutions in science suggests there is something a little rotten in the state of its subculture.

This book is very timely. The economics profession, and to some extent all the social sciences, have been caught in a narrow methodology, drawn too much from the natural sciences and inappropriate to the nature of the systems being studied. Glenn Johnson's book is an excellent corrective to this. I think it will have a substantial impact on the development of all the social sciences, and could mark a real turning point. It is no accident that Glenn Johnson comes out of the tradition of the land grant universities, which have produced a remarkable subculture of philosophers whose feet are solidly on the real world.

KENNETH E. BOULDING
Institute of Behavioral Science
University of Colorado, Boulder

Preface

This book differs from other methodological books for economists by placing equal stress on problem-solving, subject-matter, and disciplinary research rather than concentrating on disciplinary research. Though the three kinds of research are defined in the book (Chapter 2), it is worth noting that disciplinary research has to do with improving the theories, basic measurements, and techniques of economics, whereas the other two types of research are at the applied end of the economics research spectrum.

Applied research done by economists includes their contributions to the multidisciplinary studies of importance to sets of decision makers addressing sets of problems. It also includes their contributions to research designed to solve specific problems of specific decision makers. I feel that the contributions economists make in these two applied areas are so important that a book on research methodology for economists must give substantial attention to all three kinds of research.

The philosophic orientations that guide the work of economic researchers differ depending on whether disciplinary, subject-matter, or problem-solving research is being done. Closely related to differences in philosophic orientation are differences in the kinds of knowledge (discussed in Chapter 2) that the three types of research attempt to generate. The object of problem-solving research is to produce a statement about "what ought to be" done to solve a specific practical problem. Disciplinary research, on the other hand, may generate a kind of nonnormative factual knowledge that is relatively independent of values and makes no prescriptions. Multidisciplinary subject-matter research may generate both normative and nonnormative knowledge. Disciplinary economic research may also generate prescriptive knowledge since economists use maximizing or optimizing models and computations to arrive at prescriptions about what ought to be done, and to predict the behavioral consequences of changes in such variables as input prices, product prices, institutional arrangements, technological changes, improvements in the human agent, and capital accumulation. Economics is particularly concerned with the structure of optimizing theories that define "right action"—i.e.,—"what ought to be done."

Essentially, the book is three-dimensional, as described in Figure 1. The three major dimensions are (1) kind of research, (2) kind of philosophy, and (3) kind of knowledge:

- The first dimension includes disciplinary, subject-matter, and problem-solving research.

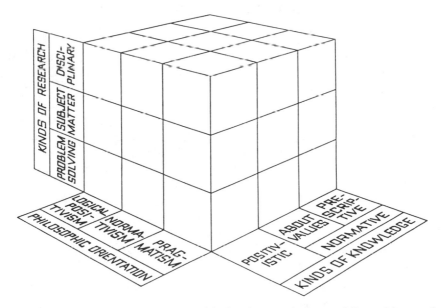

Figure 1. Interrelationships among kinds of research done, philosophies used, and kinds of knowledge generated by economic researchers.

- The second dimension mainly considers three philosophies—positivism, normativism, and pragmatism.
- The third dimension distinguishes between positivistic knowledge, knowledge about values, and prescriptive knowledge.

The three kinds of research, three philosophic orientations, and three kinds of knowledge are all treated as essential for a full understanding of the entire range of research by economists in academia, business, and government. All of the nine categories in Figure 1 are respectfully considered. However, each philosophic orientation is potentially capable of constraining the other two.

Figure 1 shows these three dimensions with each of their three subdivisions. The resultant cube has 27 constituent cubes. My task is to explain the characteristics of the 6 vertical and 3 horizontal slices, the 9 vertical columns, the 18 horizontal rows, and the 27 smaller cubes.

The first three chapters provide an overview and define the meaning of the classifications and subclassifications of figure 1. Part I concentrates on positivism, normativism, and pragmatism as schools of philosophic thought and on the roles they have played in economics.

Part II presents six case studies—two each for disciplinary, subject-matter, and problem-solving research.

Part III is practical. It deals with mobilization and accountability for support for the three kinds of research as well as with their administration, conduct, evaluation and their durability and importance. In writing Part III I drew on years of experience in agricultural experiment stations, as Director of the Economic Development Institute at the University of Nigeria and as director of or participant in several large-scale multidisciplinary subject-matter and problem-solving research projects. These experiences at the practical end of the research spectrum account for the balanced treatment of the three kinds of research.

The last chapter of Part III draws together generalizations from the earlier chapters in Part III, presents a philosophic statement to undergird the full range of research conducted by economists and, finally, deals with important issues involving methods and the scope of economics not covered in the first 16 chapters. Because Chapter 17 draws on all three philosophic orientations, it appears to be somewhat eclectic. However, it might possibly be viewed as a synthesis—a start toward a unified philosophic outlook for research economists. Chapter 17 summarizes the methodological contribution of the book to the problem-solving, subject-matter, and disciplinary research work of economists.

Acknowledgments

I am indebted to many colleagues and students—to Professors T. W. Schultz and D. Gale Johnson at the University of Chicago, where I wrote my first essay on research methodology; to the late Dr. O. C. Stine of the U.S. Department of Agriculture; to the late Professor Charles L. Stewart of the University of Illinois, Professor Kenneth Parsons of the University of Wisconsin, and Professor Rainer Schickele, formerly of Iowa State and North Dakota State Colleges who, along with Stine and Schultz, made me appreciative of Wisconsin's pragmatic institutionalism; to the late Professor Jacob Marschak and Professor T. C. Koopmans for an understanding of the positivism of econometrics; to Professor Milton Friedman and W. Allen Wallis and, again, Dr. O. C. Stine for an appreciation of the importance of empirical work and facts in economics; to those for whom I have been a consultant; to my family, my colleagues, my several Christian ministers and theological friends, and to the classical literature of economics, ethics, and philosophic value theory for an appreciation of various forms of normativism.

I am particularly indebted to colleagues and friends in the discipline of philosophy—especially to the late Professor Lewis K. Zerby, a friend and coauthor of other manuscripts, who patiently instructed me and corrected errors in my philosophic pronouncements while offering me every encouragement and help; to the late Professor Richard Rudner for help on various philosophies of science; to Professor John Taylor for help in philosophic value theory and ethics; and to Professor Philip Shepard who, following Lewis Zerby, has worked painstakingly with this manuscript to improve its philosophic content, tone, and structure.

In the last ten years, graduate students in my course on research methodology have assisted me with their encouragement, their criticisms of many early drafts of this book and my assigned readings, their suggestions of additional readings, and their willingness to be teaching guinea pigs. Important contributions from among my more immediate agricultural colleagues include those from Professors James Bonnen, Allan Schmid, the late Dr. Albert Halter, Dr. James Hildreth, Burl Back, Dean Harry Kunkel, and many others. Julia McKay has been more than a typist as she worked with me to improve this manuscript and its documentation in many, many ways.

G.L.J.

Chapter 1

Why Study Research Methodology in Economics?

Since World War II, the role of economists in the practical affairs of government and business has expanded greatly. There has also been a vast increase in the amount of public money devoted to economic research. These developments have been accompanied by rapid advances in research methods and techniques. In the same period, econometrics, operations research, cybernetics, and systems science have come into full being and have greatly extended the research capabilities of economists. There have also been rapid changes in our philosophic orientation toward research. In the late 1960s, there came an increased awareness of many policy issues involving the environment, racial equality, sexual equality, resource depletion, and a vast number of other issues that now strain our methodologies and undergirding philosophies to the limit. Relatively recent works by Machlup [1978], Georgescu-Roegen [1971], Blaug [1980], Bell and Kristol [1981], Boulding [1981], Caldwell [1982], McCloskey [1983], Eichner [1983], Hausman [1984], McClennen [1983], Sagoff [1985], Rawls [1971], Sen [1984], Sen and Williams [1982], and many others indicate that our methodological heritage from John Neville Keynes, Lionel

Robbins, Milton Friedman, and others is now in need of fundamental reexamination.

Along with greater resources have come demands for more accountability. Economists now find themselves accountable to decision makers who provide research funds for the solution of practical problems and academic peers and administrators. The question of how to create, test, and evaluate knowledge required for making practical decisions is now being pressed by activists and those who are increasingly dissatisfied with "academic science" as part of the establishment.

THE VARIETY AND EXTENT OF RESEARCH EFFORTS INVOLVING ECONOMISTS

Economists are now engaged in research efforts ranging far beyond the realm of the traditional university economics department. We now do research at all levels of government, particularly at the federal level, and in international governmental and semigovernmental agencies. We also conduct major research programs for private industry. Economic research is a major new industry. Research firms and organizations have acquired proprietary interests in major economic models and techniques whose outputs are sold on a regular basis to firms and governmental agencies.

Our research has become an immense, complex business running all the way from the most esoteric theoretical developments to extremely important, practical matters.

The extent, complexity, and variety of our research efforts make it important that we carefully examine what we do in order to know and better understand the strengths and weaknesses of our methods for doing practical problem-solving, multidisciplinary subject-matter, and basic disciplinary research.

Along with the increased size and variety of research efforts in economics has come a blurring of the line between research on the one hand and consulting, advising, and serving on the other. It no longer seems advisable or even possible to follow objective "scientific" methods in doing research while leaving consulting, advising, and service under the guidance of something less objective. Neither the clients of economic advisors and consultants nor the advisors and consultants themselves want "objectivity left in a research institute or university." Economists feel a need for objectivity in advising and consulting. Their clients and those they serve less directly are entitled to it. The distinctions between art, practice, and scientific research may be blurring much more than realized by the more isolated academicians among us. We are expected, increasingly, to be objective and rigorous in our advising, consulting, and practical research as well as in doing pure disciplinary research in economics.

WHAT IS METHODOLOGY?

Fritz Machlup [1978, Ch. 1] has presented us with an excellent discussion of the meaning of methodology. Methodology, in a sense, is the science of methods. This book places heavy emphasis on methodology so conceived. The stress is on acquiring a deeper understanding of the reasons underlying the methods economists use.

Much has been written by students of economics methodology to further the use of logically positivistic methods by economists to acquire descriptive knowledge of economies and economic activity. Yet these methods have restricted the research activities of economists concerned with values—with welfare and consumption economics. Other students of research methodology for economists have concerned themselves for decades with the possibility of acquiring, verifying, and validating descriptive knowledge about values—not only about who values what in a behavioral sense but also about the "real" value of conditions, situations, and things. There have also been important methodological discussions involving pragmatic and dialectic methods, particularly among institutional economists, members of the German historical school of economics, and Marxists. It is important to understand these varying positions if we are to understand the reasons beneath the methods and techniques we use.

In this book, the discussion ranges over methods for dealing with value-free facts, with values, and with prescriptions to solve specific problems of specific decision makers. This is a "no-holds barred" book on the foundations of methods relevant for economists engaged in research ranging from the most practical problem-solving research, advising, consulting, and administration to the most esoteric disciplinary research in economics at universities.

WHY NOT A BOOK ON RESEARCH TECHNIQUES AND METHODS?

A student impatient for assistance on which technique or method to use can be expected to ask, "Why not a book on research methods and techniques used by economists rather than a book on methodology?" Part of the answer is that specific research methods and techniques are better taught in several different graduate-level courses in economics. Research techniques and methods have become so numerous, rich, and widely dispersed in courses dealing with statistics, mathematical economics, industrial organization, operations research, input/output analysis, benefit/cost analysis, systems simulation, sampling methods, and estimation techniques (to mention only a few) that a single book dealing comprehensively with methods and techniques would contain thousands of pages. Further, a course based on such a text would duplicate much of the material now well taught in many other courses.

Our methods and techniques are simply too numerous and detailed to be compressed into a single textbook for an individual course; instead, they should be taught throughout any worthy graduate training program for economists. What is needed for the study of methodology, instead, is a book that deals with the justification of methods and with the corresponding undergirding philosophies that bear on economists' claims to knowledge.

UNDERGIRDING PHILOSOPHIES

Since before the early Greeks, philosophers have been concerned with how to acquire, validate, and use knowledge about the real world. Many different philosophies and explanations of how knowledge is acquired and tested have developed and flourished over the centuries. Many still survive. In acquiring knowledge through research, different disciplines follow methods associated with widely differing philosophies. The interests of economists in the problems of real-world decision makers compel them to deal with descriptive knowledge, including knowledge about values, decision rules, and prescriptive knowledge.

Most real-world problems are multidisciplinary. The interests of economists in real-world problems make almost all the different philosophies about the acquisition of knowledge relevant. Thus, this book will not focus on any particular underlying philosophy and its associated methods and techniques. Instead, it will consider a variety of philosophies important for economists doing the three kinds of research and for those with whom economists are likely to cooperate in doing applied research.

To focus on one philosophy would be to hamstring the economist interested in multidisciplinary, problem-solving research. It is not asserted here that economists should be multidisciplinarians. Instead, it is implied that economists involved in practical problem-solving and subject-matter research should be prepared to accept guidance from the philosophies and the different methodological views and techniques associated with the disciplines to which economists contribute.

SENSITIVITIES ABOUT PHILOSOPHIC ORIENTATIONS

People are sensitive about their philosophic orientations. In a sense, their philosophies are their intellectual foundation garments. Their philosophic orientations structure and give shape to their knowledge-producing activities. Many economists have rather specialized philosophic underpinnings as a result of accidental contacts with teachers and literature early in their careers and with professors of economics and economic literature later. Whether our philosophic underpinnings are educational accidents or the result of deliberately guided processes, our ability to function depends to a degree on the stability of our underlying philosophic orientations. So, it is not surprising that people are sensitive about having others play around with their intellectual underwear. Yet that is precisely what this book does.

All I can do is indicate that I am aware of philosophic sensitivities and hope they can be managed well enough to permit the reader to draw freely from our rich intellectual heritage in philosophy and economics. We need to draw on the different parts of that heritage as we do different kinds of research to improve our discipline, to solve problems, and to contribute to bodies of knowledge on such multidisciplinary subjects as energy shortages, poverty, racial discrimination, and environmental quality. Economic researchers have much to gain from a broad reflective understanding of the different philosophies that guide our efforts.

SEMANTIC FEARS

Along with the philosophic sensitivities discussed above are semantic fears that interfere with our ability to understand the different methods relevant for economists. It is truly unproductive for economists to converse with one another on research methods and underlying philosophies while unknowingly assigning different meanings to the same words. Machlup [1978, Ch. 1], has had a deep concern with the meanings of terms. He has examined the many ways economists use "normative," "positive," and "prescriptive," and has carefully tabulated the different meanings they attach to these terms. A person who has read these tabulations (see assigned readings for Chapter 2), will realize that two economists carrying out a conversation using these terms are likely to misunderstand each other. In this book we face up to semantic difficulties by discussing the meanings attached to philosophic terms. We do this in Chapter 2 and several other chapters, including particularly Chapter 6.

THIS BOOK IS FOR ECONOMISTS, NOT PHILOSOPHERS

It was not my intention to write a treatise for philosophers or even a book for methodologists despite the fact that philosophy, philosophers, and general methodologists have contributed substantially to it. Though the book places heavy emphasis on the important philosophies that guide the research of economists, it is primarily a book on research methodology for economists instead of a book for philosophers and methodologists. Economists do what they do—sometimes successfully—sometimes not. Philosophers and methodologists are probably of more value in examining the successes and failures of economic researchers than they are in showing economists how to do what they do. Perhaps some philosophers and methodologists may someday find this book a useful description of some of the methodological and philosophic thinking of economic researchers—some philosophers might even find it useful input for studying the philosophic underpinnings of economic research.

OBJECTIVES OF THE BOOK

The objectives of this book are (1) to help students acquire an understanding of the prominent philosophies undergirding research methods commonly used by economists; (2) to help students develop, modify, and improve their views about research methodology and philosophy by reading (both in this book and the lists of assigned readings at the end of some of the chapters) and doing case studies, recognizing fully that the students' points of view will remain quite personal; (3) to distinguish with respect to disciplinary, subject-matter, and problem-solving research (a) their main characteristics, and (b) difficulties commonly encountered in organizing, financing, promoting, maintaining support for, conducting and evaluating each of these types of research, and (4) to elucidate the special difficulties encountered in acquiring, validating, and using factual knowledge (including that about values, in some instances at least) and prescriptions.

The first objective is that of helping the reader acquire an understanding of prominent philosophies important for economists. The student should expect to acquire an understanding of what the three philosophies have to contribute to our ability to acquire, evaluate, and use the different kinds of knowledge economists seek in doing disciplinary, subject-matter, and problem-solving research. An understanding of the strengths of each philosophic orientation is needed, but so too is an understanding of how to avoid the constraints the different orientations place on each other. This objective is accomplished by studying Chapter 3 of the introductory chapters; the six chapters in Part I, which look at these philosophic positions from the standpoints of both philosophy and economics; and Chapter 17, which summarizes the first 16 chapters of the book. In addition, assigned readings contain original works from important philosophers and economists.

The case studies of Part II help by providing examples of how the various philosophic orientations have contributed and constrained economic research and of how the constraints have been ignored and overcome. In my teaching experiences I have found it advantageous to require that the conceptual and case-study reading materials be read before class so that the class sessions can be devoted to discussions of the different points of view of economists and philosophers rather than devoted to lectures or uninformed discussion covering the material in the book and assigned readings.

Readings and discussions considered in the previous paragraph should help students attain the second objective—developing, modifying, and improving their views about research methodology and philosophy. As students attain the first objective and begin to acquire knowledge of the three kinds of research, they will become increasingly aware of the strengths and constraints of the different philosophies important in the research of economists. Typically, this frustrates and creates a need for reconciliation, adjustment, and even synthesis.

Alternatively, one could avoid the frustration by specialization as to kind of research, philosophic orientation, and kind of knowledge sought, but at the expense of not dealing with the whole range of research done by economists. The need here is for students to come to terms with themselves eclectically, through synthesis, by specialization, or in some other way, while recognizing that their philosophic and methodological orientation changes and matures over a lifetime.

I have found it helpful to ask students to submit a term essay on their own philosophic and methodological orientation to economics research. In general, it has proven advantageous to assign this essay early but to postpone the actual writing to the end of the course. This gives students more opportunity to digest their readings and discussions in view of the case studies found in Part II and the discussion of administrative questions found in Part III.

The third objective—distinguishing the characteristics of disciplinary, subject-matter, and problem-solving research and the differing administrative problems encountered in conducting them—is accomplished by studying the three introductory chapters; the summaries in the chapters of Part I; the six case studies found in the three chapters of Part II; additional case studies that I recommend be carried out by students; and Chapters 13 16 of Part III, which deal with the administration and conduct of research.

The fourth objective—elucidating the special difficulties encountered in acquiring, validating, and using the three different kinds of knowledge—is accomplished by studying the three introductory chapters, the six chapters of Part I, and the articles in the accompanying book of readings.

STRUCTURE OF THE BOOK

The book is not structured in the order of these objectives, though its structure is related to the objectives.

The next chapter draws distinctions between problem-solving, subject-matter, and disciplinary research. It also indicates briefly the kinds of knowledge involved in doing each of these kinds of research and how these kinds of knowledge are related to underlying philosophic positions. Brief attention is given in Chapter 2 to financing, supporting, administering, and evaluating this research. Chapter 3 briefly presents the philosophies of positivism, normativism, and pragmatism, with incidental attention to existentialism.

Chapters 4–6 deal with philosophic positivism, normativism, and pragmatism in detail. The stress in these chapters is on philosophy. There is purposeful repetition as the three chapters that follow concentrate on the roles these three philosophies play in economics, with the emphasis on methodological issues. My teaching experience shows that such repetition is needed by students and colleagues encountering these philosophic points of view for the first time. Some instructors may find it advantageous to ask students to read the chapters of Part I twice: first in the order published, then Chapters 4 and 7, followed by Chapters 5, 8, 6, and 9.

Following the philosophical and methodological chapters of part I are the three chapters of Part II. These chapters are illustrative, using case studies. Chapter 10 presents two disciplinary research case studies. Both deal with disciplinary economic research of known relevance. Chapter 11, dealing with subject-matter research, also contains two case studies. Chapter 12, the third case-study chapter, deals with problem-solving research. At this point in using the book, I have found it helpful to break the class down into groups of four to six students, in which each student verbally presents a case study of a piece of research following the format used in Chapter 10–12. Students can also gain valuable experience learning to react constructively to suggestions and criticisms if asked to hand in a written report reflecting discussion of their verbal presentation of the case study. Meetings for the groups can be arranged and timed to permit the instructor to be present and each student to hear three or more student presentations without increasing the number of class sessions students are required to attend.

The implications of the conceptual chapters of Part I and the case-study chapters of Part II are summarized in the five chapters of Part III. Chapter 13 deals with implications for obtaining and accounting for financial and political support for the different kinds of research. Chapter 14 deals with the problems of administering and conducting research. Chapter 15 deals with review and evaluation, with special attention to relevant peers. Chapter 16 deals with implications for the durability and practical impact of research. In these four chapters the emphasis is on the differences between disciplinary, subject-matter, and problem-solving research. Chapter 17 wraps up the book by first summarizing Chapters 13–16, then drawing conclusions from Chapters 4–9, and, finally, dealing with important research issues that have escaped the systematic treatment of the first 16 chapters.

ASSIGNED READINGS

This book has assigned readings for many of its chapters. For the most part, the ideas presented in the readings are not mine. The readings come from many influential economists, philosophers, and research administrators and add philosophic depth to what would otherwise be a shallow book from the standpoint of a philosopher. The readings are not always in agreement with each other or with parts of the book.

The student of research methodology in economics should know the origin of the conflicting but often supplementary and complementary ideas presented. At the end of each chapter there arc are two lists of references—one to the required readings, the other to additional readings. The first list is essential to an understanding of the first nine chapters of the book. Literature citations in the text of each chapter may be found in either list; however, not all items in the two lists for each chapter are cited in the text.

REQUIRED READINGS

(Read in Order Indicated)

Boulding, Kenneth E. 1980. Science: Our Common Heritage, *Science* **207**(4433):831–836. (Third)

Machlup, F. 1978. *Methodology of Economics and Other Social Sciences*, New York: Academic Press, pp. 54–62. (First)

Runes, D. D. 1961. *Dictionary of Philosophy,* Paterson, NJ: Littlcfield, Adams, pp. 196–197, 284–285. (Second)

ADDITIONAL REFERENCES

Bell, Daniel and Irving Kristol. 1981. *The Crisis in Economic Theory*, New York: Basic Books.

Blaug, Mark. 1980. *The Methodology of Economics or How Economists Explain*, Cambridge, UK: Cambridge University Press.

Boulding, Kenneth. 1981. *Evolutionary Economics*, Beverly Hills, CA: Sage Publications.

Caldwell, Bruce. 1982. *Beyond Positivism: Economic Methodology in the Twentieth Century*, London: Allen and Unwin.

Eichner, Alfred. 1983. *Why Economics Is Not Yet a Science*, Armonk, NY: M. E. Sharpe.

Georgescu-Roegen, N. 1971. *The Entropy Law and the Economic Process*, Cambridge: Harvard University Press.

Hausman, David M. (ed.) 1984. *The Philosophy of Economics: An Anthology*, Cambridge, UK: Cambridge University Press.

Kirzner, Israel M. 1981. The "Austrian" Perspective, in *The Crisis in Economic Thought*, Daniel Bell and Irving Kristol, eds., New York: Basic Books.

McClennen, Edward F. 1983. Rational Choice and Public Policy: A Critical Survey, *Social Theory and Practice*, 9, (2–3):335–379.

McCloskey, Donald N. 1983. The Rhetoric of Economics, *Journal of Economic Literature* **XXI**(2):481–517.

Rawls, John. 1971. *A Theory of Justice*, Cambridge: Harvard University Press.
Sagoff, Mark. 1986. "Values and Preferences," *Ethics* **96**(2):301–316.
Sen, Amartya. 1984. *Resources, Values and Development*, Cambridge: Harvard University Press.
——— and Bernard Williams (eds.). 1982. *Utilitarianism and Beyond*, Cambridge: Harvard University Press.

Chapter 2

Three Kinds of Research

This chapter stresses three kinds of research, disciplinary, subject-matter, and problem-solving. Years of research have taught me the importance of the distinctions between them. Very different kinds of information are acquired in doing each, and acquisition of the information requires different methods. Different methods are justified by appealing to different undergirding philosophies. There are also important differences in the amount of interaction required with noneconomists. All this has important practical implications for the total research effort which is considered in Part III.

As economists contribute to all three kinds of research, a book on research methodology for economists should deal with all three. Professors teaching courses in research methodology often have a narrow disciplinary orientation. The result has been heavy emphasis in methodology texts and courses on disciplinary research to the neglect of subject-matter and problem-solving research. Partially as a result of neglecting the applied end of the research spectrum, there is often a strained relationship between economics and economists on the one hand and such applied areas as business administration, labor economics, resource economics, agricultural economics, and development, and

11

other topics on the other. In contrast with many works on research methodology, this book attempts to avoid these strains by dealing with all three kinds of research, running from the disciplinary to the applied end of the research spectrum.

This chapter first describes the three kinds of research, then relates them to different kinds of knowledge and to the methods and philosophies associated with them. Finally, the chapter indicates, very tentatively, the consequences of a balanced consideration of the three kinds of research.

DESCRIPTION OF THE THREE KINDS OF RESEARCH

We describe the three different kinds of research in the following order: disciplinary, subject-matter, and problem-solving. This is in order of increasing complexity and, unfortunately, somewhat in order of decreasing respectability in academic circles. I find it difficult to provide acceptable reasons for regarding problem-solving research as less respectable than disciplinary research, however different they are. It should be noted at the onset that (1) the three kinds or classes of research are on a continuum with pnumbra or gray areas between them and (2) many research efforts mix the three types.

Disciplinary Research

Disciplinary research is research designed to improve a discipline. In economics, it consists largely of research to develop and improve economic theories, quantitative techniques for economists, and the measurement of basic economic phenomena and parameters such as supply and demand elasticities, multiplier effects, and the gross national product. Economics, like other disciplines, has a group of ancillary disciplines that provide it with research tools. They include mathematics, history, statistics, logic, philosophy, political science, and socialogy.

Disciplinary research can be of known or unknown relevance for practical problems faced by decision makers. It is probably a mistake to refer to doing disciplinary research as problem-solving because that confuses the answering of academic disciplinary questions with solving the problems of the practical world. This assertion will become clearer as we describe the other two kinds of research, and particularly when we examine the case studies of Part II and their implications in Part III.

Subject-Matter Research

Subject-matter research is multidisciplinary research on a subject of interest to a *set* of decision makers facing a *set* of practical problems. Well-defined subject-matter research is germane to well-defined sets of decision n. practical problems. It is the relationship of the different disciplines te of problems involved that makes the multidisciplinarity of subject-. research so different from the multidisciplinarity of the relationship bet. economics and its ancillary disciplines.

The need for subject-matter research often emerges out of rather genera. issues facing society at a given time. For instance, in the 1970s and 1980s, large numbers of decision makers were concerned with the set of problems involving energy. Energy is a multidisciplinary subject drawing on engineering, geology, political science, physics, chemistry, and many other disciplines besides economics. Large multidisciplinary subject-matter research projects on energy are undertaken. Though these projects are sometimes justified as being problem-solving by project designers who refer to *the* energy problem, it is a mistake to refer to *the* energy problem as there is not simply one problem. Instead, there is a *set* of practical energy problems including literally millions of individual problems faced by millions of decision makers. This will become clearer as the reader proceeds through the book.

When economists do research on energy, they typically find themselves working with researchers from other disciplines in assembling a defined body of information relevant to a more or less well-defined set of energy problems faced by a more or less well-specified set of decision makers. For example, a carefully defined piece of subject-matter research might be specific to a set of decision makers known as midwestern U.S. maize producers dealing with the set of problems involving the use of energy to harvest, dry, store, and transport maize. After the members of the different disciplines have made their contributions to the defined set of information, the resulting body of knowledge is seldom adequate to solve a specific problem in the set of problems for a specific decision maker in the set of decision makers.

This is characteristic of subject-matter research. The practical strength of subject-matter research is that it provides a body of information useful to a great number of decision makers dealing with a large number of problems. The decision makers can accept the information made available to them by a subject-matter research effort, then use their own resources to get the additional information required to solve each specific problem.

Problem-Solving Research

Problem-solving research is research designed to solve a specific problem for a specific decision maker, though in some instances it is possible to find several decision makers with exactly the same problem. In this case, the research can be designed to solve a problem faced by more than one decision maker. Problem-solving research, like subject-matter research, is typically multidisciplinary. The practical problems of real-world decision makers respect neither the organiza-

⌐ts of universities and research institutes nor the academic disciplines
⌐hich universities and institutes are organized. Because problem-solving
⌐h is complex, it is probably the best of the three kinds of research to
⌐ine in order to ascertain the different kinds of information economists
⌐e to acquire and the different philosophic orientations essential for the
⌐search work of economists.

PROBLEM SOLVING

The complexity and generality of the problem-solving process makes it desirable
to diagram that process.

Problem Solving Diagramed

Problem-solving processes have been diagramed and outlined in many ways,
depending on the background and experiences of the authors. Figure 2 presents
contributions from a number of philosophies important to economists but is
not unduly specialized in economics. It results in part from empirical research
on the decision processes of 1,075 midwestern farmers [Johnson et al., 1961].
It has been used extensively in discussion of public problem-solving processes
and in consulting at national and subnational levels. Note that all the arrows
are two-way arrows, indicating two-way flows of knowledge and interdependencies. The process is regarded as iterative as it involves repeated trial and error.
It is also regarded as interactive when more than one person is involved in defining and solving problems and in executing decisions.

There are two information banks in the figure. One contains positivistic
information; the other, normative information. The meanings of the words
positivistic and normative are discussed in the next main section of this chapter.
At this point we stress that a part of the normative knowledge is prescriptive
knowledge for solving problems; thus, recipes, rules, laws, regulations, and
social norms and mores are found in the normative information bank as well
as information about values. In Figure 2, the decision maker is viewed as *defining* a practical problem on the basis of both knowledge about values from
the normative information bank and value-free knowledge from the positivistic
information bank.

A decision maker is envisioned in Figure 2 as being aware of a difficulty
and believing that he or she might be able to take an action that would make
the situation better. The figure portrays the decision maker as *carrying out observations* to obtain new information, both positivistic and normative, some of
which can be lodged in the appropriate information bank. The decision maker
is then seen as *analyzing* both kinds of information, with possible feedback
to get more observations or to redefine the problem. The analysis is then fed
into the *decision step*, where an attempt is made to process the two kinds of

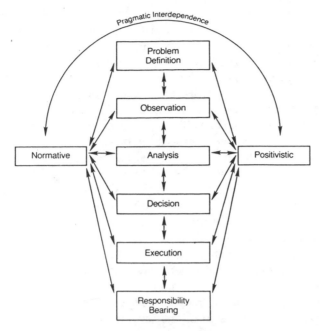

Figure 2. Problem-solving steps related to kinds of knowledge used

*Johnson, Glenn L., Philosophic Foundations: Problems, Knowledge, and Solutions, *European Review of Agricultural Economics*, 3-2/3, 1976, Part II, p. 226.

information through a decision rule into a prescription about "what ought" to be done to solve the problem. Again, feedback is possible.

When knowledge about values and value-free knowledge is imperfect among people with conflicting interests, the incorporation of existing distributions of power into decision rules permits resolutions of conflict. The role of power is considered later in this chapter in discussing the nature of prescriptive knowledge. The next step is that of executing the decision. The *final* step is bearing responsibility for both the decision and its execution.

The six steps are treated as mutually interdependent, with much feedback, iteration, and interaction between them. Some of the feedback is from the future to the present as the decision maker tries to envision the consequences of alternative decisions to carry out different acts.

Some pragmatists believe that attention to consequences in the process of solving a problem changes the value and value-free information involved. This results in an interdependence between value-free knowledge and knowledge about values that is shown in the figure with a two-way arrow labeled "pragmatic interdependence." The presence of the arrow in Figure 2 should not be taken to indicate that I regard value-free knowledge and knowledge about values as always interdependent; instead, it explicitly provides for them to be so regarded if this seems to be the case. Though the prescriptive content of the normative information bank usually depends on value-free information as well as information about values, this is not the same as interdependence between value-free positivistic knowledge and knowledge about values.

Some people express a concern that such interpretations imply more rationality than is exercised by real-world decision makers. To understand the importance of these concerns, one needs to consider the meaning of rationality. It varies a great deal from one philosophy to another and from one discipline to another as disciplines tend to specialize on different philosophies.

For some, rationality means being logical. For others it means being objective, which has as many meanings as rationality. For still others, rationality means insisting on objectivity about the acquisition and use of positivistic knowledge and knowledge about values to be processed through an explicitly stated but varying decision rule to solve practical problems. Such a conception of rationality also requires that decision rules, like the knowledge they process into a decision, be selected in an objective manner. Thus there is an infinite regression of decisions about decision rules to use in selecting decision rules. The last meaning is what I have in mind when I use the term rationality. Objectivity with respect to value-free knowledge, knowledge about values, and decision rules will be discussed in later chapters.

One cannot deny that there is a great deal of irrationality on the part of real-world decision makers. That does not prevent the interpretation presented here from being useful to students of research methodology for economists. Much research is done to improve decision-making, and research itself is supposedly one of the most rational and objective of human activities. I am aware, though, of Feyerabend's [1978] aversion to doctrinaire rationality and conformism in research methods and of his endorsement of the use of subterfuge, rhetoric, and propaganda in science.

DISCUSSIONS OF THE MEANINGS OF TERMS

It is important here to discuss the meaning of certain terms that play important roles in the remainder of this book. In this section we are especially concerned with the meaning of positivistic knowledge, normative knowledge, knowledge of values, and prescriptive knowledge. Machlup [1969] has catalogued the numerous conflicting ways in which economists use the terms normative, positive, and prescriptive. As this book places heavy stress on knowledge of values, prescriptive knowledge, and positivistic knowledge, their meanings are crucial to understanding its content.

Normative Knowledge

Normative knowledge in this book is regarded as including prescriptive knowledge as well as knowledge about values—about goodness and badness.

The adjective "normative" then covers propositions about goodness and badness as well as prescriptive propositions having to do with what ought not or ought to be done, whether the latter are stated as laws, recipes, regulations, social mores and norms, or ethical imperatives. Because the word normative has such a broad meaning, it is less useful than "prescriptive" and the expression "knowledge of values," which will be discussed next.

Knowledge of Values

Knowledge of values, a subpart of normative knowledge, is another of the three kinds of knowledge of prime concern to economists. It is knowledge having to do with the goodness and badness of conditions, situations, and things. Though logical positivism, considered in detail later in this book, holds that there are no experiences of goodness and badness as characteristics of "real"- world conditions, situations, and things from which to develop primitive undefined terms involving goodness and badness, this book does not accept that constraint in all instances. Instead, we seriously consider the idea that it is possible (1) to experience the "real" goodness or badness of such conditions as justice and injustice or of such things as the Salk vaccine for polio or the presence or lack of vitamin B-12 in our diets, and (2) to develop primitive terms on the basis of such experiences to use in describing those goodnesses and badnesses. Goodness and badness, so viewed, are undefinable but experienceable. There is also knowledge about values held by individuals and groups. Such knowledge may or may not be regarded as descriptive of characteristics in the real objective natural world.

There is a continuum of views in philosophy about the reality of values and the objectivity of our knowledge of values. At one end is an absolutist view that values are characteristics of the real world and, that there is a supreme utlimate good such as utility, which can serve as a common denominator for less ultimate values. At the other extreme is the view that values exist only in "knowing minds" and that the only empirical knowledge of value that is possible is knowledge of the values held in such minds. Economists who believe their role is not to go beyond helping people do "what they want to do" are probably reflecting this point of view. An intermediate point of view is that there are numerous goods and bads that are characteristics of the real world and are knowable, and that these are not necessarily reducible to a common denominator.

Economists or others, such as Pareto, who perceive great difficulty with the concept of utility as an interpersonally valid measure of welfare probably share this view. A second intermediate view is nearer to the view that values exist only in knowing minds. This view accepts that values exist only in knowing minds but holds that the existence of common characteristics of knowing minds makes some value knowledge universally or almost universally true. Such a view is probably held by the large number of economists who conclude that taxes should be progressive because of the widespread conviction that the bite of a tax dollar "hurts" the rich less than the poor.

The continuum of points of view about the reality and objectivity of values has been presented here because all these points of view are accorded respected positions in this book. The book does not advocate any one of these views to the complete exclusion of any of the others.

Positivistic Knowledge

Positivistic knowledge is synthetic knowledge that deals with the characteristics of conditions, situations, or things in the real world. Not all positivistic knowledge is value free; for instance, knowledge about who values what how much can be regarded as positivistic as long as it is not regarded as descriptive of real values. The possibility of descriptive knowledge of goodness, badness, rightness, and wrongness conceived as characteristics of the real world is ruled out by philosophic positivism.

Prescriptive Knowledge—Decision Rules and Power

Prescriptive knowledge is knowledge about what ought or ought not to have been done, or ought or ought not be done. Prescriptions are sometimes expressed in the future tense as goals or targets. They are also expressed as actions in the present tense; at times they are stated imperatively as laws, regulations, social mores, and norms enforced with sanctions. On still other occasions they are recipes or standard solutions for standard problems. In evaluating past actions, prescriptions are also expressed in the past tense as statements about what ought or ought not to have been done. Prescriptive knowledge can be regarded as a function of value-free knowledge and knowledge about values and, as such, is a logical consequence of them. The functions (sometimes but not always strictly mathematical) relating value-free positive knowledge and knowledge about values to prescriptions are decision-making rules. While values and the value-free characteristics of conditions, situations, and things can both be viewed as observable and experienceable, the prescriptive cannot. The prescription is a decision to act, not the act prescribed or any condition, situation, thing, or event. Prescriptions are defined, as we saw in discussing Figure 2, by applying a decision rule to knowledge of values and value-free positivistic knowledge—its rightness and wrongness is definitional but not observable.

Perfect knowledge is infinitely expensive for mortals. Indeed, some points of view about the reality of values hold that it is impossible to have any objective knowledge about values as characteristics of the real world. Thus, conflicts arise in reaching prescriptions to solve problems that are not always resolvable by acquiring more knowledge. In such instances, the decision rules used to convert knowledge about values and value-free knowledge into prescriptions are typically based on or include arbitrary distributions of power. This is nicely illustrated by the simple majority, two-thirds majority, or unanimous decision rules in political decision-making. Conflict resolution involves decision rules that trade off increments of different values against each other in attaining a more ultimate value (or common denominator) within the constraints of unredistributable distributions of power.

The exercise of power is often necessary in reaching decisions when we lack agreed-upon knowledge of a common denominator of value and/or agreement on value-free knowledge. Various social, political, market, and military covenants institutionalize distributions of power into decision rules. A few of the kinds of power distributed among individuals and groups by such covenants include those associated with ownership of income-producing resources, the possession of political and social rights, command of military and police resources and, indeed, the power of knowledge itself.

To reiterate, prescriptive knowledge deals with what it is or will be right or wrong to do. When we evaluate past decisions, we try to determine whether or not it was right to prescribe the act someone tried to carry out. When we set our goals and targets we decide or prescribe what ought and ought not to be done in the future. When we act to solve a problem we try to execute prescriptions (decisions).

It is important, as C. I. Lewis [1955] points out, to distinguish between goodness and badness on the one hand and rightness and wrongness on the other. For example, it is not always right to do what is good because often it is possible to do something still better at the same cost or sacrifice. Conversely, it is not always wrong to do what is bad. The situations we face often make it necessary to minimize losses. We find it right to do bad if it is the least bad that can be done in the circumstances. For example, doctors typically write prescriptions that minimize badness for their patients. Particularly in the case of cancer patients, many of the treatments prescribed are bad in themselves, and healthy people would not subject themselves to their side effects. However, both patient and doctor often agree that it is right for a doctor to prescribe a treatment that will, hopefully, be more lethal for the cancer than the patient.

Prescriptive knowledge—about rightness and wrongness—is the logical consequence of a decision rule applied to a body of knowledge about values and a body of value-free knowledge. Hence, prescriptive knowledge is not primitive. By contrast, knowledge of values—of goodness and badness—can be viewed as experiential. Goodness and badness will be viewed in Chapters 5 and 8 as primitive terms [Moore, 1903, pp. 6–8, 17–21]. Rightness is not experiential but definitional—it specifies "what ought to be."

The philosophic, ethical, and economic origins and implications of prescriptive knowledge will be developed at numerous points in this book; however, the word prescriptive will be used consistently to deal with what ought or ought not to be done—with what is right or wrong. The word value—about goodness and badness—will not be used to deal with what ought to be done despite the widespread tendency to define values as dealing with "what ought to be done."

Some Implications of the Above-Discussed Meanings

As we progress through the book, it will be seen that the above-discussed meanings of value-free and normative knowledge will tend progressively to destroy commonly held dichotomies between (1) facts and values, (2) the objective and the normative, (3) science and the humanities, (4) the subjective and the objective, and (5) science on the one hand and theology and the humanities on the other. The common distinction between "what is" and "what ought to be" is more a distinction between value-free positivistic knowledge and knowledge about values taken together on the one hand and prescriptive knowledge on the other, than between either facts and values or between value-free positivistic knowledge and knowledge about values.

DIFFERENT KINDS OF RESEARCH REQUIRE DIFFERENT KINDS OF KNOWLEDGE

In this section we examine how the use and pursuit of value-free positivistic knowledge, values, and prescriptive knowledge vary between the three kinds of research—problem-solving, subject-matter and disciplinary—defined in the first section of this chapter. We take up the three kinds of research in order of decreasing complexity and completeness: problem-solving, subject-matter, and disciplinary. The attention given in this book to problem-solving and subject-matter research adds an important dimension to the conclusions reached by Blaug [1980] in his admirable book on methodology for disciplinary research in economics.

Problem-Solving Research

Problem-solving research prescribes a solution to a specific problem of a specific decision maker running the practical affairs of the world. Figure 2 and the explanation of problem-solving processes presented earlier in this chapter indicate the complexity of problem-solving research. It was explained there that problem-solving research requires the acquisition and utilization of value-free positivistic knowledge and knowledge about values (with or without pragmatic interactions) to produce prescriptive knowledge based, in turn, on decision rules that may be very complex. Clearly, problem-solving research is a complex activity involving all three kinds of knowledge. Though academicans often refer to the research they do to answer important empirical and theoretical questions for their disciplines as "problem-solving," there is a difference between answering disciplinary questions and solving the practical problems of real-world decision makers. Indeed, the answering of disciplinary questions is defined later as disciplinary research, while the latter is what is defined here as problem-solving research. It is a much different thing to estimate the income elasticity of demand for blue cheese in the discipline of economics than it is to solve a multidisciplinary problem of finding the best way to organize the purchasing, storage, and sale of blue cheese in a given supermarket.

Subject-Matter Research

Because subject-matter research generates multidisciplinary knowledge of use to a set of decision makers dealing with a set of practical real-world problems, it can be simpler and less complex than problem-solving research. Subject-matter research does not produce all the knowledge required to solve all the problems in the relevant set; instead it generates a body of multidisciplinary knowledge useful in solving the problems in the set. If subject-matter research were to generate enough knowledge to solve the problems in the set, it would also be problem-solving research. Subject matter researchers can deal with value-free positivistic information without dealing with information about values and vice versa, the exceptions to this occurring when these two kinds of knowledge are found to be pragmatically interdependent. Subject-matter research can seek positivistic knowledge about who values what as well as nonpositivistic knowledge of real-world goodnesses and badnesses.

Disciplinary Research

Depending on the discipline involved, disciplinary research may seek knowledge about values, value-free positivistic knowledge, prescriptive knowledge, or any combination of the three. The decision disciplines such as economics, law, engineering, architecture, medicine, military science, and political science typically seek all three. Economics has researchers who concentrate exclusively on value-free positivistic knowledge. Similarly, economics has a long history of successful research on knowledge of values. Economics is centrally concerned with defining optima used (1) for prescriptive purposes in problem-solving research, and (2) to describe and predict the optimizing behavior of individuals and groups. These optima involve nonmonetary values in the cases of consumption, welfare and dynamic, if not static production economics.

Disciplinary research may be of known or unknown relevance. Disciplinarians produce knowledge both for the sake of improving economics and for the sake of making an indirect contribution to our capacity to solve real-world problems. One of the strengths of a university is that it has disciplinarians who devote large parts of their lives to generating knowledge to improve their disciplines, thereby enhancing the stock of disciplinary knowledge to transmit from one generation to another and for problem-solving and subject-matter researchers.

DIFFERENT METHODS REQUIRED FOR THE THREE KINDS OF RESEARCH

While there is a certain unity [Zerby, 1957] in the quest for the different kinds of knowledge, different methods and philosophies are often used in pursuing each of the three kinds of knowledge. Perhaps these differences are exaggerated by adherence to different philosophic positions and by loyalty to different disciplines. In any event, students of research methodology in economics think about different methods when seeking value-free positivistic knowledge, knowledge about values, and prescriptive knowledge. *Disciplinary* research can be positivistic, as it often is in the bio/physical sciences; about values as it often is in the arts and humanities; or prescriptive, which requires both positivistic knowledge and knowledge about values as in a decision discipline such as economics. *Subject-matter* research is multidisciplinary and involves knowledge about values and positivistic knowledge in the proportions dictated by the subject under consideration. As *problem-solving* research generates prescriptions based on both value-free and value knowledge, it involves all three kinds of knowledge.

Positivistic Methods

Positivistic methods have been advocated by such prominent general economists as John Neville Keynes, Lionel Robbins, and Milton Friedman, and by positivistic agricultural economics researchers of the 1920–1950 period [Johnson, forthcoming]. Among the positivistic researchers are empiricists, some of whom avoid the use of theory while trying to concentrate wholly on knowledge acquired from direct observation. Other positivistic researchers recognize a connection between theoretical knowledge and primitive experiential terms in generating synthetic or descriptive knowledge. It will be seen later that the philosophy of positivism tends to confine a researcher's disciplinary work to the generation of value-free knowledge and knowledge about who values what, while assigning the study of what really is valuable to what the researcher regards as the unobjective realms of the humanities and theology.

However, descriptive research about what nonmonetary values are held by what persons or what monetary values exist in an economy is acceptable to positivists. The excluded concepts are those purporting (1) to describe the value that some condition, situation or thing "really has" whether or not anyone holds that it has value; (2) to indicate what is objectively or intersubjectively valuable even though values are regarded as existing only in minds, and (3) to prescribe what ought to be done other than as a description of what some person, social group, or legal entity accepts, follows, and/or enforces. It is not necessary, however, to accept this constraint to do positivistic research and employ positivistic methods in generating positivistic knowledge important for economics.

The powerful methods of logical positivism are empirical. They entail both logical and observational testing. Generally speaking, descriptive propositions are never regarded as proven with certainty in positivism. Rather they are rejected or, conversely, only accepted as having been subjected to testing adequate for the purpose at hand. The tests are those of coherence (logic), correspondence (experience), and clarity (lack of ambiguity or vagueness). People familiar with econometrics will recognize that the test of theoretical soundness is a test of coherence, that significance and tracking tests are tests of correspondence, and that to test the identifiability of a system of equations is to test it for clarity or lack of ambiguity.

Methods for Researching Values

Economics is particularly rich in the development of methods for researching values. The history of economic thought and the history of philosophic value theory involves a great deal of common literature, including the works of Adam Smith, David Ricardo, Jeremy Bentham, J. S. Mill, Karl Marx, the Austrian school (whose members tend to deal with intrinsic values), Alfred Marshall, and the neoclassicists, who tend to concentrate on utility and values in exchange.

Logical analysis is widely employed in researching values, hence the test of coherence is an important part of such methods. However, there are also "objective researchers of values" who produce descriptive knowledge about values—nonmonetary as well as monetary, intrinsic as well as exchange, intrinsic as well as extrinsic, and esthetic as well as less esthetic. These include price, income, and expenditure analysts who work with monetary values as well as the expected utility analysts and benefit/cost analysts among economists who work with nonmonetary values. Such objective researchers use the test of correspondence with experience as one tool in their kit of methods. We will see in Chapters 5 and 8 what philosophic orientations are used to make sense of this empirical testing of knowledge about values.

Prescriptive Methods

Prescriptive knowledge, we saw at the beginning of this chapter, depends (according to a decision rule) on both positivistic knowledge and knowledge about values. Some, but not all, prescriptive methods are *pragmatic*. Pragmatism holds that the truth of beliefs depends on the consequences of acting on them.

Thus, pragmatic methods involve the test of workability of consequences (see Chapters 6 and 9) in addition to coherence, correspondence, and clarity (see Chapters 5 and 8). For pragmatists, positivistic truth and truth about value are interdependent in their practical consequences. Pragmatic methods place less emphasis than positivistic and normative ones on testing positivistic and value propositions independently of each other with the tests of coherence, correspondence, and clarity; instead, the pragmatic stress is on testing the workability of the different consequences of different prescriptions. On the other hand, the value-free positivistic knowledge and value knowledge fed into non-pragmatic decision processes can be subjected to the tests of coherence, correspondence, and clarity with less concern about workability. The choice of decision rule and the resulting prescription, however, are not easily subjected to the test of correspondence, for reasons previously discussed.

There is also a relationship between the classical literature of economics and ethical prescriptions. Alfred Marshall's *Principles* and C. I. Lewis' *The Ground and Nature of Right* are similar as both deal with optimization, though the work of Lewis is briefer and more abstract.

The maximizing techniques of economists generate prescriptive knowledge that is used for two purposes—to derive recommendations or prescriptions as to the right course of action to take, and to predict the behavior of producers, consumers, resource owners, entrepreneurs, governmental officials, and the inventors of new technology, as in induced institutional and technical change. Ethics is involved in the first of these but less so in the second.

Note that the supply and demand functions used by price analysts to predict prices assume maximizing activity on the part of producers, consumers, and resource owners. The predictive methods and techniques of econometricians are based on the assumption that individual decision makers are able to prescribe and to do what is monetarily and, even more importantly, nonmonetarily best for them.

Eclecticism Is Required and Synthesis Is Needed

Obtaining positivistic knowledge involves exploiting the strengths of positivism. Similarly, obtaining knowledge about values involves exploiting the strengths of normative philosophies. Obtaining prescriptive knowledge involves exploiting the strengths of both the pragmatic and the two nonpragmatic philosophies. As will be seen in Chapters 4–9, each of these philosophies and their variants place restrictions on one's capacity to utilize the strengths of others. But we have seen that economic research in its most complex form (problem solving) requires all three kinds of knowledge and that the subject matter and disciplinary research of economists may involve all three kinds of knowledge. As a minimum, therefore, the student of research methodology in economics needs to be eclectic with respect to the three primary underlying philosophies of economics—positivism, normativism, and pragmatism.

Ideally, a thorough-going synthesis is needed. In his book, *Beyond Positivism*, Bruce Caldwell makes a similar case for what he calls methodological pluralism; his pluralism, however, is not as closely tied to objective tests for truth as the eclecticism toward which this book leads its readers.

Later in the book, the unity of science movement will be considered in which pragmatists and positivists attempted to establish a commonality across the physical, biological, and social sciences. To me, this attempt at unity must eventually require the positivists to discard the constraints they place on ability to research values as objectively or intersubjectively valid characteristics of an objective world, and for the pragmatists to soften their position that the whole truth of differences between descriptive propositions is contained in the differences between their practical consequences. This tolerance is especially required for the unity so needed in doing multidisciplinary subject-matter and problem-solving research.

Unless the positivists give ground (which I believe is happening), there seems to be little possibility for them to cooperate with pragmatists, who hold that value-free and value propositions are interdependent in their consequences for solving practical problems [Joad, 1957, pp. 448f]. Reciprocally, pragmatists must give ground on their interdependence position in order to permit the physical scientists to pursue positivistic knowledge free of the constraint of pragmatic complexities. My late colleague, Lewis K. Zerby, and I reached this conclusion as a result of making case studies of the research done by economists, with stress on the subject-matter and problem-solving research of agricultural economists and the problem-solving activities of farmers [Johnson and Zerby, 1973; Johnson, 1961, 1977].

As noted earlier, Bruce Caldwell [1982] reached a similar position that he calls "methodological pluralism" by analyzing the disciplinary research programs of such general economists as Robbins versus Hutchinson (he might also have included Frank Knight), Hutchinson versus Machlup, and Friedman versus Samuelson. However, Caldwell's pluralism seems to place less reliance on theory and experience in generalizing knowledge of values than is found in this book. In the preface of his book, Caldwell deplores the lack of discussion of the work of economists [p. 2]; thus, Part II of this book, with its case studies and the references cited above, partially fills the gap noted by Caldwell. In so doing it stresses tests for objectivity in researching values and stresses problem-solving and subject-matter research, while preserving a crucial role for disciplinary research in economics.

IDEOLOGY IN ECONOMIC RESEARCH

Though the first definition of ideology in Webster's Third New International Dictionary indicates that ideology is the study of ideas, to state that a research effort is ideological is commonly interpreted as derogatory. In the same dictionary, the last definition of ideology is "an extremist sociopolitical program or philosophy constructed wholly or in part on factitious or hypothetical ideational bases." The dictionary does not list a word "idealology" which would probably be defined as the study of ideals. Nonetheless, the word ideology is sometimes used as if it were spelled idealology—having to do with the study of ideal systems. The last definition of ideology quoted above seems to deal more with ideas about ideals than with ideas in general. The fact that the definition mentions "extremist" programs or philosophies indicates that the ideals involved are questionable, and that to say a person is ideological is to defame that person.

There are ideals in science, research, and academic endeavors. Some of these are among the more noble and finer ideals people try to attain. Chapter 15 on review and evaluation of research will consider what is involved in measuring a research proposal or research results against scientific research ideals. Commitment to such ideals is not to be regretted. On the contrary, research, scientific, and academic communities define themselves and their activities largely in terms of ideals. Nonetheless, there are many instances in which academicians, researchers, and scientists find they have attached themselves to extremist positions and have become chauvinistic in the sense of having undue invidious attachments to that position. This kind of ideology or chauvinism is regrettable. It is anti-intellectual and out of place in objective research organizations. Throughout this book there will be a concern over what are appropriate ideals or standards for research, with attention being given to avoiding invidious attachments to inappropriate ideals.

Economists often accuse each other of being ideological in the sense of having "extremist sociopolitical programs . . . constructed wholly or in part on factitious and hypothetical ideational bases." Neoclassicists are sometimes portrayed as defenders and advocates of capitalism. Similarly, people concerned about equality in the distribution of the ownership of income-producing resources (including rights and privileges) are sometimes viewed as ideological and unobjective. In some instances, positivistic ideals are so dominant that all that is required to be regarded as ideological and unobjective is to be concerned with questions of goodness and badness and rightness and wrongness.

As in the case of academic enterprises in general, economic research can become ideological in the derogatory sense of the word. There seems to me to be an extremely important need for adhering to the ideals of science, research, and academia in doing economic research that addresses practical problems relating to justice, equality, and distribution. The need, as I see it, is to research such problems without abandoning the ideals of the academic, scientific, and research worlds by embracing extremist sociopolitical positions.

The ideals of science and academia also require that we avoid blind, unobjective adherence to various philosophic orientations. For example, we cannot let adherence to a logically positivistic approach to research cause us to avoid objective research on questions of value—monetary or nonmonetary, intrinsic or extrinsic—and on prescriptive questions about what "ought to be done" about any socioeconomic problem to whose solution the research of economists may make a contribution. One of our tasks in this book is to determine how to research values and to do problem-solving research without becoming ideological in the derogatory sense of the word.

IMPLICATIONS FOR PRACTICING THE THREE KINDS OF RESEARCH

This section sketches what will be found in the chapters to follow, particularly Chapters 13-17. As understanding of research methods and underlying philosophies is furthered through studying Chapters 3-9 and the case histories in Chapters 10-12, it will become clear that the three kinds of research call for great differences in how we:

1. Mobilize financial and public support for the research efforts of economists. (Chapter 13),
2. Conduct research—the problems of administration being much greater for multidisciplinary problem-solving and subject-matter research (where we have to cross discipline boundaries) than for specialized disciplinary research (where we do not) (Chapter 14),
3. Evaluate research proposals and results—the relevant peers are far different for disciplinary research than for problem-solving and subject matter-research (Chapter 14),
4. Assess (Chapter 15) the durability and practicality of research proposals and results for the three kinds of research. Problem-solving research tends to be ephemeral but practical, while the advances that take place in basic disciplines tend to be durable and, hence, are advantageously transferred from one generation to the next for long periods of time. Subject-matter research tends to have intermediate applicability and intermediate durability.

In Chapter 17, we will put together an eclectic philosophic position, perhaps a synthesis, of philosophic positions and associated methods to undergird our research efforts, whether problem-solving, subject-matter, and disciplinary research in nature. In that chapter we will also consider selected issues about methods and the scope of economics that seem too important to neglect despite the fact that they are not caught in the systematic nets of Chapters 4-16.

REQUIRED READINGS

(Read in Order Indicated)

Atkinson, R. C. 1980. *How Basic Research Reaps Unexpected Rewards* (Introduction), Washington, DC: National Science Foundation. (Third)

Bush, V. 1945. Science: The Endless Frontier, Washington, DC: National Science Foundation (Reprinted July 1960), pp. viii–ix, 5–9, 14–16, 18–21, 23. (First)

Handler, Phillip. 1976. The American University Today, *The American Scientist*, **64**:254–257 (May–June). (Fifth)

Lewis, C. I. 1955. *The Ground and Nature of the Right*, New York: Columbia University Press, pp. 58–77. (Seventh)

Machlup, F. 1969. Positive and Normative Economics: An Analysis of the Ideas, in *Economic Means and Social Ends*, R. Heilbroner, ed., Englewood Cliff, NJ: Prentice Hall, pp. 99–124. (Eighth)

Press, Frank. 1982. Rethinking Science Policy, *Science* **218**:28–30. (Second)

Social Science Research Council, Kenneth Prewitt, Frederick Mosteller and Herbert Simon Testify at National Science Foundation Hearings, *Items* **34**(1)March. (Sixth)

Teng Hsiao-Ping. 1979. China's Leaders Explain Views on Science, *Science* **206**:31. (Fourth)

ADDITIONAL REFERENCES

Blaug, M. 1980. *The Methodology of Economics or How Economists Explain*, Cambridge, UK: Cambridge University Press.

Caldwell, Bruce. 1982. *Beyond Positivism: Economic Methodology in the Twentieth Century*, London: Allen and Unwin. (See especially pp. 1–7 and 245–251 on methodological pluralism.)

Feyerabend, P. 1978. *Against Method: An Outline of an Anarchistic Theory of Knowledge*, Great Britain: Redwood Burn Limited Trowbridge & Esher.

Joad, C.E.M. 1957. *Guide to Philosophy*, New York: Dover Publications.

Johnson, Glenn L. (in press). Philosophic Foundations of Agricultural Economics Thought, *A Survey of Agricultural Economics Literature*, Vol. IV, Lee R. Martin, ed., Minneapolis: University of Minnesota Press.

—— 1982. Agro-Ethics, Extension, Research and Teaching, *Southern Journal of Agricultural Economics*, July, pp. 1–10.

—— 1977. Contributions of Economists to a Rational Decision-Making Process in the Field of Agricultural Policy, in *Decision-Making and Agriculture*, T. Dams and K. E. Hunt, eds., Oxford, England: Oxford Agricultural Economics Institute, Papers and Report of the XVI International Conference of Agricultural Economists., pp. 25–46.

—— 1976. Philosophic Foundations: Problems, Knowledge, and Solutions, in *European Review of Agricultural Economic*, 3-2/3, Part II, p. 226.

—— 1961. *A Study of Managerial Processes of Midwestern Farmers*, Ames: Iowa State University Press.

—— and L. K. Zerby. 1973. *What Economists Do About Values*, East Lansing: Department of Agricultural Economics, Michigan State University.

Moore, G. E. 1903. *Principia Ethica*, Cambridge, UK: Cambridge University Press.

Zerby, Lewis K. 1957. The Meaning of "The Unity of Science," *The Centennial Review of Arts and Science*, **1**(2):167–185.

Chapter 3

A Preliminary Overview of Philosophies Important in Economics

This chapter presents a preliminary overview of positivism, normativism, and pragmatism. These philosophies are given special attention because they are so actively and extensively used by research economists that none of them can be ignored in a text on research methodology for economists. There are sections on nonpragmatic prescription and other less-relevant philosophies. The purpose here is to introduce these subjects as a prelude to taking up the first three in more depth in the six chapters of Part I that follow. Chapters 4–6 examine the three main philosophies in more detail, while Chapters 7–9 concentrate on the roles these philosophies play in economics. In this chapter and the next six, we view the philosophies from the standpoint of economists rather than philosophers. This is true even when concentrating on the nature of the three philosophies in Chapters 4–6. Well-trained and well-read philosophers will not find anything new or especially insightful in these chapters. It is hoped only that the treatment is accurate and intelligible to students of economics. The accompanying assigned readings, many from respected philosophers, should offset some of the philosophic shortcomings of this book.

At this point, another disavowal is in order. This book does not survey all philosophies. Instead, it concentrates mainly on three philosophies or categories of philosophy considered of most importance in economic research. Readers of this book and the assigned readings should not assume they will learn about all philosophies or even very much about the three philosophies given special attention.

Courses are available in *the* philosophy of science. The use of the definite article *the* in this connection is unfortunate as many philosophies are relevant for science. Logical positivism tends to dominate the so-called "hard sciences"— the physical and biological sciences—which are really "easy sciences" as they deal with simple phenomena relative to the complex behavior of people studied in the social sciences. If the social sciences are soft, it is because the hardness— the great complexity—of their subject matter has not permitted the establishment of knowledge as firm as that established for the simpler biological and physical sciences. When many refer to *the* philosophy of science, they mean logical positivism. One humorous explanation of this dominance is that no self-respecting person would want to be known as an "illogical negativist."

Courses are also available in philosophic value theory and ethics, which are closely related to economics. As in the case of philosophy of science, different philosophies dealing with values and ethics are useful to economic researchers. I follow May Brodbeck's [1953] view on philosophy of science. She views philosophy of science as about science but not as science or as a part of science. Further, she does not regard philosophy of science as the science of science. Nor does she regard philosophy as the ethics of science. She also rejects the idea that philosophy of science is philosophy of nature. Instead, she is concerned with the principles in the long chain of ideas involved in "scientific concept formation," which extends from the basic abstract concepts expressed in the technical terminology of scientists (of all ilks) to what she refers to as "concrete ordinary language." She makes philosophy of science part of analytic philosophy.

Brodbeck's view seems particularly appropriate for a book about research methodology for economists. Such a title implies that we will examine underlying philosophies. In the case of economics, which has several underlying philosophies, it seems necessary to take an analytical approach to understanding the divergent philosophies relevant for economic researchers. It seems advantageous to avoid studying *the* methodology of science in general when we are interested in the methodology of one science—economics. It also seems desirable to put the ethics of science partly aside since as economists we are more pressed to understand justification for the methods economists use to acquire knowledge about values and derive prescriptions than we are in determining what "ethics" scientists follow or should endorse.

However, this book reaches into ethics and philosophic value theory as called for by the nature of economic research; indeed, as will be elaborated later, economic thought has long been part of these two closely related branches of philosophy. Similarly, we are more interested as economists in how the various philosophic orientations can be used in our work than in espousing any particular philosophic orientation. We want to understand the main contributions of the philosophies underlying economics to the methods used by economists.

We now turn to brief analyses of philosophies important for economists—positivism, various forms of normativism, pragmatism, and a little about existentialism.

POSITIVISM

Positivism is the most recent of the major philosophies to have a substantial influence on economists. One can speculate that this influence originated in the success that physical and biological scientists experienced in using positivistic methods and techniques in their work. Certainly the virtual explosion of knowledge concerning the physical and biological sciences, which was in turn translated into great technological strides, impressed the world and caused many social scientists, including economists and especially psychologists, to emulate the methods and techniques of the physical and biological sciences. This led to consideration of the philosophy of positivism, which undergirds so much of the research done by biological and physical scientists.

In positivism, the emphasis is on knowledge gained through the five senses. Some early forms of positivism (e.g., that of Auguste Comte) relied entirely on the senses, distrusting logic and theory as ways of interpretating sensory experiences. All forms of positivism sought to avoid the theological and the metaphysical, which employed the concepts of divine "will" and "purpose," "forces," and "essences" to explain phenomena. The use of will and purpose was denigrated as teleological. Forces and essences were denigrated as metaphysical. For example, positivists have argued that the statement "water wants to run downhill" has no more empirical meaning than the statement "water runs downhill." They find references to will or purpose to be empirically useless, a suspected source of bias and, at best, unnecessarily complicated. The basic argument is that there can be no genuine empirical knowledge of will or purpose (value) or of forces and essences as parts of an objective natural world. Values were widely regarded by positivists as emotive or as figments of imagination. Positivists assert that values cannot be sensed through the five senses, which rules out experiences of what is valuable. Consequently, it is impossible for positivists to conceive of value concepts as objectively grounded, let alone to conceive of values (concepts of goodness and badness) as features of the real world.

Positivism became so dominant in the second and third decades of this century that it was and still is unjustifiably treated by many as *the* philosophy of science. Consequently, it is now imbedded in the thinking of many members of research communities. Some form of positivism is held by many social scientists as well as physical and biological scientists. One of the consequences is the wide acceptance of a dichotomy between fact and value. The common tendency of positivistic philosophy is to assert that the only facts we can have are those derived from sense experience and, hence, that facts do not include knowledge of values—i.e., of the real value of anything or of value concepts that are descriptive of the real world. Positivists regard such value statements as nonfactual and ungrounded. All we can know about values, according to positivism, is about who behaves as if something were valuable or who holds something to have value.

The fact/value dichotomy of positivism is widely accepted among social scientists as well as physical and biological scientists. For positivism, it is unscientific to try to research values as characteristics of the real world or to use purpose and will as causal "forces." Scientific knowledge (i.e., logically positivistic knowledge), including knowledge of who values what, but not the real value of anything, is regarded as the only form of genuine knowledge. Positivists also identify objectivity with positivistic concepts and subjectivity with normative ones. In practice, all that is necessary to be convicted of subjectivity in the minds of some positivists is to mention value, purpose, or will as descriptive of characteristics of the real world.

Around 1920, positivism as practiced by scientists was described by philosophers and named logical positivism. In logical positivism, empiricism was combined with logic—hence the adjective "logical." In logical positivism, analytical knowledge is viewed as the underpinning for synthetic or empirically descriptive knowledge. Such knowledge also depends on the use of undefined terms based on sensory perceptions. The formal development of logical positivism as a philosophy took place at the hands of many philosophers, many of whom were associated with the so-called Vienna circle that flourished until World War II.

It should be pointed out that logical positivism is now on the wane philosophically and that even some positivists now refer to it in the past tense. A not so recent book entitled *The Legacy of Logical Positivism* [Achinstein and Barker, 1969] states on the dust cover: "Logical positivism *was* (our italics) a controversial, in some ways extreme, philosophical movement that had a profound impact on the philosophy of science—a field which the logical positivists made particularly their own. Moved by admiration for physical science and mathematical logic, they (the logical positivists) urged that all science—indeed all *legitimate* (our italics) inquiries—be patterned after these disciplines."

By contrast to past glorification of positivism, it is now widely recognized that positivism places severe constraints on the social sciences concerned with explaining the behavior of people and groups. In economics, particularly, positivism placed many maximization and minimization studies under a cloud of suspicion. Economists trying to be scientific in the positivistic sense try to purge their research and writing of all references to values as corresponding to something in the real world, in contrast to who values what in a behavioral way, a procedure tantamount to abandoning important parts of economics in its traditional, historical, and even scientific sense. Among the social sciences, psychology was heavily purged of value concepts to win it more acceptability in scientific (positivistic) circles than any other social science. Whether such purging increased the contributions of the discipline of psychology to subject matter and problem solving efforts of psychiatrists is not at all clear to me.

In Chapter 4, positivism will be discussed in considerable detail, with more attention to its present status. In Chapter 7, the implications of positivism for economics research will be explored in still further detail.

NORMATIVISM

Normativism differs from positivism by including a greater variety of substantially divergent views. Positivism was rather well unified under the logical positivists, whereas normativism finds so many different expressions that no single dominant philosophy can be referred to as normativism. Normativism is used here to designate a collection of philosophies concerned with answering questions about value and disvalue (goodness or badness) and rightness or wrongness. Many forms of normativism deal with questions of right and wrong and goodness and badness.

Normative is defined in Runes' *Dictionary of Philosophy*, but normativism is not defined. Normative is defined there [p. 212] by James K. Feibleman as: "Constituting a standard; regulative. Having to do with an established ideal. In scientific method, as concerning those sciences which have subject matter containing values and which set up norms or rules of conduct such as ethics, esthetics, politics." Runes' definition of normative clearly includes rightness and wrongness as well as goodness and badness as discussed in Chapter 2 of this book. By inference, normativism could be regarded as concerned with normative information as defined in Runes' dictionary.

In this book we draw a distinction between logical positivism and normativism that is significantly different from that between knowledge about values and value-free knowledge. While logical positivism stresses the acquisition of positivistic knowledge, it accepts the possibility of acquiring limited kinds of descriptive knowledge about values. Logical positivism accepts research on a behavioristic kind of knowledge about values that includes propositions about what values are attached to what by which person or groups of persons. Such knowledge about values is much more limited than propositions that assert that such and such a condition, situation, event, or thing really has value whether or not someone or some group holds that it does. This lat-

ter type of proposition is excluded by logical positivists from the realm of objective descriptive knowledge. The argument is that there is no basis in sense
experience to support objective claims to knowledge about values, other than
knowledge about who values what. Thus, both logical positivism and various
forms of normativism are capable of generating knowledge about values.
However, the value propositions acceptable for logical positivism are distinctly
more limited than those of normativism.

We found it advantageous in the discussions in Chapter 2 to follow C.
I. Lewis' [1955, p. 55f] and distinguish within normative knowledge between
knowledge about values and prescriptive knowledge, in part because the
prescriptive depends on positivistic knowledge in addition to knowledge about
values. It is extremely important to distinguish between knowledge of values
(about good and bad) and the prescriptive (about right and wrong) as much
confusion and controversy about research methods for economists originates
in the failure to observe this distinction consistently.

The remainder of this section deals largely with philosophic thought about
answering of questions of goodness and badness rather than about questions
as to what it is right or wrong to do. Of the classical literature common to
economics, philosophic value theory, and ethics, we are concerned here mainly with that having to do with values. Several classical economists were also
classical philosophers. This should not be surprising to economists concerned
with values (intrinsic as well as in exchange). Among classical authors common to economics and philosophy are Adam Smith, David Ricardo, Jeremy
Bentham, John Stuart Mill, Karl Marx, Vilfredo Pareto and, currently, Kenneth Arrow. Our concern here is with answering questions about the goodness
or badness of conditions, situations, and things as a basis for reaching prescriptive conclusions about "what ought to be done." Because we are concerned
with research methodology, we seek to understand the justification or basis
(rational and empirical) for descriptive statements about the goodness and
badness of conditions, situations, events, and things. One philosophic work
of particular interest is G. E. Moore's *Principia Ethica* [1903]. We follow Moore
and C. I. Lewis [1955] in distinguishing between knowledge about good and
bad as opposed to knowledge about right and wrong (i.e., between values and
prescriptions), the latter but not the former being about what ought to be.

This overview of normativism is preliminary to the more detailed development found in Chapter 4 and the interpretation of the meaning of normativism
for economic research in Chapter 8.

PRAGMATISM

As pragmatism has played such a dominant role in American public education, almost all U.S. students are significantly influenced by pragmatism. Con-

sciously or unconsciously, most U.S. economists bring to their advanced training substantial philosophic inheritances from pragmatic primary and secondary teachers as well as from the positivists who have dominated both the physical and biological sciences and the creation of the technologies so important in modern life. As the two philosophies can be made compatible only by abandoning significant parts of each, many economists have split "research personalities."

Pragmatism has a special significance and important role in the discipline of economics. John R. Commons, the father of institutional economics in the United States, was clearly influenced by the philosophy of John Dewey, the American pragmatist. Thorstein Veblen, also a founder or forerunner of institutionalism, extensively employed pragmatic ideas. It was Dewey who did so much to give impetus to practical problem solving in American public education after 1900, in contrast to the traditional educational systems of Europe and the early United States, particularly in the deep south and the east.

Dewey's pragmatism found expression in the thinking of the institutional economists, and undoubtedly contributed to their considerable skill in researching the solutions of practical problems. C. S. Peirce, one source of John Dewey's pragmatism, argued: "In order to ascertain the meaning of an intellectual conception one should consider what practical consequences might conceivably result by necessity from the truth of that conception; and the sum of these consequences will constitute the entire meaning of the conception." In Runes' *Dictionary of Philosophy*, V. J. McGill [1961, p. 246] states: "Pragmatism is first and always a doctrine of meaning, and often a definition of truth as well, but as to the latter not all pragmatists are in complete agreement." We also find [pp. 246, 247]: "The hypothesis that works is the *true* one; and *truth* is an abstract noun applied to the collection of cases actual, foreseen and desired, that receive confirmation in their work and consequences."

These quotations indicate that the truth of a concept or proposition is conditional on the problems to be solved as a *consequence* of using those conceptions and propositions.

In Chapter 2 we examined the view that problems are defined and solved on the basis of positivistic knowledge and knowledge about values. The pragmatic view is that the truth of value-free or value propositions depends on the consequences of using that knowledge to solve problems; this *makes value-free and value truths interdependent* in the context of problems. Methodologically, this important implication of pragmatism confronts the positivistic assertion about the impossibility of objective knowledge of values other than knowledge of who values what. Instead of avoiding research on value concepts and propositions as unscientific and unobjective, the pragmatist seeks to understand the interrelationships between positivistic knowledge and knowledge of values. To the pragmatist, research methods that investigate value-free truth without investigating truths about values in terms of their consequences in problematic situations are unacceptable [Parsons, 1958]. Similarly, methods by pragmatists that investigate truths about values without investigating positivistic truths in terms of their joint consequences in solving problems are also unacceptable. By implication, pragmatists reject the separation of positivistic and value knowledge.

In the lay mind, pragmatism is identified with the test of workability in ascertaining the truth of empirical propositions. This is an important characteristic of pragmatism that follows from regarding value-free truth and truth about values as interdependent in the context of the problem being solved.

A moment's reflection will indicate that workability is an irrelevant criterion for a positivist. How can a positivist know objectively whether or not a proposition works in solving a practical problem while rejecting the possibility of objective knowledge of value or purpose as characteristics of a natural objective world or an intersubjectively valid and binding feature of knowing minds?

In this book we treat pragmatism as based on the metaphysical propositions that (1) value-free truth and truth about values are interdependent as a result of their consequences in solving a problem under investigation, and (2) workability is a crucial criterion in judging the truth or falsity of any empirical statement. Pragmatism is viewed as a practical prescriptive philosophy more concerned with decisions about right and wrong that affect actions than with good and bad.

NONPRAGMATIC PRESCRIPTION

Much of ethics and economics determines rightness and wrongness without embracing the pragmatic position that value-free truth and truths about values are interdependent in the context of the problem being solved. C. I. Lewis, in his book *The Ground and Nature of the Right*, is not pragmatic in the sense that he always insists that normative and positivistic truths be regarded as interdependent. In this book, both points of view are treated as potentially relevant.

EXISTENTIALISM

Many philosophies are both conditioned by and influence economic research and economic thought. One such philosophy is existentialism, which is more a way of interpreting life than a guide for research. Basic to existentialism is the conviction that the most certain knowledge one has is knowledge of one's own existence. Along with this proposition in existentialism is the conviction that establishing and extending one's personal identity and role is one's most important activity. Thus, existentialism involves a substantial emphasis on the individual and on individuality. In a sense, one increases one's "certain" knowledge by expanding one's role and identity.

While this emphasis can be perverted to the point where one refuses to let objective knowledge (either value-free or about values) interfere with one's individuality, the emphasis of existentialism on the individual is extremely important in doing problem-solving research, consulting, advising, and carrying out programs of public education. Later, we will see that the crucial role iterative interaction often plays in problem-solving research attests to the importance of individual experiences as sources of the value-free and value knowledge used in solving problems.

REQUIRED READINGS

(Read in Order Indicated)

Brodbeck, May. 1953. The Nature and Function of the Philosophy of Science, in *Readings in the Philosophy of Science*, Feigl, H. and M. Brodbeck, eds., New York: Appleton-Century-Crofts, pp. 3–7. (First)

Cohen, M. R. and E. Nagel. 1934. *An Introduction to Logic and Scientific Method*, New York: Harcourt, pp. 392–397, 399–403. (Second)

Feigl, Herbert. 1953. The Scientific Outlook: Naturalism and Humanism, in *Readings in the Philosophy of Science*, Feigl, H. and M. Brodbeck, eds., New York: Appleton-Century Crofts, pp. 8–10. (Third)

Mitroff, I. I. and M. Turoff. 1973. Whys Behind the Hows: Effective Applications of the Many Forecasting Methods Requires a Grasp of Their Underlying Philosophies, *IEEE Spectrum*, March, pp. 62–71. (Fifth)

Northrop, F. S. C. 1947. *The Logic of the Sciences and the Humanities*, New York: Macmillan, Ch. 1. (Fourth)

Runes, D. D. 1961. *Dictionary of Philosophy*, Paterson, NJ: Littlefield, Adams, pp. 285–286, 243, 136–139, 98–100, 122–123, 327, 150, 315, 76, 245–247. (Sixth)

ADDITIONAL REFERENCES

Achinstein, P. and S. F. Barker (eds.). 1969. *The Legacy of Logical Positivism*. Baltimore, Johns Hopkins Press.

Lewis, C. I. 1955. *The Ground and Nature of the Right*, New York: Columbia University Press.

McGill, V. J. 1961. Pragmatism, *Dictionary of Philosophy*, D. Runes, ed., Paterson, NJ: Littlefield, Adams, pp. 245–247.

Mill, John S. 1936. *Principles of Political Economy*, London: Longmans, Green, (first published in 1848).

Moore, G. E. 1903. *Principia Ethica*, Cambridge, UK: Cambridge University Press.

Parsons, Kenneth. 1958. The Value Problem in Agricultural Policy, in *Agricultural Adjustment Problems in a Growing Economy*, E. Heady, et al., eds., Ames: Iowa State College Press.

Part 1

Philosophic Underpinnings and Basic Methodology

This part of the book develops the reader's understanding of the different philosophic underpinnings for disciplinary, subject-matter, and problem-solving research by economists. Chapters 4–6 treat positivism, normativism, and pragmatism (which underpin research by economists) from the standpoint of the philosopher. Though the terminology and treatment is probably not precise and detailed enough to satisfy a philosopher, it is precise and detailed enough to tax the patience of economists studying research methodology. However, the precision and detail of the philosophic treatments of these chapters are by no means as great as that displayed by research economists working in their own discipline. Chapters 7–9 deal with these same three philosophies, with the focus on the roles they and their associated methods and techniques play in research by economists.

Chapter 4

Positivism

As indicated in Chapter 3, positivism is a relative newcomer among the philosophies important in economics. Its role in economics started prior to the formalization of logical positivism by philosophers. Positivism and its related methods grew out of and, in turn, had great beneficial influence on research in the biological and physical sciences. It was the productivity of positivistic methods in bio/physical sciences that attracted the attention of methodologists in economics and other social sciences, particularly psychology. In economics, positivism's influence has been beneficial, though not without substantial adverse side effects; however, no serious study of methodology in economics can ignore positivism. It behooves economists to know something about its origin, its transformation into logical positivism, its presuppositions, its basic methods, its shortcomings and strengths, and something about its consequences for the three kinds of research with which we are concerned. In this chapter we examine positivism, including its later form (logical positivism), and its methodological implications in a general way, leaving consideration of its specific role in economics until Chapter 7.

41

A BRIEF HISTORY OF THE ORIGIN OF POSITIVISM

Two important empiricists in the history of philosophies of science were Bacon and Locke. They placed heavy emphasis on empirical observations as the source of descriptive knowledge. They opposed such rationalism as that of Descartes and Leibniz. Bacon and Locke "let the facts speak for themselves," unhampered by logic and theoretical systems of analyses they felt would tend to distort the meaning of their observations. Bacon and Locke tended to be strict positivists or narrow inductivists, by contrast with the "logical" positivists who developed later.

Auguste Comte was a philosopher who contributed substantially to the conceptual formalization of positivism as a distinct philosophy. He argued that the highest and most advanced form of knowledge was simple description based on observations from our five senses.

The first stage in the development of knowledge was regarded by Comte to be *theological,* in which explanation was based on anthromorphic (divine) wills and purposes. The second, somewhat more advanced stage in Comte's view, was the *metaphysical,* in which anthromorphic wills were converted to impersonal forces and essences. In the *positivistic* or third most advanced stage, wills and purpose (value) were supposedly removed entirely as a means of explaining observations about real-world phenomenon.

The conversion from narrow inductivism to logical positivism can be viewed as the incorporation into empirical work of the contributions made by such rationalists as Leibniz and Descartes. Scientists began to combine logic and observations in producing descriptive knowledge. With the development of symbolic logic around the turn of the 19th century, philosophers formalized what the scientists were doing. Though logical positivism as a formal philosophy is a product of the first half of the 20th century, logically positivistic research had been done by scientists for decades before its formalization. Members of the "Vienna Circle" attempted to formalize the procedures followed by practicing biological, physical, and some social scientists.

The formal structure for combining logic and experience was alluded to in Chapter 2. Briefly, it consists of using primitive empirical terms to convert uninterpreted or partially interpreted systems of logic into systems supposedly descriptive of phenomena in the real world. The intricacies of this process were studied, formalized, modified, and extended by many people including Cohen and Nagel, Carnap, Kemeny, and Karl Popper. Writings by some of these men are included in the list of assigned readings for this book. The student should read these writings as well as this book in order to better understand the meticulous care with which the underlying philosophy of logical positivism has been studied and how it attempts to specify a general methodology for science. The student should also read the other writings, which recognize the problems of logical positivism that led to the reevaluation of logical positivism and reduced its dominance of philosophy of science.

THE PRESUPPOSITIONS OF POSITIVISM

Though practicing positivistic scientists and the philosophers who formalized logical positivism have attempted to remove the theological and metaphysical from their philosophy, positivism, like all other philosophies germane to science and research, is itself based on empirically untested presuppositions. Experience, as interpreted through the senses, is the fundamental source of descriptive knowledge in positivism. Positivists attempt to confine descriptive knowledge to that which can be acquired from experience through the five senses. It is somewhat paradoxical, therefore, to discover that positivists accept an empirically untested presupposition that goodness or badness are not objectively knowable characteristics of the "real" world to be experienced.

Part of the positivistic position is that knowledge that does not countenance purpose (values) and will is superior to theological knowledge with its personalized supernatural wills, and metaphysical knowledge with its depersonalized wills, purposes, and values expressed as forces and essences. The alleged superiority of positivistic descriptive knowledge seems to be an outgrowth of believing that value concepts and propositions are only products of the mind and, therefore, not objectively knowable as characteristics of the objective natural world.

The positivists, as we will see later, seem willing to make a metaphysical leap of faith that there is something out there in the real world corresponding to their interpretations of sense perceptions insofar as the positivistic characteristics of reality are concerned, but are not willing to do so with respect to value. Instead, they posit that goodness and badness are not characteristics of the objective natural world to be experienced but that the values people attach to conditions, situations, and things are knowable only in the sense of knowledge of who values what. This view may grow out of the failure to distinguish between the good and bad and the right and wrong (which are the logical consequences of decision rules and therefore not parts of the objective natural world to be observed).

LOGICAL POSITIVISM

Three kinds of statements can be made in an "interpreted first-order language" based on standard logic. By "interpreted" we mean a language in which abstract symbols are treated as standing for something regarded as part of the real world. The three kinds of statements are (1) logically true (tautologies), (2) contingent

True Statements					False Statements
Tautological or Analytic Statements			Contingent Synthetic Statements		Contradictory Statements
Purely Logical		Descriptive			
Mathe-matical	Logic in narrow sense	Logically and empirically true—cannot be empirically false	Empirically true but not tautological	Empirically false	Logically false (also, at least partially false empirically, if empirical)
		Applied logic			
Formal Science		Factual Science			

Figure 3. An adaptation of Carnap's truth/falsity diagram

statements that may be true or false, and (3) logically false statements (contradictions). The job of empirical science is to distinguish true from false contingent statements on the basis of sense data and reason.

Carnap [1953, pp. 123f] has outlined the "truth" and falsity of various statements as shown in the following simplification of his figure (Figure 3). All statements are divided by Carnap into true and false statements [Carnap, 1953, p. 124]. Some true statements are analytic (tautologically true), some are empirically or synthetically true, some are both. Those that are empirically but not tautologically true are contingent statements whose truth depends on experience and/or nontautological reasons. On the false side, there are those that are descriptively false as well as those that are logically false.

In Carnap's truth/falsity figure, there are true analytic (tautological) statements that are purely logical and some that, though descriptive, cannot be false because of their tautological structure. Other empirical statements, however, can be descriptively false. There are also descriptive statements based on contradictory logic that are at least partially false as they contradict themselves. Finally, there are purely formal contradictory false statements.

Figure 3 is an incomplete version of Carnap's truth/falsity figure. Carnap's original truth/falsity figure can be found in Carnap [1953]. At the bottom of Figure 3 we see that the tautologically true statements constitute the realm of formal science and that the empirically true contingent statements constitute the realm of the factual sciences. Empirical science also deals with empirically false contingent or synthetic statements.

When we interpret an abstract symbol to have descriptive meaning, we replace the abstract symbol with a term whose meaning is known from experience. Such terms are undefined or experiential and are sometimes referred to as "primitive" or "undefined." They stand for our interpretation of the existential meaning of our sense experiences with something we have "faith" is out there in "reality." Though this discussion is not unique to logical positivism, it does describe much of the methodological view of positivists.

The uniqueness of logical positivism is the position that "values" are constructs of the mind, not characteristics of reality. This position precludes experience of values as characteristics of the real world. It also precludes the use of primitive or undefined experiential terms in interpreting logical systems as descriptive of values as characteristics of the real world.

It is important to note that despite Carnap's terminology positivistic descriptive knowledge is not regarded as knowable with certainty. It would be better, in a sense, to replace "true" under the contingent statement rubric in the Carnap figure with "warranted by empirical evidence though empirically still unproven." Ironically, though, positivism regards descriptive statements about what really has value as meaningless. Note that this does not exclude from positivistic knowledge, behavioristic knowledge about the values people attach to different conditions, situations, and things found in the natural objective world. By accepting the truth of such limited propositions about values, equally limited prescriptive conclusions can be reached about "what ought to be done."

Such conclusions provide the basis for (1) a positive ethics that concerned Morritz Schlick, (2) a positivistic jurisprudence in law, and (3) what we refer to in Chapter 7 as conditional normativism. In positivism, propositions about values based on observed behavior are to be regarded as descriptively true in the sense of truthfully asserting that someone holds those values, but not as true in the sense of describing characteristics of the real world or of expressing something intersubjectively knowable.

Much of the theory of economics is tautologically true and, as such, is part of formal economic science. However, there is much theory and empirical substance in economics that takes the form of empirically testable contingent statements. This portion of economics constitutes factual economic science. It has to do with questions about the numerical values of parameters whose values are not established tautologically in theory. It also has to do with non-tautological implications of the tautologies in theory, as when conclusions tautologically true under the conditions assumed in a theory are extended to situations in which the assumptions are questionable. Economists, whether builders of axiomatic systems as part of formal economic science or constructors and empirical investigators of contingent statements, have much to learn about what they do from a careful study of Carnap's original figure [1953].

Three criteria are commonly used in testing the truth of contingent statements. A statement can be disconfirmed by applying *the test of cor-*

respondence. This test can be applied to a contingent or synthetic statement by comparing it with another statement based on sensory perceptions not used in developing the statement being tested. On deeper reflection, it is evident that we cannot compare a proposition or statement directly with reality to see if there is correspondence. All we can do is use additional observations based on additional experiences to develop an independent proposition or statement about reality to use in testing the proposition being questioned. We cannot do otherwise as it is impossible to put reality into our minds to compare with the proposition being evaluated.

All we can do is experience more of reality through one or more of our five senses, then construct a new proposition on the basis of these experiences that we can compare in our minds with the proposition being tested. For example, in the work of econometricians and economic statisticians, degrees of freedom are observations in excess of the number required to produce a unique estimate of a particular parameter under evaluation. Such degrees of freedom provide the basis for a correspondence test of the parameter that is expressed, in turn, in terms of the statistical significance of the difference between an estimate and an alternative to it.

We also apply the test of coherence—of *logical* coherence. Using the Carnap figure, some descriptive statements can be at least partially disconfirmed as false because they are based on a logical contradiction.

The original positivistic philosophers and others regarded logical (analytical) propositions as provable entirely within a logical system; hence, it was possible, according to that view, to know whether a statement is tautologically true. This view became questionable when Gödel's work demonstrated that even a purely logical system is not entirely provable wholly within itself and, hence, logical truth depends on the truth of something outside the system of logic. Thus, even the portion of Carnap's figure labeled analytically true might be better labeled "not yet found to be a questionable tautology because of something outside the system, though coherence testing is thought to be adequate."

Another test is the test of *clarity* or lack of ambiguity and vagueness. This is a test for the absence of ambiguity in the propositions and concepts being tested. If a proposition or a concept has more than one meaning, it is difficult to apply the tests of coherence and correspondence. Some statements have an infinite number of meanings, others have several, some may have only two. Statements with more than one possible meaning become more difficult to test as the number of meanings increase. In economics this can be illustrated by the econometric concept of "identification" encountered in transforming estimates of the parameters of reduced-form equations into estimates of the parameters of underlying structural equations. An "over identified" system of equations allows more than one estimate of one or more parameters to satisfy the system. An "under identified" system of equations allows an infinite number of estimates of at least one parameter to satisfy the system. In either case, the system suffers from ambiguity—it is vague and, in Popper's terms, not easily falsified. For a "just identified" system there is one and only one estimate for each parameter of the structural system that can be estimated from the parameters of the reduced-form system. This eliminates the ambiguity present in the other two cases.

Karl Popper's stress on falsifiability originates in part with the realization that no universal contingent statement is ever completely provable by empirical observations. It is extremely important to realize the significance of being unable to obtain complete proof of universal contingent descriptive statements. Popper's concern is with the impossibility of ever examining all possible empirical cases. Before one can prove empirically that all swans are white, one must have observed all past, present, and future swans—an obvious impossibility. In addition we, but not necessarily Popper, stress than even singular synthetic statements are not completely provable because our only knowledge of the real world comes from our interpretations of our five sense experiences. Our interpretations can be wrong, as has been demonstrated repeatedly in the history of all sciences.

Further, there is always a *leap of faith* in making synthetic statements. This leap involves the presupposition that there is something "out there" in the real world corresponding with, for example, our interpretation of light stimuli of our retinas or of pressure stimuli of the nerve endings of our fingers. Similar statements can be made about observations based on our senses of smell, hearing, and taste. Our knowledge of the real-world meanings of our sense impressions can never be completely objective as it is always an interpretation of stimulation of our sense receptors. No matter how sophisticated our measuring equipment is, its measurements are eventually expressed in our minds as interpretations of sense impressions. In this sense, empirical science, no matter how "hard" or positivistic, is always less than completely objective.

In addition, there is always a degree of social interdependence involved in the community of scientists (or peer groups) whose agreement on interpretation is essential for the general acceptance of a factual proposition. Before an empirical term can be used in the same way by two people, they must be mutually convinced that each is experiencing the same thing and that the term refers to that experience. Two noncolorblind people can develop a mutual understanding that convinces both of them they are describing an experience with the same condition when the term red is used. Even two people—one colorblind, the other not—can both understand that the noncolorblind person can distinguish between two colors the colorblind person cannot, though the colorblind person simply cannot experience all the color differences experienced by the noncolorblind person.

The terms "validate" and "verify" are often used in connection with knowledge. To some, a statement has validity if it is the consequence of the language and presuppositions of the logical system of which it is a part [Carnap, 1953]—i.e., if it is *coherent*. Similarly, a statement is verified if its consequences are in agreement with experiences with "reality"—i.e., if it *corresponds* with other propositions about "reality" based on additional experiences.

Though these sentences are crude philosophically speaking, they convey intuitive meanings of validation (passing the test of coherence) and verification (passing the test of correspondence) in much positivistic literature. Note that some "systems scientists" and econometricians invert these meanings of validation and verification. Though the resulting pair of conflicting double meanings can be troublesome, the difficulty clears up as soon as the semantic problem is identified. We note that even greater difficulty results from using the words validate and verify to imply that positivistic knowledge is provable rather than just adequately testable for the purpose at hand.

Despite the above, many practicing scientists do not explicitly recognize and acknowledge that contingent empirical statements are never absolutely proven to correspond exactly with reality. They forget that empirical knowledge is only tested enough for coherence, correspondence, and clarity to be warranted as "true enough for the purpose at hand." This characteristic of positivistic knowledge has been amplified and described here in detail in part to make us aware of the limitations of positive knowledge and, hence, more tolerant of the attempts to develop some objective knowledge of real values as characteristics of conditions, situations, and things in the real world.

Though I took several hours of chemistry and closely related subjects in earning a bachelor's degree at the University of Illinois in the late 1930s, I am quite ignorant of the chemistry of the mid-1980s. This would not be very different had I gotten As in every course and not forgotten anything since taking them. Chemistry, as a positivistic science, has continued to develop. The theories on which it is based have been purified, extended, modified. New and powerful measuring instruments have been developed. Biochemistry has grown and developed. Some of what was regarded as true in the 1930s is now regarded as false, and much that was unknown in the 1930s is now included in chemistry or in such related but then virtually nonexistent fields as molecular biology.

The point is that positivistic knowledge is not immutable. Furthermore, it is culturally dependent, generally not completely provable, and results in part from inspiration more akin to revelation than to the process of amassing knowledge through systematic observation and analysis. Value-free positivistic knowledge is fundamentally judgemental in character. Sense impressions are interpreted using the theoretical constructs and logic available at the time in the scientific cultures of scientists. At one time, for instance, scientists generally agreed that the earth was flat. At another time, they believed in two physics—one celestial, one terrestrial—rather than one, as they do now. Neither the observations themselves nor the logic employed in interpreting sense impression is beyond question in the positivistic sciences.

The concept of paradigm, which has gained prominence from the writings of Thomas Kuhn [1970], also challenges us to examine the limitations of scientific and, particularly, positivistic objectivity. Each discipline devises general patterns or ways of acquiring knowledge and of viewing the phenomena of concern to it. Such a "disciplinary matrix" (or paradigm), once established, persists for a substantial time, during which it structures the thinking of the people in the discipline who share it. As Kuhn used the term in his early writing (Blaug, 1980, pp. 31–32), it refers to major patterns within a discipline—for instance, the neoclassical and Keynesian patterns of thought and work within economics. In his later writings, Kuhn preferred the term "disciplinary matrix" to paradigm, and discussed more or less continuous changes in the disciplinary matrix [Blaug, 1980, p. 30].

Paradigms or disciplinary matrices are eventually exhausted in the sense that they yield the answers they are capable of providing and are unable to answer some of the questions that continue to arise in a discipline. The frustrations experienced when an old paradigm confronts insurmountable anomalies leads to the creation of a new paradigm. Kuhn refers to the introduction of a new paradigm into a science as a scientific revolution. Here we see another way in which scientific disciplines and the knowledge they generate are time- and culture-dependent and, indeed, how disciplinary research depends fundamentally on problem-solving and subject-matter research to reveal the shortcomings of paradigms.

When the above difficulties are recognized, disciplinary researchers expect that what is accepted as true today may be disproven tomorrow, as their discipline improves its logic, experiential base, and observational ability or as it responds to new challenges and struggles with old anomalies. A characteristic of positivistic and other scientific methods is that the results are always uncertain to some degree and properly regarded as not completely proven. The strengths lie not in the absence of subjectivity, avoidance of revelation and empathy, lack of metaphysical leaps of faith, or infallibility but lie, instead, in recognition of fallibility, provision for improvement, and provision of forgiveness for being wrong. This self-correcting or self-healing nature of positivistic and other scientific methods is a great strength.

Positivistic and other scientists do not vilify and scourge each other for accepting hypotheses that are later disproved, because positivistic methods and their underlying philosophy indicate that mistakes are inevitable and to be expected. This leads to the self-healing process of correction and improvement. Being incorrect is not really regarded as a sin even if regrettable. About the only sin not forgiven by scientific positivistic cultures is that of "playing God"—asserting that one has perfect knowledge and is such an authority that one's results need not be questioned and tested by fellow scientists. This offense results in excommunication from scientific societies. Again, this stresses the subjective, basically unprovable nature of positivistic knowledge.

POSITIVISTIC DIFFICULTIES WITH VALUES

Positivistic scientists keep encountering arguments that they cannot avoid value judgments. Richard Rudner [1953], in an article entitled "The Scientist Qua Scientist Makes Value Judgements," has examined four such arguments. The first is that having a science at all involves a value judgement. The second is that scientists use value judgements in the process of selecting the problems on which they work. The third is that every scientist as a human being is a mass of predilections and that the value predilections among them must inevitably influence all of their activities including their scientific ones. Rudner, correctly in my opinion, rejects these three arguments as irrelevant to what the scientist does as a scientist.

The fourth argument Rudner examines, however, leads him to the conclusion that scientists (positivistic or otherwise) must make value judgements *as scientists*. Because of the probabilities of being wrong and the different risks involved in accepting various uncertain empirical statements, scientists have to determine what level of evidential support is sufficient to warrant acceptance. In statistical terms, they have to specify confidence intervals for their estimates. They deal with what is an acceptable degree of confirmation "for purposes at hand" by specifying confidence intervals for parameter estimates. Such specification entails matching the cost (sacrificed value) of marginal improvements in such estimates against the value of such marginal improvements. Thus, a scientist's specifications for the test of correspondence of the acceptability of an estimate are based on values.

Rudner points out that the "scientist qua scientist" cannot avoid this by letting the director of his or her research institute or the head of the department set the specifications for the test as this is merely one step in an infinitely long regression. Once an administrative superior sets a specification to be met, the scientist still has to set his or her "own specifications" as to when she or he has met the supervisor's specifications. Regardless of how many supervisors one has, one has to develop specifications as to when the specifications of ones most immediate supervisor are met, and these specifications have to be based on the marginal *costs* and *benefits* for the scientist doing the work of getting more accuracy. Thus, argues Rudner, making value judgements is an inherent part of the work of a scientist as a scientist. Positivism, however, encounters other fundamental difficulties with knowledge about values. As we will see later, Rudner's argument constitutes an argument for pragmatism over logical positivism or, at least, for an eclecticism utilizing both pragmatism and logical positivism.

Rudner's argument is significant in part because of the positivistic assertion that there can be no objective knowledge of what "really" has value beyond behavioristic knowledge of who attaches what value to what. That assertion has had considerable impact beyond constraining the methods of positivism.

Combined with the eminence of positivism (almost as *the* philosophy of science), this assertion has led (unreasonably, it will be argued) to widespread rejection of research on real-world values as unscientific and unobjective. Partly because of this, positivism became a wedge that has for too long separated the sciences from the humanities, while exerting pressure on the decision disciplines to become narrowly behavioristic.

Nonetheless, the concept of objectivity in positivism and positivistic methods has a practical and operational significance going far beyond positivistic research on value-free propositions.

POSITIVISTIC OBJECTIVITY

Two kinds of objectivity can be distinguished—the objectivity *of propositions or concepts* and objectivity of *investigators*.

A *proposition or concept can be regarded as objective* in a particular context if it has been subjected to and has not failed tests of coherence, correspondence, and clarity sufficient for the purposes at hand. Following Rudner, what is "sufficient for the purposes at hand" depends on the marginal cost of getting better evidence for the statement in question. This, in turn, depends on the importance or value of the consequences of accepting and acting on a false statement or of rejecting and not acting on a true one.

A *researcher or investigator can be defined as objective* in a particular context if he is willing to subject his statements to the tests of coherence, correspondence, and clarity sufficient for the purposes at hand and to abide by the results. Conversely, an investigator or researcher not willing to subject his propositions and concepts to the same tests and to abide by the results can be defined as unobjective.

OTHER DIFFICULTIES WITH POSITIVISM

Logical positivism, which flowered in Europe between 1920 and 1940 and in the United States after World War II, is no longer widely accepted by philosophers, even philosophers of science, though it is still widely adhered to by scientists and many who administer research. In addition to the problems referred to above, philosophers have become concerned about the distinction between the analytic and synthetic [Achinstein and Barker, 1960, pp. 229–236]. There are also difficulties with the idea of a purely analytic truth truly independent of prior empirical knowledge. In turn, there are also philosophic difficulties with the supposed certainty of sense impressions apart from interpretive concepts. Nonetheless, scientists in their work use both theoretical concepts and sense experience, though perhaps not exactly as idealized by the logical positivists. This makes it extremely important that the student of methodology be aware of logical positivism's account of scientific method and its philosophic shortcomings.

Gödel demonstrated that no logical system is completely provable entirely within itself, thereby adding logical uncertainty as well as empirical uncertainty about the truth of synthetic knowledge. Page 392 of the *International Encyclopedia of Social Sciences* indicates the importance of the limits Gödel set out formally in the early 1930s when he showed that a formal system capable of being expressed arithmetically does not preclude statements unprovable entirely within the formal system. This difficulty is important for the disciplinary scientists among economists who work on the crucial logical tautologies of concern in formal economic science.

Besides the criticisms mentioned above, students of research methodology should be aware of the destructive arguments of Feyerabend [1978] that oppose the strict methodological views of the logical positivists. Feyerabend identifies the methods of science with logical positivism; hence, he sometimes conveys the impression of being anti-science in his book entitled *Against Methods: An Outline of an Anarchistic Theory of Knowledge* [1976].

Karl Popper's ideas were discussed at some length earlier in this chapter. There is some disagreement as to whether or not Popper is a positivist. His stress on falsifiability and the unprovability of positivistic knowledge makes him appear (1) as antipositivistic to those who tend to regard the positivistic knowledge of science as proven and immutable, but (2) as a mature positivist to those who understood more about the weaknesses and strengths of positivism. Either way, he does not get far beyond positivism as he offers little that is constructive about how to research values and prescriptions in an objective empirical manner. In this respect, he is positivistic.

IMPLICATIONS OF POSITIVISM FOR THE THREE KINDS OF RESEARCH

There is, of course, positivistic disciplinary research in the more positivistic biological and physical science disciplines. Even economists do positivistic disciplinary research. There can also be positivistic research at the subject-matter level. Scientific methods as viewed by positivism have much to contribute to both disciplinary and subject-matter research. Positivism, however, constrains scientists from doing subject-matter research that purports to describe "real" values, though research can be done on who attaches value to what, including the monetary (exchange) values people in economies attach to goods and services. This imposes even severer constraints on problem-solving research as completely objective problem-solving research cannot be done if there can be no objective synthetic knowledge of values as opposed to behavioristic knowledge about who attached what value to what. This seriously constrains researchers engaged in defining and finding solutions to problems.

REQUIRED READINGS

(Read in Order Indicated)

Barker, S. F. 1960. Logical Positivism and the Philosophy of Mathematics, in *The Legacy of Logical Positivism*, P. Achinstein and S. F. Barker, eds., Baltimore: The Johns Hopkins Press, pp. 229–236. (Fifth)

Carnap, Rudolf. 1953. Formal and Factual Science, *Readings in the Philosophy of Science*, Feigl, H. and M. Brodbeck, eds., New York: Appleton-Century Crofts, pp. 123–128. (Second)

Feyerabend, P. 1978. *Against Method: An Outline of an Anarchistic Theory of Knowledge*, Great Britain: Redwood Burn Limited Trowbridge & Esher (Preface, Analytical Index and Introduction). (Fourth)

Rudner, R. 1953. The Scientist Qua Scientist Makes Value Judgements, *The Philosophy of Science* **20**(1):1–6, January. (Third)

Runes, D. D. 1961. *Dictionary of Philosphy*, Paterson, NJ: Littlefield, Adams, pp. 280, 118, 45. (First)

ADDITIONAL REFERENCES

Ayer, A. J. 1959. *Logical Positivism*, New York: Free Press.

Feigl, H. 1969. The Origin and Spirit of Logical Positivism, in *The Legacy of Logical Positivism*, P. Achinstein and S. F. Barker, eds., Baltimore: The Johns Hopkins Press, pp. 3–24.

Kaplan, A. 1968. Positivism, *The International Encyclopedia of the Social Sciences*, Vol. 12, D. L. Sills, ed., New York: Free Press.

Kuhn, T. S. 1970. *The Structure of Scientific Revolutions*, 2nd ed., Chicago: University of Chicago Press, Vol. II, No. 2, pp. 43–51.

Popper, K. R. 1959. *The Logic of Scientific Discovery*, New York: Harper and Row, pp. 40–42, 72–75, 81–84.

Chapter 5

Normativism

Economists have been concerned for centuries with public and private decison-making involving the maximization of both nonmonetary and monetary values. As students of public and private decision-making, economists are deeply concerned about ethical questions. Answering questions about what it is right or economical to do, what it was right or economical to have done, or what ought to be done in the future involves answering preliminary questions about what is good to try to attain or bad and should therefore be avoided. Questions of what is good and bad are fundamentally different from questions of rightness and wrongness [Lewis, 1955]. Acts can also be viewed deontologically, as when the goodness or badness of an act itself is considered, regardless of the goodness or badness of its results relative to the situation modified by the act. For instance, people generally agree that the act of taking a human life is bad regardless of its consequences.

As pointed out in Chapter 2, classical economists have contributed to the classical literature of philosophic value theory and ethics. In addition to this close historical relationship between philosophy and economics, there is a close relationship between ethics and the decision and game theories of economics, both of which are concerned with what constitutes a right decision. This latter relationship seems to be intensifying [McClennen, 1983]. Thus, it is more difficult in the case of normativism than for positivism to separate philosophy from its applications and implications for research in economics and this chapter touches on economics more than Chapter 4.

Normativism in Chapter 2 deals with answers to questions about goodness and badness, with prescriptive questions about rightness and wrongness, and with prescriptions as expressed in laws, rules, recipes, social norms and mores, and regulations.

Our concern in this chapter is not with all normative philosophies. It is with those considering the generation of knowledge about goodness and badness, with lesser attention to those concerned with answers to questions of rightness and wrongness. Economists deal with intrinsic goodness and badness (values) as well as values in exchange. Almost throughout the history of economic thought, economists have been concerned with values— nonmonetary versus monetary and intrinsic versus extrinsic (exchange). Values in exchange are determined by trading off one value against other values in deciding what is right and wrong to do. Further attention to questions of right and wrong will be found in Chapter 6 on pragmatism, and in Chapters 8 and 9, which are concerned with both nonpragmatic and pragmatic prescriptions in economics.

The classical literature common to both economics and philosophic value theory includes the works of Adam Smith, David Ricardo, Jeremy Bentham, N. W. Senior, J. E. Cairnes, J. S. Mill, Vilfredo Pareto, Karl Marx, and the intuitionist Sidgwick. The methodological pronouncements of several classicists advocated a positivistic approach to economics that avoided prescription. However, even people with strong positivistic orientations, such as Senior and Cairnes, became prescriptive in advising and consulting on practical matters.

In classical economic thought there was a tendency to explain value in one of two ways. Some argued that value originates in the effort or cost involved in obtaining a thing or in establishing a condition or situation. Others, such as the utilitarians, argued that value originates in the capacity of conditions, situations, and things to satisfy the needs and demands of people. On the cost of production side, value theories have often been highly specialized, including those of the physiocrats, who tended to build their concepts and propositions around the costs or sacrifices entailed in using land. In another line of thinking (also on the cost side), value was regarded as originating in and as being measurable in terms of the labor used to produce things and to establish conditions and situations. This line of thinking generated the labor theory of value. That theory was important in the thinking of David Ricardo, and was probably brought to its highest stage of development by John Stuart Mill before being extensively used by Karl Marx.

On the demand side, an important development in economics and in philosophic value theory was the development of utilitarianism. Utilitarianism treats the capacity or utility of commodities, services, situations, and things to satisfy human ends (sometimes, but not always, just happiness) as a good to use as a common denominator in solving problems. Utilitarianism is associated with the name Jeremy Bentham. Sidgwick was a somewhat more intuitive utilitarian than Bentham. Utilitarianism in various forms [Hare, 1982] is still a relevant but far from wholly accepted normative philosophy. The many variants of utilitarianism include hedonic (pleasure/pain), nonhedonic, act- and rule-utilitarianism, and individual and social forms. Perhaps it is its flexibility that makes utilitarianism, like the English language, so widely used and criticized.

Until about 1939, many neoclassical economists treated utility as knowable or measureable in an interpersonally valid way. The value or utility of money was taken to be so well-known that one could safely conclude that the utility of an extra dollar was much greater for a poor person who cannot satisfy his material needs for food, clothing, and shelter than for a rich person who can [Cooter and Rappoport, 1984]. Reliance on the empirical validity of this conclusion led to the establishment of many programs in western capitalistic democracies to redistribute the ownership of rights and privileges (wealth) from the advantaged to the disadvantaged on the grounds that total welfare would be increased because the poor could derive more utility from an increment in wealth than the rich who were thus deprived of a unit of wealth. Progressive income taxation is perhaps the most important example. A. C. Pigou's book *Welfare Economics* [1932] was a significant piece of literature that accepted the interpersonal validity of our knowledge of the cardinal utility of wealth and income transferred from the rich to the poor through the power of the state.

In an earlier work, Vilfredo Pareto [Samuels, 1974] raised serious questions about the ability of economists and others to make interpersonally valid measurements of the utility of wealth and income or anything else. He was willing to grant intrapersonal validity of utility or welfare measurements but not interpersonal validity. In 1932, Lionel Robbins also questioned the interpersonal validity of utility measurements. In the late 1930s, John R. Hicks [1939] redid consumption economics in his *Value and Capital* on the assumption that utility was measureable ordinally but not cardinally. He also redid welfare economics on the assumption that utility and welfare are intrapersonally measureable in an ordinal sense but not interpersonally measureable even in an ordinal sense.

His reformulation greatly reduced the self-perceived capacity of economists to reach conclusions favorable to the forcible redistribution of the ownership of all rights and privileges, including the ownership of wealth from the rich to the poor. Cooter and Rappoport [1984] now question this development. They hold that Pigou (and Marshall) may have been factually correct in concluding that the marginal utility of income for the poor is cardinally greater than for the rich and that this justifies redistribution.

OBJECTIVE NORMATIVISM

Of the normative philosophies, the ones of most interest to people concerned with economics are those that provide some help or hope, at least, of being able to do objective descriptive research on the values that conditions, situations, and things "really have." In Chapter 4 we saw that positivism, despite its reputation for being objective and impersonal, is culturally dependent, judgemental, and subjective. In discussing positivism in Chapter 4, we noted the subjective nature of our interpretations of sense impressions, Gödel's question about the provability of logical systems wholly within themselves, and the roles of faith, insight, group approval, and intuition in positivistic methods. Still further, Rudner's analysis [1953] demonstrated that value judgements are an essential part of value-free positive investigations. Recognition of these characteristics of value-free positivistic knowledge and research has an advantage. The advantage is that it then appears less ambitious to aspire to objective descriptive knowledge of "real" values. One can even aspire to combining logical positivism, normativism, and even pragmatism into an eclecticism or a synthesis that deals objectively with both values and value-free positivistic knowledge.

Fortunately, considerable progress has been made toward an objective normativism. One path involves the work of G. E. Moore [1956] who, at the turn of the century, made substantial contributions to this end. He partially opened the door to use of the methods and techniques of positivism in investigating goodness and badness by arguing that propositions about goodness are always synthetic and never analytic.

Moore believed that good and bad are not defined terms; instead, he treated them as primitive terms whose meanings are known from experience. In doing so, he implied that individuals in a group experiencing the goodness of a given condition, situation, or thing eventually learn to communicate about goodness and badness and to know and understand what is meant when the characteristic of goodness or badness is ascribed to a particular condition, situation, or thing. However, he did not regard goodness and badness as characteristics of the natural objective world though, as will be discussed later, his reasons for not doing so are not entirely clear to me. It is interesting that Pirsig, who wrote *Zen and the Art of Motorcycle Maintenance: An Inquiry Into Values* [1974], treats quality or value much as G. E. Moore does, though there is little evidence in his book that Pirsig ever read Moore's *Principia Ethica*. Pirsig has an interesting account of how to demonstrate that quality in writing is undefinable but demonstrable and experienceable. From page 200 and the following pages, we print, with the permission of William Morrow, the publisher,

> Quality is a characteristic . . . that is recognized by a nonthinking process. Because definitions are a product of rigid, formal thinking, quality cannot be defined . . . you know what Quality is.

His students protested

"Oh no, we don't!"
"Oh yes, you do."
"Oh *no*, we *don't*!"
"Oh yes, you *do*!"

and he was

> . . . ready to demonstrate it to them. He had selected two examples of student composition . . . [He] read both, then asked for a show of hands on who thought the first best. Two hands went up. He asked how many liked the second better. Twenty-eight hands went up.

> "Whatever it is, he said, "that caused the overwhelming majority to raise their hands for the second one is what I mean by Quality. So *you* know what it is."

Similarly, Moore rejected all attempts to define goodness, holding instead to the position that we know different goodnesses and badnesses by experiencing them rather than as a result of definitions.

Undefined value terms make it possible to proceed in a manner parallel to that of the positivist to interpret formal nondescriptive logical statements as descriptive synthetic value statements by substituting primitive value terms for the formal terms in analytical statements. These resultant interpreted statements lead in turn to contingent statements about values that can be tested by the rules of logic and by appeal to experience.

There is a parallel between what takes place in forming value perceptions and value-free positivistic perceptions. A first step in perceiving redness is to experience certain stimuli of the nerve endings in the retinas of our eyes. Similarly, a first step in perceiving the badness of a burn is to experience certain stimuli of the nerve endings of the area of our body that is burned. In the case of redness, the next step is to interpret the meaning of the stimuli of our retinas in terms of a mental formulation (or view of the world) about differences in color and the different consequences of such color differences. Similarly, in the case of the badness of a burn, the next step is to interpret the meaning of the stimuli of nerve endings in terms of a mental formulation about the different amounts and kinds of good and bad consequences of different amounts of heat applied to the skin.

Admittedly, the mental formulations are different, one being evaluative, the other not being evaluative, but both are mental and products of the mind and both require a leap of faith that there is something "out there" in "reality" to correspond to a mental formulation.

The tests of correspondence as well as coherence stressed by the positivists become applicable to contingent-value statements. As on the positive side, comprehensiveness becomes important because the more experiences with values that can be explained, the greater the coherence and the greater the degree of correspondence. Also as on the positive side, clarity is important as it is difficult to apply the tests of coherence and correspondence to ambiguous statements about values.

The above extension of Moore's position receives general support from Michael Scriven, who argued [1969, p. 199f] in *The Legacy of Logical Positivism* against the positivistic idea of a value-free social science. He found that the idea is an incredible gaffe originating in several mistakes. He argued, contrary to those seeking value-free social sciences, that the preferences of people not only provide a basis for concluding that value is attached to conditions, situations, and things but also a basis for factual judgements about the superiority of, say, the Salk vaccine over physical therapy for preventing infantile paralysis even for a group of people who do not know and, hence, do not hold that Salk vaccine is good.

Scriven implies that value judgements can be as factual as judgements about the value-free positivistic nature of reality. Both, of course, have to be based on "leaps of faith" that there is something in the real world corresponding to our perceptions and our mental formulations or "views of the world" employed in interpreting the sense impressions of scientists and lay people.

The real question that has to be settled by anyone taking seriously the idea that our knowledge of values can be descriptive of characteristics of the objective natural world is whether or not we experience the goodness and badness of such things as injustice, justice, a healthy well-developed body, the badness of a lingering death from cancer or starvation, Salk vaccine, the beauty of a colorful sunset, or the goodnesses of family and friends. If one answers this question negatively, saying instead that such goodnesses and badnesses are not experienced but are just matters of emotion and that there is no reality corresponding to such propositions and concepts, one has to remain a positivist and reject methods for deriving objective descriptive knowledge of values from experiences. If, on the other hand, one believes that we experience goodness and accepts the above-described parallel, then methods very similar to those employed by the positivists can be used to develop objective knowledge about values conceived as real.

With respect to value-free positive knowledge, it is important to recall that methods used in acquiring such knowledge involve the subjectivity of sense impressions, the necessity of interpreting sense impressions, leaps of faith from sense impressions to reality, insight, intuition, and the need for interpersonal acceptance of perceptions of reality. This leads to the position that objective descriptive knowledge about the value of conditions, situations, and things is fundamentally similar to knowledge on the value-free positivistic side, and that both value-free positivistic and value propositions are judgemental in nature. We also note that on both sides we have to put up with both probability distributions and the possibility of making mistakes in interpreting our sense impressions and in employing our logic. Further, it should be kept strictly in mind that we are only considering knowledge of values here and are excluding prescriptive knowledge of rightness and wrongness.

Rightness and wrongness are more complicated matters involving value-free positivistic knowledge as well as knowledge about values, not to mention (1) decision rules for deriving conclusions about rightness and wrongness from both kinds of knowledge, and (2) the conflict-resolving role of power distributions in decision rules. Self interest and distributions of power are inherent in making decisions about rightness and wrongness in a manner not inherent in either research on value-free positivistic or value questions other than in the decisions of positivistic and value researchers as to whether their knowledge has been adequately tested [Rudner, 1953]. There is, of course, the problem that arises from being able to see the consequences of either value-free positivistic or value knowledge for prescriptions as to what is right. Ability to see such consequences can be a source of bias whenever positivistic or value researchers view the prescriptive consequences of objective knowledge as adverse to their own interests.

With respect to values, communities of objective scholars are no more tolerant of people who assert they have perfect knowledge of values than are the corresponding communities of positivist scholars tolerant of those who assert they have perfect value-free positivistic knowledge. To assert one has perfect knowledge is to "play God" and to risk excommunication by communities of scholars attempting to maintain objectivity whether the knowledge sought is value-free or about values. On both sides, the objectivity of researchers can be understood to be a willingness on their part to subject synthetic descriptive propositions to the tests of coherence, correspondence, and clarity, and to abide by the results.

As I believe is the case for value-free knowledge, I believe that society improves its knowledge about values over time. For example, I have often reflected about family accounts of my grandfather, who took part in the Civil War. Grandfather was a young volunteer on the Union side. Family accounts indicate that his knowledge of the goodness of many aspects of racial equality was limited, and that he did not conceive of the goodness or badness of many things, conditions, and situations in the relationships between races that we now treat as factually good or bad. It is probably fair to say that grandfather thought a black person should be treated at least as well as a horse and that neither should be unduly punished, overworked, or deprived of such rights and privileges as food, water, and protection from the elements.

It appears that the rate at which American society has been learning about values in relation to race has increased rapidly since the early 1960s. Our knowledge of the goodness and badness of the many complex dimensions of racial inequality and equality has deepened greatly as a result of our experiences and logical thinking since 1864. There seems to have been an explosion of knowledge of values in this area in recent years resulting from making our values logically more consistent with each other and especially with the goodnesses and badnesses we have experienced in differing relationships between races.

In considering the possible objectivity or lack of objectivity of value statements, it is important to consider two fallacies G. E. Moore regarded as important. He distinguished between the naturalistic and metaphysical fallacies in connection with knowledge of good and bad. According to Moore, the naturalistic fallacy consists of defining goodness to be that which possesses the characteristic of goodness—e.g., the mistake of defining goodness to be life because life possesses the characteristic of goodness. The metaphysical fallacy consists of asserting something to be good without regard to experience—e.g., of designating a vaccine as good without first experiencing its goodness.

It seems that a logical or semantic difficulty may exist with respect to Moore's naturalistic fallacy. For instance, he wrote, " 'Good,' then, if we mean by it that *quality* (our italics) which we assert to belong to a thing, when we say that the thing is good, is incapable of any definition . . ." [Moore, 1959, p. 9]. Two pages earlier he wrote ". . . propositions about the good are all of them synthetic and never analytic." Note that he is writing about the use of the word good as an adjective—i.e., as when we say that a healthy body is good, or state that something possesses the characteristic of goodness just as some varieties of ripe apples may be described as possessing the characteristic of redness.

The naturalistic fallacy consists of defining that which possesses the quality of goodness to be not merely good but to be goodness itself. Whether life or justice "naturally" or "really" possess the characteristic of goodness is a different question than whether either is goodness (a noun). A "yes" answer to the latter question would enable life or justice to serve as a common denominator for the goodnesses possessed by other entities. Moore writes that the "naturalistic fallacy . . . consists in identifying the simple notion which we mean by 'good' with some other notion" [Moore, 1959, p. 58].

The confusion about the naturalistic fallacy that seems to need clarification is not one of regarding the goodness one experiences to be a characteristic of the natural world. Instead, the naturalistic fallacy is one of mistaking that which possesses the characteristic of goodness for goodness itself. Though it may be empirically true that an apple is red (an adjective), it is not true that red (a noun) is an apple. Similarly, while it seems experientially true that cancer of the colon is bad (an adjective), it is not true that bad (a noun) is cancer of the colon. Both the redness of apples and the badness of cancer, however, appear to me to be viewable as describing characteristics of the natural world without committing the fallacies of regarding an apple as redness or cancer of the colon as badness.

Moore's justified aversion for the naturalistic fallacy seems to have led him to reject somewhat inconsistently the related important possibility that goodness and badness may in some instances be regarded as "real world" natural attributes. To so view goodness is consistent with Moore's position that goodness is undefinable but experienceable, with his concept of the naturalistic fallacy, and with his view that goodness as a primitive undefined term is always synthetic and never analytic. In this book we extend Moore's ideas about the undefinable synthetic nature of knowledge about values to include the possibility of objective knowledge of the "real" values of conditions, situations, and things in the empirical world we know through our five senses while continuing to deplore and trying to avoid Moore's naturalistic fallacy.

In doing this it is important to stress (1) that we are using methods and procedures already in the tool kit of the logical positivists, and (2) the uncertain nature of positivistic knowledge. To do what is proposed here requires a leap of faith that there is a reality about values to be known—a leap, however, that seems no more drastic with respect to the goodness of Salk vaccine and the badness of leukemia, poverty, and starvation than it is with respect to a positive proposition about the level of the sea or the straightness of a specific road.

Conversely, the agreed-on superiority of one line of Bach's music with respect to another seems as certain or more certain than an assertion in physics that one of the various competing value-free positivistic propositions about the fundamental particle of matter is the empirically true one. Similarly, the cultural dependency; the fundamental unprovability of descriptive propositions; the roles of insight, empathy, and inspiration; and the questions raised by the pragmatists are as troublesome for those researching value-free positivistic as for those researching value questions.

IMPLICATIONS FOR THE THREE KINDS OF RESEACH

Moore's arguments in support of objective experiential knowledge of values and our extension of his arguments have major implications for the three different kinds of research. Moore's arguments have largely been ignored by the western world for several decades, probably because of the position of logical positivism as *the* philosophy of science and, in the United States for an additional reason—the tendency of pragmatism to dominate American education. Because of positivism, attempts to answer questions about values as characteristics of the real world have often been denigrated as unobjective, unscientific and, hence, as an unsuitable activity for a scientific researcher. Now that logical positivism is in substantial intellectual trouble, however, it is becoming more "respectable" to consider the possibilities of objective knowledge of values and to do empirical research on questions about the values of different conditions, situations, and things. This development, in my view, comes none too soon, for we are in serious disarray about how to deal with values in making public choices on major problems involving minorities, poverty, injustice, the exhaustion of fossil energy, starvation and malnutrition around the world, food chain contamination, science policy, and environmental quality.

Implications for Disciplinary Research

The implications of the above discussions suggest that it may be possible to do empirical disciplinary research on the values conditions, situations, and things really have in the decision disciplines. There are reasons for believing that questions about values can be researched and answered following methods implied by the Moore argument as extended here. Thus, empirical disciplinary research on the real values of conditions, situations, and things tends to be legitimized.

Implications for Subject-Matter Research

Subject-matter research, as we have previously seen, can seek value-free positivistic knowledge, knowledge about real values, or both. Our extension of Moore's legitimizing arguments concerning objective knowledge of goodness and badness opens the way for objective subject-matter research on either values alone or in combination with value-free positivistic inquiries.

Implications for Problem-Solving Research

It is with respect to problem-solving research that the possibility of objective research on values as characteristics of the real world has its greatest implication. Research on values (beyond who holds what values about what) is necessary if problem-solving research is to deal with the attainment of more than emotive, arbitrary, or unreflective and unexperienced values. The goodness and badness of the consequences of alternative prescriptions to solve a problem can be investigated using positivistic methods according to Moore's arguments as extended here. Further, the goodness and badness of decision rules used to process value-free and value information into prescriptions about which decision rule to use can also be objectively investigated.

REQUIRED READINGS

(Read in Order Indicated)

Bentham, Jeremy. 1950. An Introduction to the Principles of Morals and Legislation, *Ethical Theories*, in A. I. Meldon, ed., Englewood Cliffs, NJ: Prentice-Hall, pp. 248–263. (Second)

makes value-free knowledge and knowledge about values interdependent with their empirical truth determined by the consequences). The Oxford empiricist, F.C.S. Shiller, is quoted in Runes [p. 246] as stating, "In validating our claims to truth . . . we really transform . . . [realities] by our cognitive efforts, thereby proving our desires and ideas to be real forces in the shaping of the world."

John Dewey's pragmatism is often called instrumentalism. Runes' dictionary also quotes [p. 246] Dewey as stating:

> When the claim or pretention or plan is acted upon, it guides us *truly* or *falsely*: it leads us to our end or away from it. Its active, dynamic function is the all important thing about it, and in the quality of activity induced by it lies all its truth and falsity. The hypothesis that works is a true one and truth is an abstract noun applied to the collection of cases actual, foreseen and desired that receive confirmation in their work and consequences.

Thus we see that the two underlying tenets of pragmatic philosophy are (1) the interdependence of positivistic and value propositions because of the mutual dependence of their truth on their practical consequences in real-world problem-solving situations, and (2) the importance of the test of workability, which makes truth dependent on use as an instrument in attaining ends determined by the context of the problem at hand.

The pragmatists are interested in "scientific" problem solving. A typical pragmatic statement or outline of the problem-solving processes follows [Whitney, 1946, p. 14]:

1. The existence of a felt difficulty (note: This indicates a practical problem, not a disciplinary question).
2. Defining the difficulty.
3. Finding a tentative solution.
4. The development of hypotheses concerning solutions to the problem, leading to the elaboration and investigation of alternative solutions to the problem, leading to (note: the hypothesis is prescriptive),
5. the belief that the solution (a hypothesized one) is appropriate.
6. An experimental verification.
7. Evaluation of the results of that experimentation to determine if the hypothetical solution really works. If not, the process is repeated until a solution is reached.
8. A forward look or simulation of future situations in which the solution would be used.

Though this outline of the problem-solving process is similar to the figure presented in Chapter 2, there are important differences. It contains no separate information or data banks for positivistic and normative information, since pragmatists would be uneasy with the separation of knowledge into positivistic value-free and value components however much they may appreciate the figure's "pragmatic" loop between them. Furthermore, because the truth of propositions depends on their practical consequences, the likelihood of data or information retaining truth from one problem to another would tend to be viewed by the pragmatists as justifying less data banking than practiced by logical positivists.

The hypotheses generated by the pragmatists are mainly prescriptive, in contrast to the positivistic value-free and value hypotheses of concern to positivists and normativists. I have observed pragmatists and positivists agree on the importance of testing hypotheses in research without realizing that their primary concerns were with sharply different kinds of hypotheses. A thoroughgoing positivist, for instance, would not be able to conceive of objectively testing the value propositions on which a prescription is based if those propositions are interpreted as representing knowledge of the values that conditions, situations, and things really have. Indeed, even the pragmatic test of workability is relatively meaningless or arbitrary to a positivist because he does not conceive of an objective way of knowing whether a consequence is really good or bad and, hence, whether a practical problem really existed and whether it was solved.

In pragmatism, one of two competing hypotheses is treated as a thesis, the other as its antithesis. The dialectics of pragmatism thus involves a conflict between competing prescriptions. Conflict resolution has to do with testing one prescriptive hypothesis against another. Positivism, too, is dialectic in that whatever is accepted as true at one point in time and in one culture is always to be challenged by an opposing hypothesis. It is this special form of dialecticism in positivistic science that makes it self-correcting. The difference between positivism and pragmatism is not so much that one is dialectic while the other is not as that they are dialectic about different things. Pragmatism is dialectic about prescriptive hypotheses. Positivism is dialectic about positivistic hypotheses. There is, of course, a corresponding dialectic about values in various forms of normativism.

LACK OF CLARITY ABOUT INTRINSIC, INSTRUMENTAL, AND EXCHANGE VALUES IN PRAGMATISM

Philosophers and economists distinguish between intrinsic and extrinsic values. A condition, situation, or thing can be said to have intrinsic value when it has value independent of the value it has as a means of attaining or acquiring something else. For example, a gold coin in a country on a gold standard has intrinsic value as gold that is not characteristic of paper currency of the same denomination, though both have the same exchange value. The exchange or extrinsic values of concern to economists may or may not be monetized. Exchange or extrinsic values of particular importance for economics include the extrinsic values that arise because things are instruments for attaining other things of more intrinsic value—for example, when the value of nitrogen arises because it is a means of producing corn.

It seems to me that the distinction between intrinsic and instrumental or exchange values is sometimes partially lost by the pragmatists, perhaps to the extent of abandoning the idea of intrinsic value entirely. When the consequences of a proposition are regarded by pragmatists as constituting the whole truth about it, the idea of intrinsic values or values independent of problematic situations becomes tenuous.

I find it significant that Runes' *Dictionary of Philosophy* contains no references to monetary values in exchange or to Alfred Marshall's and Clark's combination of cost of production and demand explanations of value into a single explanation of values in exchange. Marshall and Clark deduced that equilibrium values in exchange are determined in markets (large and small, monetized and nonmonetized) in the process of balancing off intrinsic as well as extrinsic or instrumental values against each other in the trades that take place in markets and in the totality of society.

PRAGMATIC TESTS FOR TRUTH

The prescriptive hypotheses of pragmatism are tested as to their workability, coherence, and clarity. The test of workability determines whether the prescriptive hypothesis best solves the practical problem under investigation. The clarity test (important for using the coherence or correspondence test in positivism) is also important in pragmatism. Clarity or the lack of ambiguity is important in testing for logical coherence and does not lose its importance because truth is regarded as determined by the consequences of prescriptions determined in part by decision rules and, hence, not observable. Before the pragmatic test of workability can be applied to a pragmatic prescriptive hypothesis, the nature of the expected consequences of the hypothesis must be unambiguously stated. The test is one of determining whether the hypothesis is or is not the logical consequence within the decision rule of the interdependent positivistic and value knowledge accepted as true for purposes of solving the problem.

Note that it is difficult to regard the pragmatic test of workability as a test of correspondence. Testing the workability of value and positivistic judgements conceived to be interdependent is more complex and involved than when they are conceived as independent. In addition, all prescriptions (pragmatic or not) are complex and difficult to evaluate because prescriptions depend on both positivistic and value knowledge from many disciplines, with the prescriptions not being experiential.

Prescriptive hypotheses are difficult to verify with the test of correspondence *prior* to acting on the prescription, as the test of correspondence cannot be applied *ex ante*. Prior to the act, all that can be done is apply the correspondence test to the value-free and value knowledge entering into the decision process that produced the decisions. This, however, is not satisfactory to pragmatists, who hold that value-free and value truths are interdependent and determined by their consequences, which include those of the prescriptions they generate. Pragmatists, therefore, are constrained in their ex ante evaluation of prescriptions to the use of the coherence test and a consideration of the simulated expected consequences of the prescribed act. Ex post (after the act), pragmatists can apply the correspondence test to consequent goodnesses attained, badnesses avoided, and positivistic circumstances that evolve, but hardly to the rightness and wrongness of the prescription that was determined as the consequence of using a decision rule rather than being something that can be experienced.

Another difficulty for pragmatic evaluators of prescriptive hypotheses is that pragmatists regard the observable value-free and value consequences of actions as interdependent in the context of the problem the act is designed to alleviate. Nonpragmatic prescribers are freer than pragmatic ones to apply independent correspondence tests to value-free positivistic and value knowledge (if they are not so positivistic as to believe that the part of the latter pertaining to "real" values cannot be tested for correspondence). However, like pragmatic prescribers, they must await the outcome of prescribed acts before testing the value-free and value outcomes of a prescription for correspondence. Ex post, both encounter the definitional nonexperiential nature of the rightness and wrongness of prescriptions.

In this connection, it is worth recalling the Rudner argument, presented in Chapter 4, that scientists as scientists unavoidably encounter the need to use values as an integral part of their work. Fundamentally, Rudner's argument is pragmatic because it makes what is warrantable as true dependent on the problem(s) it is to be used to solve.

The prescriptions of pragmatists, like all prescriptions, are relatively ephemeral. Consequently, pragmatists tend not to accumulate banks of tested value-free and value information to be stored and applied repeatedly in the solution of problems. Instead, they conceive their interdependent value-free and value information as problem- and time-dependent. This makes history and case studies more important than data banks and leads to the "story telling" on the part of the pragmatic institutional economists so deplored by Blaug [1980, p. 127]. The difficulties noted in Chapters 4 and 5 that are created for the positivists and normativists by the cultural dependency of their knowledge, and the roles that faith, empathy, and intuition play in the creation of knowledge, are multiplied manyfold for the pragmatists, who extend dependency to problems as well as cultures.

THE PRAGMATIC INTEREST IN TIME AND IN WHO IS BENEFITTED AND HARMED: INTERACTION AND ITERATION

The pragmatic insistence that the truth of a proposition depends on its consequences implies an interest both in time and in who is benefitted and harmed through time. Pragmatic economists are interested in history, time-series analysis of the past, case histories or stories, and informal, if not formal, simulations of the future. Some of the important economic historians such as O. C. Stine of the U.S. Department of Agriculture and Wesley Mitchell were pragmatic institutionalists in their training. Their work and that of the German historical school are closely related. Initially, solutions that are prescriptive and depend on both value-free and value knowledge of problems are stated as goals or targets—as states of affairs to be brought about. Knowing the consequences of a prescription requires knowledge of who it will hurt and benefit, how, when and where.

This interest in time, space, and the incidence of benefits and damages often makes it important that there be an interaction between investigators, decision makers, and those likely to be affected by the prescriptions of decision makers. Such interaction is extremely helpful in more fully envisioning the future consequences of any proposition (value-free or about values) or prescriptive hypothesis. Hence, interaction is a source of knowledge for pragmatists and others as well. Interaction of researchers with decision makers is important as the latter bear responsibility for executing prescriptions. The same is true for interaction with people who are affected by the consequences of decisions executed.

Iteration is also important because the interactions between investigators, decision makers, and affected people often result in the rejection of poor prescriptive hypotheses and the acceptance of superior ones. This is recognized with the two-way arrows in Figure 2 of the problem-solving process presented in Chapter 2. The interests of pragmatists in time, space, and in who is benefitted and damaged, where, and how, makes interaction important in pragmatism. This iterative/interaction is part of the dialectics of pragmatism. Later it will be seen that there is a close though not well-recognized relationship between the iterative/interaction of pragmatism and the simulation techniques used by applied systems scientists.

PRAGMATISM AND DIALECTICAL MATERIALISM RELATED

While pragmatism and the dialectical materialism of Marxism are not identical, there are important similarities. Both are dialectical with respect to prescriptions. Both are concerned with material consequences, though pragmatism less exclusively than dialectical materialism. Both regard the world as in a continual process of change. Both are interested in time, history, and the future. Both are interested in solving social problems, yet pragmatism has not become a part of a political movement as has the dialectical materialism of Marxism.

It is also interesting to note the similarities in the roles played by dialectical materialism in Soviet society and by pragmatism in American education. In both, heavy emphasis has been placed on solving practical problems. The Soviet state embraced dialectical materialism, and with it attempted to focus the attention of academicians on solving the practical problems of the state. The government has tried to insist that art be devoted to the evolution of societies desired by Marx and Engels. Dialectical materialism tends to eliminate disciplinary positivistic research in the biological and physical sciences and investigation of values in the humanities except as they are relevant to the purposes of a Marxist state.

In American education, pragmatism, or what came to be called modern education in the first half of the 20th century, has tended to downplay the roles of the scientific (positivistic) and humanistic (normative) disciplines and to concentrate the attention of educators and students on the solution of practical problems of individuals and the state. Pragmatic intellectuals in colleges of education have favored vocationalism and problem solving over the classical disciplines of the sciences, arts, and humanities.

The interesting thing is that neither the dialectical materialism of the Soviet government nor the pragmatism of American education has been able to carry the day completely in the universities of their countries. The independent positivistic sciences and the humanistic disciplines of the Soviet Union have at least partially survived, and through their survival have made substantial contributions to Soviet society and the Soviet state. Similarly, the positivistic and normative disciplines in the sciences, arts, and humanities of American universities have not become completely subservient to the pragmatic solving of the problems of decision makers in U.S. society. There continues to be an important role in U.S. education for disciplinarians who concentrate on positivistic and normative disciplines independently of each other without major emphasis on practical problem-solving research, and that role has permitted them to make important disciplinary contributions to U.S. society.

THE UNITY OF SCIENCE, PRAGMATISM, AND POSITIVISM

The unity of science movement has included such pragmatists as C. W. Morris as well as leading positivists. The stress has been on the unity of the language of science, the need to adapt terminologies in different sciences to each other, and the hope for a fundamental set of laws applicable across the sciences. The late Lewis Zerby [1957] examined "The Meaning of the Unity of Science" with respect to laws, methods, and language. He concluded that there was little unity of science as far as scientific law and method were concerned, but that the unity that existed was in the language of science, a conclusion that still seems to hold.

The methods of different disciplines are still related to their underlying philosophies and the phenomena they study. Thus, methods vary widely from the positivistic biological and physical sciences at one extreme to esthetics at the other. Pragmatists, with their interest in decision-making (ethics), are philosophically equipped to deal with both value-free and normative knowledge, but in a way that partially denies the methods of positivists and many normativists. The quest for unity in method is a quest for a unity in philosophic orientation, a goal not easily achievable given the diversity of views in the history of philosophy.

Members of the decision disciplines—e.g., economics, medicine, law, architecture, engineering, military science, dentistry—feel a particularly intense need for unity of the sciences. Some of the decision disciplines are pragmatic, the institutionalist part of economics being an outstanding example. Some of the nonpragmatic decision disciplines involve so-called "scientific (positivistic)" and "art" phases. The latter phase includes the work of substantial numbers of nonpragmatic economists. Again, we find a lack of unity, even among the decision disciplines, on methods for providing the information needed in making decisions.

Though the unity of science movement seeks a methodological unity that could be useful to the decision disciplines, it appears that these disciplines will have to get along without this unity for some time. In this book on research methodology for one of the decision disciplines—economics—we have to get along with a tentative mixture of methods and philosophies useful in acquiring, testing, and analyzing different kinds of knowledge—positivistic value-free, about values, and prescriptive. Pragmatism certainly provides a necessary component for this mixture and probably contributes to the needed unity. The contribution of pragmatism to the unity of science is apparent from Rudner's pragmatic analysis of the essential role played by values in science and by the gap left for pragmatism to fill in problem-solving research when mainly positivism and normativism is used.

In Chapter 9, it is noted that the econometrician, Georgescu-Roegen, argues that entropy makes physics—the crown jewel of positivism— fundamentally pragmatic. There is hope that we may be acquiring the ingredients for synthesizing a more unified approach to science than we now have. At present, eclecticism seems more assured than a synthesis.

STRENGTHS AND WEAKNESSES OF PRAGMATISM

It seems worthwhile now to discuss some of the strengths and weaknesses of pragmatism. As will be seen in Chapter 9, the strengths of pragmatism for economics are substantial. A textbook on research methodology for economists should sympathetically consider the major contributions of the pragmatic institutional economists, though recent books by Blaug [1980] and Caldwell [1982] give little sympathetic attention to the pragmatism of institutional economics. The low regard of these two authors for institutional economics, with its pragmatic underpinnings, seems to be based on (1) a high regard for disciplinary contributions they fault institutional economics for not producing, and (2) a lack of attention to the substantial practical contributions of the institutionalists. At the same time, the obvious weaknesses of pragmatic methodologies cannot be ignored.

Strengths

The first strength of pragmatism is that it addresses real-world problems and their solutions. Pragmatism was attractive in American education because Americans needed solutions to problems and were dissatisfied with traditional education, which placed disciplinary emphasis on religion, law, sciences, humanities, and arts, to the neglect of the practical problems faced by producers (farmers, manufacturers, tradesmen), consumers, and public decision makers.

A second strength of pragmatism is that it breaks down the barriers between the traditional academic disciplines and tends to force them to pool their knowledge in subject-matter and, especially, problem-solving efforts.

A third strength is that it provides a method for working objectively on both the value-free and value sides of particular problems.

A fourth strength is that pragmatism is eclectic enough to mesh with several forms of normativism and positivism. Perhaps it was this eclectic tendency that made pragmatism a part of the unity of science movement despite what appears to me to be an inherent antipathy between pragmatic and positivistic philosophies. However, pragmatism has not been sufficiently eclectic to avoid conflict with disciplinarians and to play a dominant role outside of colleges of education.

A fifth strength is that pragmatism has been holistic enough to deal with the complex multidisciplinary domains of practical problems and important issues.

Weaknesses

Probably the greatest weakness of pragmatic methods is their complexity. The testing of truth in terms of consequence makes it necessary to deal with many kinds of knowledge and to deal with them interactively and iteratively, while the emphasis on problems makes it necessary for most pragmatic investigations to be multidisciplinary and rather holistic.

A second weakness of pragmatism is that interdependent value-free and value knowledge, whose truth is conditional to specific problems, does not accumulate very rapidly; instead, the knowledge produced is regarded as ephemeral and problem-specific. Data and information banks are not rapidly filled with much more than historical case studies of problematic situations, problem-solving efforts, prescriptions, and consequences. Information retrieval systems for nonhistorical knowledge are not very relevant for pragmatic institutional economists.

A third weakness is that pragmatism is inconsistent with the advantages to be gained on occasion from subdividing the pursuit of knowledge and tackling one aspect at a time. Because positivists and normativists believe in greater stability of their knowledge despite its cultural dependency, they can subdivide in the pursuit of positivistic subjects independently of normative ones and vice-versa, and subdivide both in much more detail. The advantages of such specialization are denied by the holism of a more pragmatic philosophy.

A fourth weakness of pragmatism is that it denies us the demonstrated benefits both of positivistic methods in addressing positive questions in the hard sciences and the demonstrated effectiveness of normative philosophies in addressing value questions, independently of each other.

IMPLICATIONS OF PRAGMATIC METHODS FOR DOING THE THREE KINDS OF RESEARCH

Again, as in Chapters 4 and 5, we look at the importance of a philosophy for the purposes of doing problem-solving, subject-matter, and disciplinary research—in this case, pragmatism.

Problem-Solving Research

Obviously, pragmatism is at its best when used to undergird problem-solving research. Its methods concentrate on problem solving. Of the three philosophies examined, pragmatism is the most specialized in problem-solving research. As we said in Chapter 3, not all problem-solving research has to be pragmatic.

Subject-Matter Research

Though it is possible to conceive of pragmatic subject-matter research, it is probably less commonly encountered than nonpragmatic subject-matter research. Because subject-matter research deals with a multidisciplinary subject important to a group of decision makers facing a set of problems, it is possible to investigate concepts and propositions that have their truth established in the context of a set of problems and the corresponding sets of concerned decision makers and affected persons as well as in the context of a single decision maker and problem. Truth can be regarded as relative to consequences in solving sets of problems for sets of decision makers as well as for individual problems and individual decision makers.

Disciplinary Research

With the exception of research in the decision disciplines, pragmatism tends to downplay disciplinary research. This is especially true of the biological and physical disciplines, with their emphasis on positivistic knowledge, and the arts and humanities, with their emphasis on normative knowledge. Even for the decision disciplines, pragmatism has weaknesses and strengths, and is therefore more constraining than a freely eclectic philosophy for such disciplines. This point will be more fully developed in Chapter 9 (also on pragmatism), in the case studies of Part II, and in the chapters of Part III up to Chapter 17, which summarizes the eclectic view (possibly a synthesis) to which this book leads.

REQUIRED READINGS

(Read in Order Indicated)

Dewey, John. 1950. The Continuum of Ends-Means, *Ethical Theories*, A. I. Melden, ed., Englewood Cliffs, NJ: Prentice Hall, pp. 360–366. (First)
———. 1964. *Logic: The Theory of Inquiry*, New York: Holt, pp. iii–v, 159–171. (Second)
Runes, D. D. 1961. *Dictionary of Philosophy*, Paterson, NJ: Littlefield, Adams, pp. 245–247. (Third)
Whitney, F. L. 1946. *The Elements of Research*, Englewood Cliffs, NJ: Prentice-Hall, pp. 14–15. (Fourth)
Zerby, L. K. 1957. The Meaning of "The Unity of Science," *The Centennial Review of Arts and Science*, 1(2):167–185. (Fifth)

ADDITIONAL REFERENCES

Blaug, Mark. 1980. *The Methodology of Economics*, Cambridge, UK: Cambridge University Press.
Caldwell, B. J. 1982. *Beyond Positivism: Economic Methodology in the Twentieth Century*, London: Allen and Unwin.
Kaplan, Abraham. 1968. Operationism and the Unity of Science, in *International Encyclopedia of the Social Sciences*, Sills, David L., ed., Vol. 12, New York: Free Press, p. 393.
Thayer, H. S. 1952. *The Logic of Pragmatism*, New York: Greenwood Press, pp. 9–12, 194–211.

Chapter 7

Positivism in Economics

In Chapter 3, we surveyed positivism as one of the three broad philosophies important in economic research. In Chapters 4–6, we looked briefly at normativism and pragmatism. We now start a repeat consideration of the three philosophies, this time emphasizing the roles they play in economics. This chapter looks at the role of positivism. Chapter 8 will consider normativism, Chapter 9 pragmatism.

THE RISE OF POSITIVISM IN ECONOMICS

Positivism is a latecomer among the important philosophies guiding research in economics. Economics was strongly guided by such normative philosophies and outlooks as utilitarianism, mercantilism, physiocratic thought, the labor theory of value, and intuitionism throughout its classical decades. In the classical period, so many scholars contributed to the literature of ethics, philosophic value theory, and economics that students of the histories of economic and philosophic thought have difficulty separating their fields of study.

As positivism increasingly demonstrated its productivity in the biological and physical sciences, some economists were very attracted to it. One of the most important early proponents of positivism in economics was John Neville Keynes [1963, originally 1890]. His positivistic methodological pronouncements were made in the hope that economics might become a science like physics, chemistry, and biology. Even though he preceded the logical positivists of the Vienna Circle, J. N. Keynes' positivism was of the "logical" variety rather than the purely empirical variety. In a footnote discussion Keynes drew heavily on an illustration produced earlier by W. E. Johnson in the "Method of Political Economy," which Keynes states was published in Palgrave's *Dictionary of Political Economy*. The following methodological *scheme* of the chief departments of economic science is from Keynes' footnote.

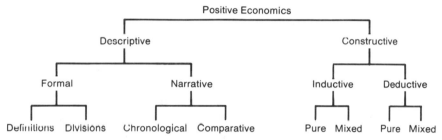

Observe that the divisions under the heading constructive economics relate to the method of reasoning adopted, which Johnson regarded as predominantly inductive or deductive, while in each case a mixed method is recognized in which induction is modified by deduction, or deduction by induction.

In discussing Johnson's illustration narratively, Keynes noted that more than description is involved. "Political economy does not . . . deserve the name of a science at all, if the economist is not competent to reason about the phenomena of wealth and discover laws of causal connexion. Mere description cannot constitute a science . . . The detection of causal connexion needs the assistance of some apparatus of reasoning . . ." It is interesting to note that this was written in the 19th century, long before the peak of logical positivism in philosophy and long before the marriage of theory and empirical work in econometrics. Ironically, Mini's book *Philosophy and Economics* [1974] still stresses the need for this marriage despite econometric's earlier and successful marriage of theory and data. Apparently, the rationalistic or analytical approach of Descartes and Leibniz has died slowly among neoclassical English economists and their followers around the world.

J. N. Keynes regarded the British classicists and neoclassicists as "positive abstract and deductive" and the German historical school as "ethical, realistic and inductive." Positive, as the elder Keynes used the word, was far from empirical despite the present-day identification of logical positivism with empiricism [Runes, 1961]. Actually, the German historical school and the pragmatic

monetary ones), and are generatable with the methods of positivism and acceptable to positivists. Though statements about monetary values are acceptable to positivists, it is also clear that monetary values are normative—i.e., they *are* descriptive statements about values, in this case monetary exchange values. Further, they are not inherently prescriptive, though economists often do prescribe equilibrium prices. Similarly, cost, supply, and demand functions are forms of knowledge about values that are acceptable to positivists.

Several false dichotomies further confuse the terminology [Machlup, 1969]. Positivism seems to be responsible for the fact/value dichotomy, which is, of course, fallacious as even the positivists accept facts about such behavioristic monetary values as prices, income, expenditures, and price-weighted indexes of production and consumption not to mention the possibility of empirical knowledge about nonmonetary values as characteristics of the "real" world. In the latter case, propositions about monetary values and such nonmonetary goodness as the goodness of Salk vaccine or the badness of slowly burning to death seem as factual as many value-free positivistic propositions accepted as factual.

Another questionable positivistic dichotomy is that between objectivity and knowledge of values. Again, this is an unreasonable positivistic dichotomy that is reasonable for part of positivism but unreasonable for other parts because of the inclusion of behavioral knowledge of values in positivism. The falsity of this dichotomy is easily illustrated with monetary values. It is simple to be objective in measuring the price (value) of wheat on the Chicago Mercantile Exchange at a point in time or of a particular stock on the New York Stock Exchange at the same time. It is also possible to be objective in measuring gross national product, national income, consumer expenditures, and many other price or price-weighted variables of the economy.

The objective/value dichotomy simply cannot survive examination in light of some of these important value measurements made by economists. Even on the nonmonetary side, the dichotomy cannot survive the large amount of empirical work being done with the expected utility hypothesis, which has resulted in the cardinal measurement of utility.

Another false positivistic dichotomy is the fact/value judgement one, which differs from the equally false fact/value dichotomy as it opposes facts to judgements. We saw in Chapter 4 that positivistic facts are really judgements which, like value judgements, are time- and culture-dependent. A more appropriate and truer dichotomy seems to be that between value and value-free positivistic judgements, both more or less factual but judgemental nonetheless, as Popper recognizes when he writes about acceptable corroboration of unprovable but falsifiable knowledge [Popper, 1959, pp. 269f].

Economists also deal with values in a nonbehaviorist sense. They ascribe goodness and badness (as well as rightness and wrongness) to balances between governmental regulation and the extent of free choice in society and to the resulting equilibrium prices. Many economists also recognize the "inherent" or intrinsic as well as the instrumental or exchange value of the goodness of such things as food, clothing, shelter, and animal protein or vitamin B-12 in the diets of non-nursing children. Prices, of course, grow out of the behavior of individuals and organizations and, hence, are behavioral. This does not preclude their being based on experienced goodnesses and badnesses in the objective natural world of diseases, health, nutrition, and hunger.

It is inconsistent to reject conclusions as meaningless and metaphysical about experienced goodness and badness as characteristics of conditions, situations, and things of the natural objective world while accepting conclusions about their value-free characteristics. Descriptive conclusions about values seem to be based on interpretations of either direct sense experiences of badness (as when one burns one's finger) or goodness (as when one enjoys a healthy body) and indirect interpretations in which goodness and badness are parts of a larger whole. The inconsistency arises when interpretations of sense impressions of value-free characteristics of conditions, situations, and things are accepted, while interpretations of sense impressions involving values are rejected as metaphysical and meaningless because they are interpretations.

The tendency not to distinguish carefully between goodness or badness and prescriptions about rightness or wrongness has also generated confused thinking and statements. This confusion can be materially reduced by following C. I. Lewis in distinguishing between values and prescriptions as components of normative knowledge. Lewis' distinction is particularly meaningful to economists, who maximize the difference between revenue (a good) and expenditure (a bad) to find an optimum to prescribe as the right action to take and to use in predicting the behavior of maximizers.

Harry Johnson (1975, p. 150), following Popper in part, encountered some of the inconsistencies noted above when he agreed with Popper's argument and stated somewhat inconsistently that the difficulty with values is not to be overcome by researching values and trying to create value-free social sciences. Instead, he argued for empirical tests and logical proof. One wonders how to apply the tests of scientific experimentation and proof to value concepts and propositions without researching values. If that is not what is meant, how are values to be handled if one does not research them but, instead, applies the tests of scientific experimentation and proof only in investigating value-free variables? One also wonders about what happens to Popper's falsifiability criterion and the general conclusion that descriptive positivistic knowledge can never be completely proven anyway.

In Chapter 4, we saw that positivism has passed its zenith in philosophy and is referred to in the past tense—as having "left a legacy." In economics, positivism has become very important—perhaps too important. However, it has never attained the dominance it has in the biological and physical sciences and in the philosophy of science. Perhaps this is because the inconsistencies noted above are more apparent to economists, with their classical interests in values and the use of maximization as a basis for making prescriptions and predictions of the behavior of producers, resource owners, and consumers.

POSITIVISM IN AN APPLIED SUBJECT-MATTER AREA: AGRICULTURAL ECONOMICS

As this book stresses problem-solving and subject-matter research as much as disciplinary research, it is appropriate to examine an applied area. Wassily Leontief in his presidential address to the American Economic Association spoke very highly of the quantitative work done by agricultural economists, and made reference to their extensive application of econometric techniques and to their disciplinary contributions to the development of those techniques. Thus, agricultural economics, my applied area, is an appropriate area to examine with respect to the role of positivism and empirical work. Many of the agricultural economists who have applied quantitative techniques from econometrics have regarded themselves as positivistic. Econometrics is logically positivistic in the sense of combining theory or logic with observational data to produce descriptive knowledge. It was Leontief's satisfaction with the way agricultural economists worked with data and theory that led to his laudatory comments. On the other hand, he has joined Mini in recent issues of *Science* to criticize general economists for failing to produce and work with data [Leontief, 1982]. He applies this criticism more to the disciplinary research of economists than to subject-matter and problem-solving resarch for which empirical knowledge is relatively more important.

Agricultural economics originated not from general economics but from biological and physical scientists working on the practical problems of agriculture in such multidisciplinary subject-matter areas as agronomy, soil science, animal husbandry, and crop science. These positivistically oriented scientists were working on practical problems, about which most of the unanswered questions were positivistic and for which the relevant value questions had simple, relatively well-known answers. Their main task in the USDA/land grant system was to develop and transfer knowledge to help farmers, agro-related private decision makers, and public officials solve practical problems involving agriculture.

These scientists soon became aware that answering a technical fertilization question about wheat or a nutrition question for dairy cattle did not necessarily result in improved wheat or dairy production. Some of them took what would now be termed a "systems" view of, say, dairy or wheat production, and became students of dairy production or wheat production management. Before long, meetings were being organized for farmers and college courses were being taught about such subjects as the management of beef, dairy, wheat, and sheep enterprises. This, in turn, led to the realization that cash crop, feed crop, and livestock enterprises are generally parts of still larger systems known as farms. Before long, the field of farm management emerged.

While economics was germane to farm management, early farm management professors were primarily biological and physical scientists by origin who carried with them substantial amounts of philosophic positivism. It is also true that some of the leaders in this area, including Mitscherlich in Germany and Spillman in the United States, were outstanding in their own biological fields. Perhaps this is why they carried so much positivism over into the field of farm management. In time, farm management departments were established, later to be renamed departments of agricultural economics and at several universities combined with the general economics departments.

Between the two world wars, Cornell University had one of the strongest farm management research and teaching programs in the United States and in the world [Johnson, in press]. Its students, in turn, became department heads at many other major land grant universities. Early Cornelian farm management thought was positivistic in nature. Furthermore, it tended to have a purely positivistic slant rather than a logically positivistic slant. Theory and logic were avoided in true Baconian and Lockeian style. It was not until after World War II that a substantial amount of economic theory was introduced into farm management work at Cornell, so that Cornellian farm management became logically as well as purely positivistic. It should be also stressed that the introduction and greater use of neoclassical economic theory in Cornellian farm management eventually carried farm management researchers into more normative work.

Positivism also impacted agricultural economics in many universities at the same time it was impacting general economics. Again, the impact came from the desire to be "scientific" and as productive as the biological and physical scientists. Most departments of agricultural economics were located in agricultural faculties. Thus, the impact of positivism came more naturally in agricultural economics than in general economics because of the continual contact of agricultural economists with their positivistic colleagues working on biological and physical questions in the colleges of agriculture.

Agricultural economists took up statistical, mathematical, and econometric techniques with alacrity, dedication, and the success approved by Leontief. In the 1960s, agricultural economists began to distinguish between normative supply functions and supply behavior, a questionable distinction, but one that reflected a growing awareness of positivism and a desire "to be scientific and objective" in a positivistic sense. Students and professors of farm management as well as students of consumption economics within agricultural economics tried to be behavioristic. They wanted to predict and explain the behavior of farm managers and consumers in positivistic terms without resorting to "unscientific" normative propositions (about both values and prescriptions) concerning utility, profit, and maximization.

Some asserted that all value propositions were teleological and not sub-

ject to empirical investigation. C. I. Lewis' distinction between goodness and
badness (values) as opposed to rightness and wrongness (of prescriptions) was
not known or utilized. When the normative (about both values and prescriptions) came to be regarded as unscientific and unobjective, the problem-solving
and subject-matter responsibilities of agricultural economists suffered. Fortunately, attention was paid to the behavioristic knowledge of values (monetary
as well as nonmonetary), which is acceptable in positivism. Research on
goodness and badness as characteristics of the natural objective world was unacceptable in positivism and neglected.

RETROGRESSION FROM ECONOMETRICS TO THE
RATIONALISM OF LOCKE AND LEIBNIZ

Those who originated econometrics had a high regard for both economic theory
(logic) and empirical knowledge, including measurement. This is implied by
the name "econometrics." The logical underpinnings of econometrics are in
economics and its ancillary disciplines—mathematics, logic, and statistics. Its
empirical underpinning is in data derived from measurements. This combination of the empirical and the logical made econometrics much more than
mathematical economics and statistics. Econometrics is the offspring of the
marriage of the two underpinnings [Marschak, 1950]. Unfortunately, economists
have now given Leontief what he regards as sufficient grounds for complain-
ing that economists (including many regarded as econometricians) neglect data
and measurement [Leontief, 1982] while concentrating on abstract logic.

Some who regard themselves as econometricians (but perhaps might be
better labled mathematical economists) have tended to neglect empirical work
and to become mathematical economists. The axiomatization of economic
theory and the use of set theoretics has led to the substitution of hypothetic
deductive methods for econometric's joint use of logic (theory) and experience
(data) in economic research. The analytical is often glorified by such
econometricians or mathematical economists, while the synthetic (descriptive
or synthetic) is neglected. Perhaps no one has been more forthright in his
criticisms of this development than Leontief, one of whose articles is in the
assigned list of readings.

POSITIVISM AND QUANTITATIVE METHODS ARE
NOT SYNONYMOUS IN ECONOMICS

Positivism and quantitative methods in economics are not synonymous, though
they are sometimes so treated. The term quantitative methods is used here to
include econometrics, statistics, mathematical economics, programming, systems

analysis, etc. The tendency of some to regard positivism and quantitative methods as synonymous, however, appears to have enhanced the role of positivism among economists as quantitative methods have increasingly demonstrated their usefulness and productivity in economics.

Regarding the two as synonymous also weakened the position of the normativists and pragmatists among economists. Instead of pointing out and demonstrating that quantitative techniques have great potential for them, normativists and pragmatists have tended to accept the position that quantitative methods are positivistic and, hence, have avoided their use and opposed quantification. This is ironical in view of the large amount of research done by econometricians, price analysts, and researchers on monetary *values*—i.e., on such normative but positivistically acceptable measures of value as prices, productivity, income and expenditures, consumer surpluses, and expected utility. Further, it is ironic that pragmatic institutionalists have made major contributions to the data bases of the discipline of economics.

PARETO'S POSITIVISM

Pareto is difficult to fit into the structure of this book. He was a positivist in the sense that he wrote formally in literature that knowledge about values is nonlogical and nonexperimental (not based on experience) in contrast to the logical experimental knowledge of the positive world [Samuels, 1974, pp. 26–31]. Pareto, like Weber and T. Parsons, was part of the movement to make sociology positivistic—to cleanse the science of sociology of nonlogical, nonexperimental, nonbehavioristic research on values. However, Pareto's impact on economics has not been entirely positivistic because his treatise, as Warren Samuels and others have pointed out, uses knowledge about values in a logical experimental manner. In economics, the concept of Pareto optimality grants logico-experimental status to an individual's knowledge of values but does not grant such status to value statements purporting to have interpersonal validity. Pareto optimality is discussed in Chapter 8 on normativism in economics. Only his positivism was discussed here.

Conditional Normativism

Conditional normativism can be regarded as a variant of positivism in economics. It includes research that solves problems either by assuming or taking answers to questions about values as given, or by regarding value questions as behavioristically answerable. It is particularly crucial for positivists wanting to do problem-solving or subject-matter research to have value premises. They need value "premises" in the same way the positivistic ethicist or those practicing positivistic jurisprudence need them. To positivists, these value concepts are only premises (something less than descriptive knowledge of values as characteristic of the real world) such as assumptions, behavioristic knowledge of values held by individuals or groups, and givens.

These premises are used both to define and solve problems. The techniques of conditional normativism have been used repeatedly in the past, particularly since positivism began to dominate western thinking. A very explicit treatment of the conditionally normative method is found in Appendix 2 of Myrdal's *American Dilemma* [1944], a portion of which is in the assigned readings for this chapter. Students should read the Myrdal assignments with care in order to supplement the brief discussion that follows.

Myrdal has argued that explicit statement and treatment of value premises permits one to acquire a kind of positivistic objectivity. Positivists identify concern with values as characteristics of the real world with lack of objectivity; so does Myrdal. Myrdal's objectivity consists of honestly stating value premises (which he assumes are arbitrary and emotive, or at best merely statements of who values what in an emotive way). Myrdal wants this done so that everyone will be able to see the "value premises" that lead to prescriptions and recommendations rather than leaving them hidden. In so doing he draws a distinction between value premises and prescriptions or policy conclusions similar to the one drawn by C. I. Lewis between values and prescriptions. Myrdal wrote [1969, p. 55f] " . . . the value premises that actually and of necessity determine social science research are generally hidden . . . The only way in which we can strive for 'objectivity' . . . is to expose the valuations to full light, making them conscious, specific and explicit and permit them to determine the theoretical research. In the practical phases of the study, the stated value premises, together with the data (established by theoretical analysis with the use of the same value premises) should then form the premises for all policy conclusions."

Because Myrdal does not apply the test of correspondence to his explicitly stated value premises, one finds in reading his books, *The Asian Drama* and *Objectivity in Social Research*, that he tends to exhort decision makers to "believe in" the goodness of life and equality rather than researching them directly. Myrdal does not attempt to demonstrate objectively that enough people have experienced goodnesses of equality and life to conclude with confidence high enough for "purposes at hand" that life and equality do "in fact" possess the characteristic of goodness.

Conditional normativism has the distinct merit of permitting a positivistically inclined economist to engage in problem-solving and subject-matter research. However, its shortcoming is that it still regards one to be "sinning" against positivism when one attempts objective, descriptive research on values as characteristics of an objective "real world." Note that the conditional normativist approach, limited as it is, does permit the maximization procedures of economics to be used to define solutions to practical problems of decision makers.

Problem solvers, consultants, and advisors of the practical world probably pay less attention to conditional normativism than intellectuals. Like Myrdal, practitioners can often see that they can neither define nor solve problems without values. Apparently, they simply draw on experience and logic to reach conclusions about what "really has value." Also, some of them interact repeatedly with decision makers and affected people to deepen their knowledge of values.

One of the difficulties for conditional normativists shows up when their value assumptions are questioned. If they argue that the values they use are realistic—that they correspond with reality—they find themselves going beyond positivism to try to test their descriptive, synthetic, value statements against experience (correspondence) and logic (coherence). If, on the other hand, they elect to remain true to positivism, they must admit that their value assumptions are either arbitrary, or mere statements about who values what that their positivism prevents them from regarding as objective knowledge of what really has value. In the latter case, their solution is not demonstrably better than another based on the same positive knowledge but different arbitrary value propositions. According to conditional normativism, prescriptions based on one set of arbitrary values would be as objective and acceptable as those based on another. This dilemma reveals the consequences of positivism's rejection of conclusions about what really has value whether or not anyone else perceives that value.

Kenneth Parsons [1958], a pragmatic, institutional agricultural economist, has expressed his dissatisfaction with conditional normativism as follows: "Ancient thought assured itself of its ends of conduct and allowed these to determine the world which tested its hypotheses. We insist such ends may not be formulated until we know the field of possible action." Parsons also quotes Knight from his *Ethics of Competition* [1935], "Society cannot accept individual ends . . . as data . . . they simply are not data, but are historically created in the social process." At another point in his article, Parsons [1958, p. 295] wrote "In rigorous statements in economic theory, ends (values) are often accepted as given. In the most rigorous statements, ends are treated as given in order to provide the conditions for defining the equilibrium position of an economic system." Such a position, he writes [Parsons, 1958, p. 296], entails two points:

> (1) ends and means are separated; ends are data which stand alone so to speak, independent of the means of realization. (2) Whatever evaluation, whatever judgment, which exists about the worth of an end is made antecedent to, or independently of, any act of economizing or any analyzing by economists. [paragraph] At least this much can be said about such positions. They do not touch the problem of value; indeed they avoid it . . . this current practice . . . holds the possibility of opening the way for a reversion to the medieval view that the world of thought and action should be organized around social values presented to mankind as dogma. Actually, however, the position is in a sense worse than either dogma or reversion to the assured ends of conduct, as it makes answers to questions a matter of accident.

Myrdal himself has had difficulties with his conditional normativism. In his book *Objectivity in Social Research* [1969, Chapters XVII, XVIII] he is mystified by the widespread, long-continued attachment of value to equality by people in so many different societies. That attachment appears to be more than accidental, more than a matter of chance. Unfortunately, Myrdal's positivistic conditional normativism does not permit him to investigate whether people in these societies have experienced the "actual" goodness of more than less equality, and whether their experiences justify concluding that equality really has value (whether anyone in the practical world holds that it does) with enough confidence for the purpose at hand. Both the objective normativists and pragmatists would argue that Myrdal might find such an approach fruitful even if the reality of experience with values as characteristics of the real world is ruled "out of bounds" by positivism.

THE IMPACT OF THE LATE 1960s AND EARLY 1970s

Economics and related more applied fields such as labor economics, agricultural economics, monetary/fiscal policy, trade policy, regional development, and economic development have been heavily influenced by the social issues of the late 1960s. Racial unrest, minority issues, resource exhaustion, OPEC operations, environment pollution, world hunger, war, the North/South dialogue, and East/West tensions reflect some of the issues that burst on society in the late 1960s and early 1970s when both young and older people became disillusioned with science and the academic establishment.

The value neutrality of positivistic science and the divisiveness positivism promotes between science on the one hand and theology and the humanities on the other reduced our ability to address practical problems. Positivists refused to address the value aspects of these issues beyond concern with who holds what values about what. Positivistic science is viewed as denigrating knowledge of values, while theologians are sometimes viewed as addressing value questions but neglecting relevant positivistic knowledge. Scientists, humanists, and theologians seemed artificial and irrelevant to people concerned with values and the major issues and problems of those two decades.

Many fell into the trap set unwittingly by the positivists and those who have accepted the division between science and the humanities and religion. The trap involves a supposed inability to work objectively with logic and experience in generating knowledge about "real" values to use in defining and solving the practical problems inherent in the issues of the late 1960s and early 1970s.

Demands have arisen for courses in medical ethics, on the ethics of world hunger and malnutrition, on biological ethics, etc. Church groups organize conferences. Activists carry out demonstrations. Song writers write "instant folk music" about the values involved. Many without access to Lewis' distinction between values and prescriptions unrealistically treat values as goals—i.e., they confuse goodness with rightness while ignoring the positivistic constraints of reality. The outstanding characteristics of most of these efforts are (1) the absence of systematic use of logic and experience in arriving at value propositions to use in defining and solving problems, and/or (2) a distrust of the systematic use of logic and experience in developing value-free and value propositions for use in defining and solving problems. The trap set earlier by the positivists caught many victims in the late 1960s and early 1970s.

Recently, positivism has come under increasing criticism in intellectual circles from economists such as McCloskey, Caldwell, Kirzner, and others. McCloskey [1983] attacks what he calls modernism. He characterizes modernism as associating scientific economics with positivism and unscientific economics with the normative. He further argues that modernism is philosophically obsolete as its tenets are now unacceptable to many philosophers. His arguments are similar to those found in the Achinstein/Barker book considered in Chapter 4. Caldwell's book *Beyond Positivism: Economic Methodology in the Twentieth Century* examines positivism in detail and concludes that though it has important contributions to make to methodological pluralism (referred to in this book as eclecticism), positivism is by itself an inadequate undergirding for much economic research. While Kirzner does not attack positivism per se, his Austrian orientation takes him beyond the reductionism of positivistic economics to a more holistic view of economics than is common among positivistic neoclassical economists. These developments seem symptomatic of the early 1980s.

CONSEQUENCES OF POSITIVISM IN ECONOMICS

The consequence of the extreme form of positivism is the lost ability of economists to be objective in solving practical problems faced by public and private decision makers. One is restricted to the laws of chance, arbitrary assumptions, and what is regarded by positivists as unreliable emotive knowledge of goodness and badness, as sources of knowledge of values for the solution of practical problems.

In its less extreme form, positivism fosters disciplinary excellence in positivistic economic research. Positivism also promotes excellence in quantitative skills. Economists, particularly econometricians, have developed great skill in combining logic with observational data to acquire descriptive, synthetic knowledge, some value-free, but much measuring the behaviorally revealed value positions of individuals, groups and the economy as a whole. Furthermore, economists have greatly increased their capacity to apply the tests of coherence in validating and of correspondence in verifying positivistic propositions. Still further, the skill of economists in applying the clarity test has been greatly improved, as evidenced by the attention given to the identification of the parameters of systems of equations for purposes of estimating those parameters from the parameters of reduced-form equations.

The rigorous quantitative methods and techniques of positivism have made a major contribution to research excellence in economics, particularly on the value-free side, but also with respect to knowledge of behavioral values. This excellence has appeared in research on monetary values (prices, production, demand, income, consumer expenditures, and investments). When economists have investigated values, positivism has steered them to investigation of monetary rather than nonmonetary values and away from the investigation of intrinsic values to the investigation of who attaches what value to what.

However, much of the work of economists using the expected utility hypothesis, Pareto optimality, and consumer surplus is positivistic with respect to method and philosophy even if devoted to the estimation and description of nonmonetary behavioral values. Another major influence of positivism on the work of economists has been the impetus it has given to conditionally normative methods and techniques.

Though Pareto optimality will be discussed in the next chapter on normativism, positivism has also supported the tendency to use methods and techniques associated with the concept of Pareto optimality. Positivistic questioning of the validity of all empirical research on values established a fertile environment in which extremely relevant questions have flourished about the interpersonal validity of welfare measurements and the validity of cardinal utility measurements for individuals.

Positivism has also encouraged benefit/cost analysts to convert nonmonetary values into monetary ones rather than vice-versa. This practice is often followed even by otherwise pragmatically oriented institutionalists working as resource economists. When such resource economists use monetized benefit/cost analysis to study redistributive public choices, the prices they use as weights in aggregating costs and benefits are functions of the distributions of rights and privileges being redistributed. A consequence of this is that these analysts have to stop short of prescriptions to redistribute as their benefit/cost measures lack validity across the different distributions being considered. Historically, pragmatic institutionalists were less constrained by logical positivism and felt freer to proceed more confidently toward redistributive prescriptions.

Generally, positivism in economics has led to the neglect of research on values as characteristics of the real world and, hence, has tended to reduce much of the prescriptive capacity of economists. This has reduced ability to work toward the solution of practical problems and made economic research more disciplinary at the expense of problem-solving and subject-matter research.

Fortunately, in my view, positivism has been its own worst enemy and appears to be in the process of destroying its own negative influence. The *Encyclopedia of Social Sciences* has an article by Kaplan [1968]. In it he placed the beginning of the end of logical positivism as a philosophy at the end of World War II. While he notes that the logical positivists were scattered by the war, he also notes the importance of diverging views among logical positivists and the consequent misunderstandings and lost cohesion of the group. The breakdown started with World War II and continued to the point at which logical positivism was no longer the dominant point of view among philosophers of science. This breakdown and loss of dominance is less evident in economics than in philosophy.

CONSEQUENCES OF POSITIVISM FOR THE THREE KINDS OF RESEARCH

Despite this somewhat adverse evaluation, positivism as it is practiced, if not as it is often described and prescribed, has much to contribute.

The combined use of theory (logic) and experiential data continues to be productive in disciplinary, subject-matter, and problem-solving research. It is important that the union of theory and experience be preserved and extended to research on values. Positivistic methods are productive when value-free knowledge can reasonably be expected to be independent of knowledge about values. It will be argued in the next chapter that the methods of positivists can be used to research questions about goodness and badness as characteristics of an objective real world.

In general, the analytic/synthetic distinction of positivism is useful, if somewhat questionable. So is the idea of primitive, undefined experiential terms, which permit application of the tests of correspondence, while logic provides the test of coherence. The test of clarity or lack of ambiguity is important as clarity makes the tests of correspondence and coherence possible. All of these tests remain useful and, as we are seeing in our examination of normativism, applicable in researching value as well as value-free questions. Nothing in positivism prevents the use of the analytic/synthetic distinction, the concept of undefined primitives, and the three tests of objectivity in doing empirical research on values except the untested presupposition that we do not experience the goodness and badness of conditions, situations, and things as characteristics of the objective natural world. The next chapter critically considers that presupposition.

Positivism restricts disciplinary and subject-matter research to value-free and to behavioristic information about who values what. In so doing, it seriously constrains problem-solving research.

REQUIRED READING

(Read in Order Indicated)

Friedman, M. 1953. *Essays in Positive Economics*, Chicago: University of Chicago Press, pp. 3–15, 39–43. (Third)

Keynes, J. N. 1963. *The Scope and Method of Political Economy*, 4th ed., New York: Augustus M. Kelley, Bookseller, pp. 9–20. (First)

Myrdal, G. 1944. *The American Dilemma*, New York: Harper, pp. 1041–1045. (Fourth)

—— 1969. *Objectivity in Social Research*, New York: Pantheon Books, pp. 73–76, 94–96. (Fifth)

Robbins, L. 1949. *An Essay on the Nature & Significance of Economic Science*, 2nd ed., London: Macmillan, pp. xi–xiii, 24–28, 38–39, 151–152, 157–158. (Second)

Scriven, Michael. 1969. Logical Positivism and the Behavioral Sciences, in *The Legacy of Logical Positivism*, Achinstein, P. and S. F. Barker, eds., Baltimore: Johns Hopkins Press, 1969, pp. 195–209. (Sixth)

ADDITIONAL REFERENCES

Caldwell, Bruce. 1982. *Beyond Positivism: Economic Methodology in the Twentieth Century*, London: Allen and Unwin.

Cohen, Jacob. 1982. Empirical Research in Economics, *Science*, **218**:1070.

Frazer, William J., Jr. and Lawrence A. Boland. 1983. An Essay on the Foundations of Friedman's Methodology, *The American Economic Review*, Vol. 73, pp. 129–144.

Johnson, Glenn L. (in press). Philosophic Foundations of Agricultural Economics Thought, *A Survey of Agricultural Economics Literature*, Vol. 4, L. R. Martin, ed., Minneapolis: University of Minnesota Press.

Johnson, H. G. 1975. *On Economics and Society*, Chicago: University of Chicago Press, pp. 129–139.

Kirzner, Israel M. 1981. The "Austrian" Perspective, in *The Crisis in Economic Thought*, Daniel Bell and Irving Kristol, eds., New York: Basic Books.

Knight, Frank H. 1935. *The Ethics of Competition*, New York: Harper.

Leontief, Wassily. 1982. Academic Economics, *Science*, **217**:104–107.

Machlup, F. 1969. Positive and Normative Economics, in *Economic Means and Social Ends*, R. Heilbroner, ed., Englewood Cliffs, NJ: Prentice-Hall.

Marschak, Jacob. 1950. Statistical Inference in Economics: An Introduction, in *Statistical Inference in Dynamic Economic Models*, Tjallings Koopmans, ed., New York: Wiley.

McCloskey, Donald N. 1983. The Rhetoric of Economics, *Journal of Economic Literature* **XXI**(2):481–517.

Mini, P. V. 1974. *Philosophy and Economics*, Gainesville: University of Florida Press.

Myrdal, G. 1944. *The American Dilemma*, New York: Harper, pp. 1057–1064.

Parsons, K. H. 1958. The Value Problem in Agricultural Policy, in *Agricultural Adjustment Problems in a Growing Economy*, E. Heady et al., eds., Ames: Iowa State College Press, Ch. 18.

Popper, Karl. 1945. *Open Society and Its Enemies*, London: Routledge and K. Paul.

Runes, D. D. 1961. *Dictionary of Philosophy*, Paterson, NJ: Littlefield, Adams.

Samuels, Warren J. 1974. *Pareto on Policy*, Amsterdam: Elsevier.

Schultz, T. W. 1959. Omission of Variables, Weak Aggregates, and Fragmentation in Policy Adjustment Studies, *Problems and Policies of American Agriculture*, Ames: Iowa State College Press.

Chapter 8

Normativism in Economics

We have already seen that normativism was prominent throughout the classical and neoclassical portions of the history of economic thought. Normativism in economics goes back at least to the physiocratic doctrines involving the primacy of land and agriculture as sources of value. Classical economics includes attempts to explain value on the cost-of-production side, one prominent attempt being the labor theory of value of such classicists as David Ricardo, J. S. Mill, and Karl Marx. On the demand side, economists attempted to explain value in a number of ways including, particularly, the utilitarianism of Bentham, Sidgwick, and Senior. Most of neoclassical economics is concerned with the definition and determination of optima for use as prescriptions and in predicting the behavior of producers, consumers, resource owners, governmental officials and, more recently, the generators of (induced) technical, institutional, and human change.

Classical economics is viewed here as ending when Alfred Marshall in England and John B. Clark in the United States independently combined attempts to explain value on the cost or supply side with attempts to explain value on the utility or demand side to produce a single explanation of value *in exchange.* While Marx had earlier distinguished between "the value" and the "exchange value" of a commodity, his exchange value was far different from the equilibrium price established at the intersection of supply and demand curves. The measurement of Marx's exchange value has to do with "the labor time" necessary to produce the commodity under the distributions of technical skills, institutional rights and privileges, and human competence existing in a society. By contrast, the later Marshallian/Clark synthesis generated an explanation of values in exchange, nonmonetary as well as monetary, that has been very useful in analyzing the price and income consequences of market operations. It has largely been ignored by philosophers despite its usefulness in explaining extrinsic values, both nonmonetary and monetary.

The neoclassical synthesis of cost-of-production and demand theories into an explanation of exchange values was one of the great intellectual accomplishments in the history of economic thought. It matches in many ways the melding of terrestrial and celestial physics by Newton into a unified conception of the laws of space and motion.

PARETO OPTIMALITY

In the early neoclassical period it was assumed that enough was known about utility to state safely that the marginal utility of money is empirically less for rich people than poor people. Partly as a consequence of this conviction, the neoclassical period prior to 1939 was a period of substantial redistributive change through progressive taxation and social programs to help the poor. Such redistributive changes were sustained in the conviction that nonmarket redistributions of income and wealth to the poor were justified by our empirical knowledge of utility. Widespread progressive income taxation in northern Europe and North America became a means of redistributing the ownership of wealth and incomes more equally. A. C. Pigou's book on welfare economics [1932] summarized the intellectual basis for such nonmarket redistributions.

The state of our descriptive empirical knowledge of utility came under severe questioning largely as the result of the work of Lionel Robbins [1932] and John R. Hicks [1939]. Once Hicks had placed Pareto's earlier questions about the interpersonal validity of welfare or utility measures on the agenda of economists, considerable uncertainty arose about the conclusion that we know enough descriptive truth about utility functions to justify either an existing distribution of wealth and income or to change it. As a result of Pareto's questions, John R. Hicks redid consumption economics on the assumption that utility was measureable ordinally but not cardinally. He also redid welfare economics on the assumption that utility and welfare are intrapersonally measureable in an ordinal sense but not interpersonally measureable in either cardinal or ordinal senses. Hicks' reformulation greatly reduced the confidence of economists in conclusions either to redistribute or to defend the existing pattern of ownership of rights and privileges, mainly by raising questions about the interpersonal validity and cardinality of our knowledge of welfare and utility.

In a sense, the Hicksian posing of Pareto's question came at an unfortunate time. Philosophic positivism had already expanded from J. S. Mill's attempt to eliminate metaphysical and supernatural explanations to attempts to eliminate the description of values, except the description of who attaches value to what, in contrast to describing the values that conditions, situations, and things "really" have. The early neoclassical conviction that we know enough about utility that is interpersonally valid to justify prescriptions to redistribute was questioned by Robbins, who also questioned the validity of our knowledge of goodness and badness.

Many logical positivists, as we saw earlier, claimed that there is no objective, descriptive knowledge of good and bad as characteristics of the real world. While Hicks' questions made it necessary to use Pareto optimality, it did not eliminate investigations of utility. Raised when it was, however, Hicks' question strengthened the positivistic case against normativism in economics, a development that would probably have pleased Pareto. Further, it was an extension of the disagreement between the English school of "a positive abstract deductive science" and the German school of "an ethical, realistic, and inductive science," to use the elder Keynes' words.

In the preceding chapter we looked at conditional normativism as a variant of positivism. As indicated by the writings of Gunnar Myrdal, conditional normativism accepts the positivistic point of view that there can be no objective descriptive knowledge of values other than behavioristic knowledge. Apparently, Myrdal believes positivistically that one can assume, and perhaps even know objectively, what values are held by people, but that one cannot know objectively what conditions, situations, and things "really" are valuable. Myrdal avoided objective study of "real" values as well as the metaphysical and supernatural kinds of knowledge about the positivistic world.

Post-Hicks neoclassical economics was severely constrained by the joint impact of positivism and Pareto optimality. Cooter and Rappoport [1984] now argue that the Hicksian ordinalist revolution and the abandonment of cardinal utility was a mistake. Positivism and conditional normativism left answers to descriptive questions about what really has value up to intuition, emotion, and arbitrary assumption. In other words, positivism made objective knowledge of real values, per se, impossible.

The conditional normativist can test descriptive value propositions about the natural objective world for coherence but not correspondence. When Myrdal attempts to explain why so many societies attach value to equality, positivism prevents him from applying the test of correspondence between perceptions based on the experiences of people in those societies and the proposition that equality is a condition really possessing the characteristic of goodness. In his book, *Objectivity in Social Research*, Myrdal could have noted that empirical observation indicates that many individuals and groups have experienced the goodness of equality and the badness of inequality. Had he done so, his mystification about the widespread acceptance of the proposition that equality possesses the characteristic of goodness would have been reduced. I believe that adherence to positivism kept Myrdal from conceiving that the widespread acceptance of the proposition that equality is good is based on experiences of different societies with equality (and inequality) as well as logic.

THE WORK OF PRACTITIONERS

Economists as private and governmental decision makers, advisors, and consultants have tended to disregard both Pareto optimality and conditional normativism. Somehow or other, when economists are removed from the protective walls of their academic environments, the shackles of positivism and its two variants (conditional normativism and Pareto optimality) tend to fall off and they regain a measure of operational common sense [Cooter and Rappoport, 1984]. In these circumstances, some economists *use both logic and experience* to help answer questions about real values, thereby arriving at more or less objective, descriptive, synthetic propositions about values to use in defining and solving problems permitting only non-Pareto optimal redistributional alternative acts.

The constraints of Pareto optimality and conditional normativism indicate the great need of practicing economists for objective descriptive knowledge of values. Pareto optimality stresses this need by pointing out the difficult measurement questions involved in attaining interpersonal validity of our measures of value. Conditional normativism, à la Myrdal, stresses it by demonstrating the bankruptcy of positivism with respect to the development of objective descriptive knowledge of values as characteristics of the real objective world. Practitioners, as distinct from disciplinary economists, stress it by ignoring both Pareto optimality and conditional normativism and doing informally what can be done on the basis of experience and logic.

Our first task as disciplinarians and applied subject-matter researchers and problem solvers is to free ourselves from the shackles of logical positivism and of Pareto optimality and conditional normativism. We need to do this to get on with the important task of increasing our stock of objective disciplinary knowledge about the goodnesses and badnesses experienced as characteristics of the real world. More such objective knowledge of values is crucial if we are to improve and prevent deterioration in the structure of our economies and societies. Without this knowledge we cannot know objectively whether improvement or deterioration is taking place.

OBJECTIVE KNOWLEDGE OF VALUES

Chapter 5 on normativism considered the important work of G. E. Moore. His book, *Principia Ethica*, was a crucial point in the intellectual life of John Maynard Keynes, who stated [Moore, 1903, dust cover, 1959 printing] "I went up to Cambridge at Michaelmas 1902 and Moore's *Principia Ethica* came out at the end of my first year . . . , its effect on *us*, and the talk which preceeded and followed it, dominated, and perhaps still dominates everything else."

John Maynard Keynes' effectiveness as an advisor to governments and governmental leaders, including Franklin Roosevelt, displayed a conviction that he knew enough descriptively true about answers to relevant questions of value to produce prescriptions about right and wrong—about what ought and ought not to be done. Further, he was able to support his recommendations with sufficient logic and appeal to experience to convince those leaders to take his advice. Errors in his prescriptions were to be expected, as all human knowledge, including the value-free positivistic knowledge of the "hard" scientists as well as knowledge of values, is so tentative and culture-bound that we must expect some of it to be in error and to lead to errors in prescriptions.

G. E. Moore argued that good is always synthetic and never analytic. Good and bad are primitive, undefined terms describing the goodness and badness of various things, conditions, and situations. Such primitive terms can be used to convert abstract, formal, logical sentences into synthetic propositions about values. We saw in Chapter 5 a way out of Myrdal's conditionally normative mystification and out of the constraints positivism and Pareto optimality impose on the research economists do on "real" values. This "way out" involves accepting the reality of experiences with the real goodnesses and badnesses of such conditions, situations, and things as equality, health, cancer, life, injustice, and inequality. This permits us, like Moore, to conceive of goodness as a primitive term to use with logic to generate synthetic descriptive statements about goodness or badness that can be subjected to the tests of correspondence (experience).

The obvious test of correspondence is that of repeated observations to determine whether or not a condition, situation, or thing alleged to possess the characteristic of goodness or badness can be experienced to have that characteristic. It should be recognized that in doing this we go beyond Moore, but mainly in a manner that seems to me to clear up the meaning of Moore's naturalistic fallacy. This fallacy consists of asserting that something possessing the characteristic of goodness is itself goodness. This is far different from asserting that it is a naturalistic fallacy to say something really possesses the characteristic of goodness. Moore might have regarded the latter as a naturalistic fallacy, but it is not so regarded here.

Value observations are obtainable by economists from the ongoing experiences of individuals and society. These can be recorded continuously in the case of both monetary and nonmonetary values—i.e., as verbal and partially quantified accounts of experiences with the goodnesses of such conditions, situations, and things as more racial and gender equality, less poverty, or the badnesses of war, cancer, social disorder, environmental pollution, and starvation. Also, observations on values are obtainable from experiments such as those conducted by the "expected utility hypothesis analysts" and "product acceptability researchers." The measurement of "consumer surplus" as well as research on "social indicators" should also be mentioned as examples of objective research on values.

When preferences stated in the form of prescriptions in contrast to statements about value are recorded, there is the difficulty of distinguishing statements about underlying values from preference statements of the form "I ought to do so and so" or "all things considered I prefer to have this or that because it is what I ought to have." The difficulty is similar to the "identification problem" encountered by econometricians in estimating supply and demand curves from price/quantity data.

Prescriptions and preferences are not based solely on values. They are based on value-free positivistic information as well, and are arrived at by trading off different goods against each other or attaining a good at the expense of incurring a bad (see Figure 1, Chapter 2) under the constraints imposed on a decision maker by knowledge of positivistic reality. If a decision maker's value-free perception of reality changes while his perceptions of value hold constant, the resultant changes in his preferences will reveal his value perceptions. If, on the other hand, his value perceptions change while his value-free perceptions remain unchanged, the consequent changes in his preferences tend to reveal his positivistic perceptions. When both value-free and value perceptions change, it is difficult to find anything accurate to say from changes in preferences about either underlying value or value-free perceptions.

Methods for handling a similar difficulty have been developed by econometricians to estimate the parameters of supply and demand functions from price/quantity observations [Marschak, 1950; Koopmans, 1945]. A similar method is needed to determine whether one can derive information about perceived values from stated preferences or even observed behavior.

Experiential value observations make the methods of positivism available for use by economists to generate knowledge of nonmonetary values as well as the positivistic and monetary value knowledge long regarded as attainable. While philosophers have conceptual difficulties with the theoretical/observational or analytic/synthetic distinction in the logical positivists' account of science [Shapere, p. 118f], positivistic methods are demonstrably operational both in economics (with respect to monetary values) and in the biological and physical sciences (with respect to value-free knowledge). Positivistic methods can also produce knowledge about nonmonetary values as demonstrated by the utility measurement techniques explicated by Friedman and Savage and used extensively by present-day "expected utility" analysts.

KNOWLEDGE OF VALUES
VERSUS PRESCRIPTIVE KNOWLEDGE

In Chapter 2, we presented C. I. Lewis' distinction between right and wrong (the prescriptive) on the one hand and goodness and badness on the other. Machlup's work indicates that many economists and sociologists do not make this distinction, particularly those trying to make their discipline "scientific" in a positivistic sense. Failure to maintain this distinction perpetuates the idea that value propositions are unstable, arbitrary and, perhaps, merely emotive. Moore has argued that goodness is always synthetic, never analytic. By contrast, prescriptions are the consequences of decision rules and, hence, not experienceable and not synthetic.

Some economists, sociologists, and anthropologists observe very different prescriptive rules, "norms," and mores between different cultures about right and wrong sexual behavior, and questionably conclude for this reason that answers to questions about the goodness of sex are emotive and mere matters of opinion. They should be more careful. It is true that different societies prescribe and proscribe different sexual behavior as right or wrong, but this is quite different from knowledge of the goodness of sex. I have traveled and lived extensively in both the more developed and less developed worlds but have yet to find a society whose members do not act as if they experience sex to be good despite wide differences in what are acceptable sexual practices.

Rightness and wrongness, as Lewis stresses, are not the same as goodness and badness. Rightness and wrongness—the prescriptive—are always conditional and dependent on decision rules devised by humans (see Figure 1, Chapter 2), value-free knowledge, and knowledge of goodnesses and badnesses. Because rightness and wrongness are prescriptive, they are much more time, place, and culture-dependent than either value or value-free knowledge. Further, because they are basically functions of decision rules, they are fundamentally different from Moore's undefined, primitive "goodnesses" and "badnesses." Prescriptions are hardly amenable to the test of correspondence, as they depend on decision rules. When decision rules are changed, rightness and wrongness change, even though perception of goodness and badness and of value-free characteristics of the real world do not.

What "ought to be" is prescriptive. Both value and value-free propositions purporting to describe "what is" can be viewed as synthetic. What "ought to be" (the prescriptive) is not synthetic or descriptive. Its value-free and value bases may be tested for correspondence but the prescriptive itself cannot be so tested. However, prescriptive knowledge is at least partially the logical consequence (within a decision rule) of value-free and value knowledge; hence, its coherence can be tested. We should note, though, that there are value-free positivistic and value consequences of a decision as to what "ought to" be done that become "what is" after the decision is executed and that can then be tested for correspondence. The "ought to be" or the prescription, however, seems to escape any direct correspondence test both before and after execution. Only the resulting "what is" can be so tested. And, the "what is" that can be tested can describe either value-free positivistic or value phenomena.

It should be recalled that value-free or positivistic knowledge was also seen to be culture, time, and place-dependent in Chapters 4 and 7. So is knowledge about values. But neither value-free positivistic knowledge nor knowledge about values are as culture, time, and place-dependent as prescriptive knowledge, which is also specific to problems and the decision rule used to define it.

It is interesting to me that the New Testament of the Christian Bible has many parables, accounts, and stories illustrating the above distinction. Christ found it "right" to get an ox out of a ditch on the Sabbath despite Judaic law and customs proscribing labor on the Sabbath as bad. Christ also permitted his feet to be washed by a prostitute and dried with her hair, again despite proscribing laws and customs. He found it "right to do" these things in view of the circumstances and of the badness of letting an ox die and the goodness of the prostitute's desire to receive His teaching.

NONPRAGMATIC PRESCRIPTIVE KNOWLEDGE AND DECISION MAKING

Because the pragmatists have been so effective in doing problem-solving work, advising, and consulting. Chapter 5 on pragmatism may have given the reader the impression that problem solving, prescriptions, and decision processes are always pragmatic. Thus, it is appropriate to observe here that neoclassical economists have long engaged in nonpragmatic, prescriptive research to solve problems. By a nonpragmatic prescription we mean a prescription based on value-free and value knowledge that are treated as independent of each other even though the prescription resulting from processing them through a decision rule depends on both. Also, conditional normativism, which can be a part of neoclassical economics, generates nonpragmatic prescriptive knowledge.

The normativism of Chapters 3 and 5 and the positivism of Chapters 3 and 4 treat value and value-free positivistic knowledge as independent. Traditionally, neoclassical English economics has concentrated on the logic of nonpragmatic prescriptions. When the beginning student of economics is taught how to transform a physical production function into a value productivity function, then to subtract total costs from that value productivity function to be able to maximize profit as the difference, he is taught *nonpragmatic* prescription and problem solving. The prescription indicates one "ought to use" the amounts of the factors that maximize the difference between total value product (goodness) and total cost (badness). Of course, economists also have larger systems of analyses for reaching nonpragmatic prescriptions about optimal organizations of entire economies.

There are four preconditions for using maximization to locate optima: (1) the availability of a common denominator between the goods and bads whose difference is being maximized, (2) interpersonal validity of the common denominator when the maximization affects more than one person, (3) a means of arranging possible acts (which may be disparate) in the order of their decreasing net advantage per unit of cost, and (4) an agreed-on decision rule. (When knowledge is imperfect, as it always is in practical circumstances, rule (4) has to be more complex than the maximization of returns less costs.)

In static neoclassical economics, these preconditions are ensured or made unnecessary by the laws of diminishing utility and production, by assumptions to eliminate the possibility of non-Pareto optimal change or by assuming interpersonal validity of welfare measures, and by assuming perfect knowledge under which the decision rule is simply one of maximizing the difference between good and bad.

Economists use nonpragmatic maximization extensively. Its two important common uses are for reaching prescriptions and predicting the behavior of resource owners, producers, consumers, and governmental decision makers. Behavioral predictions are, of course, easily subjected to the test of correspondence even if the prescriptions on which the predictions are based are not.

A RETURN TO RESEARCH ON VALUES IN ECONOMICS

The shortcomings of positivism, Pareto optimality, and conditional normativism for economists interested in problem-solving and subject-matter research seem to be prompting some economists to return to research on values. Evidence of this includes work currently being done with the expected utility hypothesis. This hypothesis has provided the basis for cardinal measurement of utility. Many economists are now researching the measurement of utility using this technique. However, the use of the expected utility analysis has gone much beyond the estimation of cardinal utility functions into the areas of investment and disinvestment theory and portfolio analysis.

On another front, Kenneth Boulding in his AAEA presidential address [1969] embraced pragmatism, as did Georgescu-Roegen in his *The Entropy*

Law and the Economic Process [1971]. The work of Karl Fox and others on "social indicators" [1974] to be reviewed in Chapter 11 of this book should also be mentioned. Further evidence of the return to research on values is project design and evaluation research. Benefit/cost, present expected value, and net present value analyses are used extensively in appraising and evaluating the consequences of nonmarket changes by monetizing many nonmonetary values. General systems simulation and industrial organization studies deal with values in the form of "criteria" and "performance" variables, respectively. All of these efforts represent attempts to work objectively with values.

Further evidence of increased interest and progress in researching values is found in the works of scholars such as Amartya Sen [Sen and Williams, 1982], R. Nosick [1974], J. Rawls [1971], and J. Harsanyi [1977a, 1977b]. An excellent review of these and other related works has been provided by E. F. McClennen [1983]. Though these works tend to be more analytic than synthetic, they represent progress in the area. Nosick argues for organizing a society in such a way that a person would choose to be in it even if one's position in the society were to be randomly determined. On first consideration, this appears to be an argument for equality. However, further reflection indicates that the need for decisiveness in decision-making under stress and uncertainty would make it undesirable to live in a completely equal society. Who, for instance, would want to serve on a battleship without a captain? Or fly in a commercial airplane without a pilot in command?

As we saw in Chapter 2, distributions of power (and unequal ones, at that) are essential components of decision rules. The point of this discussion is that the reasoning of people like Sen, Rawls, Harsanyi, and Nosick is providing a basis for potential empirical work on values, decision rules, power (market, administrative, political, social, police and military) distributions, and prescriptions.

There also seems to be some basis for hoping that economists will distinguish more sharply, following C. I. Lewis, between values (about goodness and badness) on the one hand and the prescriptive (about rightness and wrongness or what ought or ought not to be) on the other. This optimism also includes some basis for hoping that economists will acquire increased capacity along the lines discussed to use both logic and experience in developing and testing propositions about goodness and badness. It also provides hope that the results of research on values will take on increasing interpersonal validity as a basis for reaching more objective prescriptions about how to solve the major structural and redistributive issues facing society. In any event, it is clear that research on values is not dead; conditional normativism, Pareto optimality, and their parent, positivism, have proven to be inadequate grave diggers and pall bearers for research on values. Such research is an increasingly lively part of modern as well as part of classical economics and the pre-1939 neoclassical welfare economics of A. C. Pigou.

IMPLICATIONS OF NORMATIVISM FOR THE
THREE KINDS OF RESEARCH

The revival of interest in research on values and prescriptions has substantial implications for the three kinds of research considered in this book. The first is that it helps develop a more complete kit of positivistic and normative methods to undergird nonpragmatic *problem-solving* research that is different from the pragmatic problem-solving research the institutionalists never lost.

With respect to *subject-matter research*, it is now possible to consider research on values as characteristics of the real world in addition to doing positivistic research about who attaches value to what. Such research, combined with research on value-free positivistic subjects, is crucial for solving the problems of our time. Research is needed on the values of energy, environmental quality, equality in the ownership of rights and privileges, the exhaustion of natural resources, technological change, world hunger, monopolies and oligopolies, and institutional change.

On the *disciplinary side*, the revival makes it respectable for economics to focus again on prescriptive, value, and value-free positivistic knowledge.

REQUIRED READINGS

(Read in Order Indicated)

Eastman, Max (Ed.) 1932. *Capital: The Communist Manifesto and Other Writings by Karl Marx*, New York: Modern Library, pp. 29-33. (These pages were also assigned in Chapter 5.) (Third)

Hicks, J. R. 1939. *Value and Capital*, Oxford: Oxford University Press, pp. 11-25. (Sixth)

Hymer, S. and F. Roosevelt. 1972. Comment, *Quarterly Journal of Economics*, **XXXVI**, 4:644-657. (Fourth)

Marshall, A. 1946. *Principles of Economics*, London: Macmillan, pp. 348-350. (Fifth)

Mill, J. S. 1936. *Principles of Political Economy*, London: Longmans, Green (first published in 1848), Book III, Chs. I and IV. (Second)

Reder, M. W. 1948. *Studies in the Theory of Welfare Economics*, New York: Columbia University Press, second printing, Ch. 1. (Seventh)

Whittaker, E. 1940. *A History of Economic Ideas*, New York: Longmans, Green, pp. 715-730. (First)

ADDITIONAL REFERENCES

Boulding, K. 1969. Economics as a Moral Science, *American Economic Review*, **59**:1-12.

Cooter, R. and P. Rappoport. 1984. Were the Ordinalists Wrong About Welfare Economics? *Journal of Economic Literature*, **XXII**:507-530.

Fox, Karl. 1974. *Social Indicators and Social Theory*, New York: Wiley.

Georgescu-Roegen, Nicholas. 1971. *The Entropy Law and the Economic Process*, Cambridge: Harvard University Press.

Harsanyi, J. C. 1977a. "Non-Linear Social Welfare Functions: A Rejoinder to Professor Sen," in *Logic, Methodology and Philosophy of Science*, R. Butts et al., eds., Boston: Reidel.

—— 1977b. *Rational Behavior and Bargaining Equilibrium in Games and Social Situations*, New York: Cambridge University Press.

Keynes, J. N. 1963. *The Scope and Method of Political Economy*, 4th ed., New York: Augustus M. Kelley, Bookseller, pp. 9–20.

Koopmans, T. C. 1945. Statistical Estimation of Simultaneous Economic Relationships, *Journal of the American Statistical Association*, Vol. 40, No. 232, Part 1, pp. 448–466.

Marschak, J. 1950. Statistical Inference in Economics, in *Statistical Inference in Dynamic Economic Models*, T. C. Koopmans, ed., New York: Wiley.

McClennen, Edward F. 1983. "Rational Choice and Public Policy: A Critical Survey," *Social Theory and Practice*, 92–3:335–379.

Moore, G. E. 1903. *Principia Ethica*, Cambridge, UK: Cambridge University Press.

Nosick, R. 1974. *Anarchy, State, and Utopia*, New York: Basic Books.

Pigou, A. C. 1932 (originally 1920). *Economics of Welfare*, 4th ed., London: Macmillan.

Rawls, J. 1971. *A Theory of Justice*, Cambridge, MA: Belknap Press of Harvard University Press.

Robbins, Lionel. 1949. *An Essay on the Nature & Significance of Economic Science*, 2nd ed., London: Macmillan.

Shapere, Dudley. 1969. "Notes Toward a Post-Positivistic Interpretation of Science," in *The Legacy of Logical Positivism: Studies in the Philosophy of Science*, P. Achinstein and S. F. Barker, eds., Baltimore: Johns Hopkins University Press, pp. 115–160.

Chapter 9

Pragmatism in Economics

Pragmatism, as described in Chapters 3 and 6, finds expression in economics largely in the institutional school of thought prominent in the United States, though there is also a relationship between institutional economics and the German historical school and some relationship to the dialectical materialism of Marxist economics. Both the institutionalists and the German historicists shared a common uneasiness about classical and neoclassical economics [J. N. Keynes, 1963 (originally 1891)]. The American institutionalists place heavy emphasis on individuals, and in so doing make it unlikely that their thinking will give any aid and comfort to authoritarians. By contrast, the role the thinking of Hegel played in German historicism made German historicism more capable of supporting both rightist and leftist authoritarian movements.

JOHN R. COMMONS AND PRAGMATISM

In his book on institutional economics, John R. Commons [1934] was clearly influenced by the pragmatism of Peirce and Dewey as indicated by the following quotation from him:

> We therefore . . . follow most closely the social pragmatism of Dewey; while in
> our method of investigation we follow the pragmatism of Peirce. One is scientific
> pragmatism—a method of investigation—the other is the pragmatism of human
> beings—the subject matter of the science of economics.

Commons did not explain the difference between scientific pragmatism and
the pragmatism of human beings.

As Commons stressed solving practical problems, pragmatism was attractive to him and greatly affected the methods he used. From Chapter 6, we recall
that the truth of propositions in pragmatism depends on their practical consequences for a particular problem. Thus, as truth depends on practical consequences, it is not acceptable to treat value-free positivistic and value knowledge
as independent. Similarly, neoclassical economics makes values in exchange
unique to individual circumstances, especially with regard to the distribution
of the ownership of power, including income-earning rights and privileges.
However, neoclassicists tend to leave intrinsic values (as opposed to exchange
values) independent of positivistic knowledge.

Institutional economics growing out of the work of Veblen and Commons
reached a crescendo in the 1920s, which Martin Blaug [1980, p. 87] states was
virtually over by the early 1930s. While this historical assessment may be accurate from the standpoint of disciplinary economics, practicing institutional
economists played important roles in the major restructuring of the U.S. government and its policies that took place from the early 1930s well into the 1950s.
They still wield considerable influence in resource and regional economics as
well as in the related practical affairs of government.

Institutionalism also had great impact on public affairs in Wisconsin from
1910 to 1930 through World War II and beyond. Some of these years were years
of extensive institutional reform in both the Wisconsin and national governments. Institutionally oriented economists combined forces with neoclassicists,
who felt early in the period that they had enough knowledge of values with
interpersonal validity to introduce redistributive reforms including progressive
taxation.

In agriculture, which was then a proportionally more important part of
the U.S. economy, institutionally trained agricultural economists were instrumental in developing many of the agricultural programs of the 1920s and especially the 1930s. In this applied area of agricultural economics, institutional
economics was dominant at the first two post-World War II national conferences held in Wisconsin. Thus, institutional economics made its impact felt
in problem-solving and subject-matter activities long after people asserted that
it failed to contribute to the disciplinary hard core of economics. For those
years, it is difficult to doubt the importance and the significance of the
pragmatism that found expression in Wisconsin institutionalism.

Reciprocally, it is understandable that pragmatism would make institutionalists uneasy about a neoclassical economics that takes utility (a measure

of value) as a given, independent of problems. However, neoclassicists were justified in thinking that institutionalists should be able to perceive of dynamic situations in which utility and cost functions are viewed as dynamically independent even in the context of the problem-solving activities of producers and consumers. Neoclassicists would expect this to help institutionalists recognize that changes in exchange values can be legitimately conceived to result from changes in the cost of producing goods and services independently of changes in the usefulness or *intrinsic* values of goods, services, conditions, and situations.

The pragmatists reject the methods of the positivists, who regard value-free knowledge as autonomous and regard it as impossible to have knowledge of values as characteristics of the real world. Conditional normativism probably offends the pragmatists more than positivism in general as it is a form of positivism particularly distasteful to pragmatists. The conditional normativist assumes answers to value questions, then attempts to reach prescriptions on the basis of positivistic investigations alone. This offends the pragmatists because it leaves values unchanged and uninfluenced by the processes of investigation [Kenneth Parsons, 1958, p. 296f]. Conditional normativism, as noted in earlier chapters, simply does not subject the value propositions it uses to the test of workability—of determining the truth of value propositions in terms of their consequences for solving a practical problem. Instead, it assumes the truth of value premises.

The institutionalists also practice the dialectics of pragmatism. Pragmatic hypotheses (which are typically prescriptive) are confronted by alternative prescriptions. A problem-solving pragmatic investigation confronts each hypothetical solution with its antitheses and determines which prescription is better in terms of its consequences. As pointed out in Chapter 6, the difference between pragmatism on the one hand and positivism and normativism on the other is not that the first tests hypotheses while the other two do not. The difference is that pragmatism tests prescriptive hypotheses, whereas the other two test value-free and value hypotheses. All three are interested in disproving hypotheses. All three expect that the surviving hypotheses will eventually be disproven or displaced by superior hypotheses. Pragmatic institutionalism seeks prescriptive knowledge to solve practical problems as opposed to answering disciplinary questions, with the truth of those prescriptions regarded as depending on their anticipated consequences as determined by both logic and experience.

In Chapter 6 we saw the roles played by the tests of coherence (logic), correspondence (experience), and clarity in pragmatism. We also saw that the pragmatic test of workability can be regarded as a special case of correspondence with experience—but only in the sense of experience (actual or anticipated) with the value-free positivistic and value consequences of the action that executes the prescription. It is far more complicated to test a prescriptive hypothesis under the pragmatic presumption that truth is to be determined by the total value-free positivistic and value consequences of that prescription than it is to test a simple value-free positivistic or value hypothesis.

The complexity arises out of the implied interdependency of value-free positivistic and value knowledge, the question of whether the decision rule (with its inevitable incorporation of power distributions) is appropriate, and the multidisciplinary nature of the knowledge required to solve real-world problems. Pragmatic methods for acquiring knowledge are also complex. Pragmatically, truth is dependent on consequences. It makes a difference who is benefitted or hurt, when, where, and how. To determine such consequences is complex, difficult, and holistic rather than simple, easy, and reductionist.

In pragmatism, feedback (both actual and conceptual) is important as there are time lags from prescriptions to execution to the bearing of responsibility for actions taken. In obtaining the benefits of feedback, interaction between investigators and decision makers and/or affected people is important. Even when feedback from the relevant decision makers and/or affected people is impossible, it is helpful to simulate the incidence of different costs and benefits in time and space and among groups of people to be able to study empathetically the consequences of different scenarios.

Commons, we noted at the beginning of this chapter, followed both the *social* pragmatism of Dewey and the *scientific* pragmatism of Peirce. Because value propositions emerge out of and are clarified by considering the consequences of prescriptive hypotheses, much of a pragmatic investigation is likely to involve premaximization instead of the direct maximization characteristic of so many linear programming and econometric analyses. Premaximization research helps establish the preconditions for optimization noted in Chapter 8 to be necessary in discussing nonpragmatic prescription. Perhaps this explains the apparent aversion to maximization of institutionalists who cannot really be averse to maximization as they seek the prescription that best solves the problem at hand. Pragmatic methods tend to be problem-specific and, hence, unstable and ephemeral. In addition to being complex, they often lack elegance and tidiness.

PRAGMATISM UNDER ATTACK

The upsurge of pragmatism in the 1920s and 1930s seemed to create its own opposition. Part of the opposition grew up among disciplinarians, some of whom were offended by the antagonism of the institutionalists toward neoclassical economics. Even more fundamentally, some disciplinary economists (including Keynesian and other nonneoclassical economists) regarded institutionalists as opposing the hypothetico-inductive method characteristically used by but not necessarily limited to the logical positivists of the so-called hard sciences. Such opposition to pragmatism cannot be unambiguously ascribed to neoclassicists, some of whom were and are too analytic to proceed to the descriptive and synthetic from the analytic. Also, neoclassicists often felt that the solutions institutionalists advocated for the problems of the time left something to be desired in terms of their likely influence on the productivity of the economy by disrupting price and market mechanisms.

Groups of hypothetico-deductive opponents to pragmatic institutionalism included the economists who were developing sophisticated and advanced disciplinary skills in mathematical economics. Also, economists interested in quantification and econometricians were attracted to the relatively straightforward methods of the positivists and were dissatisfied with what they viewed as an unnecessarily complex pragmatic, holistic institutional view of the world. When the quantitatively oriented neoclassicists dealt with values (monetary or nonmonetary), they did not deal with them in a pragmatic way. The utility functions underlying their neoclassical demand equations were regarded as measures of rather stable instrinsic values even though the econometric analyses often equate supply functions with demand functions to determine fluctuating prices or exchange values.

From the standpoint of econometricians, it appears unnecessarily complex to regard utility functions as functions of the process of solving problems. In economics there was a natural antipathy between the pragmatic institutionalists and econometricians that was probably more intense than the antipathy that has prevented complete unity between pragmatists and positivists in the unity of science movement, as discussed in Chapter 6.

By the early 1930s, and especially after World War II, pragmatism and Wisconsin institutionalism were under severe attack. Even though neoclassical economics had been badly hurt by Pareto's question as translated by John R. Hicks in 1939, a Pareto optimal, more market-oriented, neoclassical economics became increasingly dominant. It was reinforced by the increased capacity of the econometricians and other quantitatively oriented economists to translate theoretical structures into mathematical models and to estimate the parameters of such models. Individuals in both groups wanted to do disciplinary work and fill data banks and information systems with stable enduring theories, models, observations, and parameter estimates. The pragmatic institutional point of view produced mainly ephemeral knowledge, often with a half life less than the time it takes to solve a problem.

It was in this period, that Kenneth Boulding is alleged to have characterized institutional economics as a mixture of poor economics and bad sociology—or was it bad economics and poor sociology? Even today, Blaug and Ward [1972] refer to institutionalism disparagingly as unrigorous "story telling" lacking logic and difficult to disprove presumably because of its ambiguity and the lack of degrees of freedom in relevant data series [1980, p. 127]. Institutionalism was also criticized by Robbins for failing to contribute laws and quantitative knowledge to the discipline of economics [Robbins, 1932, p. 114]. Institutionalists focused on solutions to multidisciplinary problems, while their protagonists, who displayed more interest in economics as a discipline, derided institutional work for failure to make disciplinary contributions.

Disciplinary economists, interested in economics as a positivistic and/or normative but not pragmatic discipline, want enduring theoretical concepts, quantitative techniques, and basic measurements whose truth does not depend on consequences in solving particular short-term problems. A related conflict between pragmatists and nonpragmatists involves the holism of pragmatism versus the advantages of specialization for disciplinarians. The holism of pragmatism involves the need to look at the many relevant disciplinary dimensions of practical problems and generate interdependent positivistic and normative knowledge in researching prescriptions. This holistic approach to problem solving is at variance with the desire of a disciplinarian to subdivide economics and to work on it one part at a time.

The disciplinarian finds an advantage in methods and philosophic points of view that permit one to specialize and to attack one particular part of the discipline until it is thoroughly mastered and knowledge of potential enduring value is generated. This knowledge can then be carefully appraised by disciplinary peers and, if acceptable, made a permanent part of the information banks of economists. By contrast, disciplinarians find themselves uncomfortable with the ephemeral holism and multidisciplinarianism of pragmatism.

In a sense, the conflict between pragmatism and other philosophies within economics is a part of a wider American conflict between pragmatism and more traditional academic and disciplinary points of view. John Dewey's pragmatism had an even greater influence on American primary and secondary education than it did on economics via John R. Commons. In American education, the pragmatists were basically dissatisfied with the academic disciplines of the European and traditional east coast American universities of the 19th century.

The traditional disciplines tended to focus on either value-free positivistic or value knowledge. There were the sciences with their positivistic empirical orientation and the humanities with their normativistic orientation. The pragmatists felt it was important for education to be oriented to the practical problems of society. This pragmatic reorientation was consistent with the politics of the land grant movement, which insisted that universities and institutions of higher education address the practical problems of agriculture, industry, and society or, more generally, problems involving technology, people, and institutions.

Pragmatic educators wanted to teach the process of problem solving. The traditional disciplinarians wanted to teach their academic subjects undisturbed by the cares and difficulties of farmers, businessmen, and communities, and in a way that mostly did not regard truth as dependent on consequences but regarded value and value-free positivistic truths as independent and enduring.

Important in the conflict between pragmatic and nonpragmatic points of view was the confusion of quantitative work with positivism, a confusion shared by both positivists and pragmatists. Though the pragmatists have regarded themselves as empiricists and have been prominent in the unity of science movement, pragmatic institutionalists in economics have been critical of what they regard as the "quantitative technicians" they feel employ methods too simple to capture the subtle, interdependencies between value-free knowledge and knowledge of values in the contexts of particular problems. The pragmatists distrust the quantitatively oriented economists, particularly the econometricians, who combined neoclassical logic with empirical observations in positivistic ways.

RESURGENCE OF PRAGMATISM AND INSTITUTIONAL ECONOMICS

The post-World War II period included counteroffensives by the pragmatists. As positivism drove neoclassicists interested in problem solving toward conditional normativism, a chink appeared in the armor of the opposition that was exploited by the pragmatists. A strong counterattack, discussed in Chapter 7, was mounted by Professor Kenneth Parsons [1949], an agricultural economist from the University of Wisconsin. Parsons disagreed (see Chapter 8) with the positivistic conditionally normative method of taking values as given and feared it would lead to a reversion to medieval reliance on authority and dogma. His case against conditional normativists in agricultural economics applies as well to the conditional normativism of Gunnar Myrdal as expressed in Appendix II of the *American Dilemma* [1944] and reexpressed in Myrdal's more recent book, *Objectivity in Social Research* [1969].

Parsons wanted values to be explicit as did Myrdal but also wanted values to be researched. Parsons went beyond the normativists and wanted values to be viewed as functions of problem-solving experiences in which their truth depends upon their consequences. He did not want unobjective, arbitrarily assumed values to determine prescriptions to problems without examining the truth of those values in the context of the problems they are used to solve.

In agricultural economics, but also in general economics, the pragmatic position taken earlier by Parson's found much support in the late 1960s among the younger general and agricultural economists concerned with the issues of the times. They were dissatisfied with neoclassical economics as modified by the introduction of the concepts of Pareto optimality and other positivistic views and methods. They were also dissatisfied with positivistic presuppositions that there is nothing objective to be known about values as characteristics of the real world. It should be noted, however, that not all of those dissatisfied with neoclassical economics in the late 1960s and early 1970s sought objective knowledge of values. Indeed, some activist economists displayed considerable unwillingness to submit their value concepts to the tests of logic (coherence) and experience (correspondence), whether or not those tests were pragmatically conceived.

Nonetheless, problem-solving became more important when U.S. society was shaken to its roots in the late 1960s by issues involving the races, minority rights and privileges, the Vietnam war, and the rising demands of the third world. Then in the early 1970s, came the reduced availability of fossil fuels and OPEC's effect on energy prices. Problem solving became increasingly important as the complacencies and self-satisfactions of the 1950s and early 1960s were shattered. With the loss of complacency and self-satisfaction, there was less to be said in favor of disciplinary points of view and disciplinary research whether or not of known relevance, while the problem-solving orientation of pragmatism became more attractive.

In 1968, Kenneth Boulding, who is often forward looking and imaginative, delivered his presidential address to the American Economics Association. In that address, Boulding took an obviously pragmatic approach to economics. He wrote in *The Image* that the processes by which the normative and positivistic images of reality are formed are similar [1956, p. 11]. In writing *The Image*, Boulding was becoming pragmatic, though not so much so that he was unable to envision separate positivistic and value images of reality. He was pragmatic, however, in the sense that he began to view the processes by which these two separate images are created as essentially the same and pragmatic.

Perhaps the greatest conversion to pragmatism in this period is revealed in Georgescu-Roegen's book, *The Entropy Law and The Economic Process* [1971]. Georgescu-Roegen demonstrated that physics, the prime example of positivism for the logical positivists, is essentially pragmatic and far from purely positivistic. In effect, Georgescu-Roegen challenged the logical positivistic interpretation of science. He argued that entropy and the second law of thermodynamics cause a pragmatic interdependence between knowledge of values and value-free positivistic knowledge, even in physics. In close agreement with Frank Knight [1946, pp. 205–208] and Kenneth Boulding [1981, p. 153], Georgescu-Roegen noted that a category or classification of events contains events that are similar with respect to "important" characteristics and dissimilar with respect to unimportant characteristics. What is important and unimportant depends on values defining problems at hand.

Georgescu-Roegen stressed the penumbra that exists between classes. There are always individual events that are hard to classify because they are on the edges of their class and differ with respect to less "important" variables. He points out that physicists and society place high value on low-level entropy. (For the student unacquainted with physics, a low level of entropy has to do with the greater availability of energy or with more forms and substances that can be created and/or maintained only at the expenditure of energy.) Georgescu-

Roegen then demonstrated that the classifications used and measurements made by physicists are determined by changes in value associated with changes in levels of entropy. Thus, as the values of society shift in accordance with changes in the availability of low-level entropy, the classifications of physics and the variables in which physicists are interested also change. Consequently, the propositions and measurements of physics, the showpiece of the positivists, become dependent, in Georgescu-Roegen's view, on the values society places on different levels of entropy to make the truths of physics depend pragmatically on consequences.

The social crises and the unrest of the late 1960s and early 1970s brought so many important issues and problems to the forefront, it was necessary for economic researchers to address themselves to solutions to these problems. Pragmatic institutionalism at least had an ability to define and solve problems however cumbersome and complicated that ability was. The stress on problems and issues in the 1970s also strengthened the position of normativism as evidenced by the much greater interest in such subjects as medical ethics, bioethics, women's rights, agroethics, environmental ethics, and racism. As the problems and issues of the time also entailed substantial dissatisfaction with the distribution of the ownership of rights and privileges, the position of Pareto optimality was weakened while the case for pragmatism was strengthened. However, these same issues also strengthened the case for nonpragmatic forms of welfare economics based on objective research on values regarded as independent of value-free positive knowledge, as discussed in Chapter 8.

There has been a recent expansion of literary contributions dealing with the concerns of pragmatic institutionalists. Part of this literature makes the case, perhaps unintentionally, for pragmatic institutionlism by expressing dissatisfaction with neoclassical economics. Other parts of the literature make the direct case for institutional economics, if not pragmatism. Examples of this literature include several of the chapters in Robert Heilbroner's *Economic Means and Social Ends* [1969], Kenneth Boulding's *Evolutionary Economics* [1981], the chapters in Daniel Bell's and Irving Kristol's *The Crisis in Economic Theory* [1981], Bruce Caldwell's *Beyond Positivism: Economic Methodology in the Twentieth Century* [1982], Richard R. Nelson's and Sidney G. Winter's *An Evolutionary Theory of Economic Change* [1982], and chapters in Alfred Eichner's *Why Economics is Not Yet a Science* [1983]. The *Journal of Economic Literature* consistently publishes pragmatic institutionalist articles, including one by Donald McCloskey entitled "Rhetoric of Economics" [1983].

In a sense, the resurgence of institutional economics is more disciplinary than the institutional economics that crested in the 1920s (later in applied spheres). Critics of the earlier institutionalism, such as Robbins, criticized it for not contributing to the hard core of neoclassical economics. Those with an institutional-like approach to economics are redefining the discipline away from what McCloskey refers to as modernism—in his view, a logically positivistic, mechanistic mixture of neoclassical market economics, econometrics, and mathematical economics—to include in economics the dynamics of technical, institutional, and human change.

Pragmatism, General Systems Simulation, and Industrial Organization

Perhaps unknown to many pragmatic institutionalists is the effect of iterative, interactive methods for modeling subject-matter and problem-solving domains developed by systems scientists. Though systems science evolved out of cybernetics, which was greatly influenced by positivism, some of the applied systems-science resaerch has become very pragmatic. As systems scientists contributing to the efforts of multidisciplinary teams have attempted to model the domains of different subjects and problems, they have found it important to interact iteratively with decision makers and affected people. This interactive iteration turns out to be an important source of value-free positivistic and value information. Often, it has been clear that the truth or acceptability of propositions being incorporated into systems science models has depended on their consequences over time in terms of who is hurt and benefitted, how, and why.

Systems scientists often use iterative scenarios to investigate these consequences interactively with affected people and decision makers. The acceptability of model components and policy alternatives often proves to be dependent on these consequences, as interaction with decision makers and affected people often makes it necessary to redo the models repeatedly as faults in their structures are revealed. This iterative interactive nature of systems science analyses of subjects and problems proves to be rather pragmatic despite the positivistic origins of systems science in cybernetics. Pragmatic institutionalists seem to be slow in recognizing this pragmatic tendency in systems science analysis, probably because of the antipathy that developed earlier between the pragmatists and positivistically oriented economists who employed quantitative methods that did not admit the possibility of interdependence between value-free positivistic and value propositions.

Industrial organization studies are also compatible with pragmatism and the general systems simulation methods just discussed. Industrial organization studies are concerned with "structure," "conduct," and "performance" variables, while general systems simulation studies are concerned with corresponding similar "state," "behavioral," and "criterion" variables. Both study time and process. Both tend to be multidisciplinary. Both are more closely related to problem-solving and subject-matter research than disciplinary research, and perhaps for this reason fail to appear in the index to Martin Blaug's [1980] important book on economic research methodology, which is oriented to disciplinary economic research.

General systems simulation studies probably involve the technical changes generated by the biological and physical sciences more than either institutional or industrial organization studies. Human change, by contrast with changes in agencies, organizations, and firms, may be more neglected in institutional economics and industrial organization research than in general systems simulation research. Both are pragmatic in seeking truth through consequences, which leads them to deal with positivistic and value propositions interdependently. Industrial organization adherents appear to share the institutional economist's distrust of the quantification of general systems simulation research for similar reasons.

IMPLICATIONS FOR THE THREE KINDS OF RESEARCH

The resurgence of pragmatism and the development of general systems simulation and industrial organization research have substantial implications for problem-solving, subject-matter, and disciplinary research.

Pragmatism provides methods often appropriate for *problem-solving research*. However, pragmatic methods need not be confined to problems involving institutional change. Pragmatic methods are appropriately used in solving complex practical problems involving technical and human change where interdependent answers to value-free and value questions are required. The experiences of institutional economists researching problems involving institutional change in both public and private sectors can advantageously be supplemented by the experiences of industrial organization researchers dealing with problems involving the private sector.

While general systems simulation researchers also investigate problems involving public and private institutions, they have had relatively more valuable experience researching problems involving technological and human changes to complement the experiences of the institutionalists and industrial organization people researching institutional change. Importantly, the general systems simulators have developed substantial skill in using quantitative methods and computers not possessed by many institutionalists and industrial organization analysts.

Pragmatic methods tend to be unduly complicated for problems whose solution turns on answering relatively independent positivistic or value questions. In such cases, simpler, less complex methods are adequate.

With respect to *subject-matter research*, pragmatism and its two variants have distinct advantages when interdependent value-free positivistic and value knowledge are involved. Instances involving relatively independent value and value-free positivistic knowledge are better handled with simpler normative or positivistic methods. Subjects involving changing decision rules often need to be handled pragmatically in ways well understood and practiced by institutionalists despite their frequent aversion for quantification. The holism of pragmatism makes it amenable to the multidisciplinary nature of subject-matter research.

Disciplinary research in economics is another matter. Many disciplinary questions are questions of logic, where logic takes precedence over the empirical quarrels between pragmatists, normativists, and positivists, who differ far more over empirical methods than questions of logic. Other disciplinary questions have empirical answers. If these answers are obviously of enduring value to economics, they will not be affected by ephemeral problematic contexts and can probably be obtained by positivistic and normativistic methods—and I doubt increasingly that there is much difference between the two—that treat value-free and value knowledge as independent.

At a deeper level, the question can be raised as to whether economics, as a discipline concerned fundamentally with optimization, decision making, and prescription, should ever be regarded in other than pragmatic terms. John R. Commons thought it should not, and developed a pragmatic form of institutional economics. Members of the German historical school had similar convictions. Marxists also share the conviction at least partially, Hegel and dialectics being part of the heritage of both the German historical school and the Marxists. Even if one agrees with Commons, it seems that more flexibility to incorporate the accomplishments of positivism, normativism, and systems science will be required than is normally present among pragmatic institutionalists.

REQUIRED READINGS

(Read in Order Indicated)

Boulding, K. E. 1969. Economics as a Moral Science, *The American Economic Review*, **LIX**(1):1–12. (Tenth)

Bressler, R. G., Jr. 1964. Research on the Structure of Agricultural Markets, in *Market Structure Research: Theory and Practice in Agricultural Economics*, Paul L. Farris, ed., Ames: Iowa State University Press, Ch. 1. (Eighth)

Churchman, C. W. and R. L. Ackoff. 1969. Purposive Behavior and Cybernetics, in *Modern Systems Research for the Behavioral Scientist*, Walter Buckley, ed., Chicago: Aldine, pp. 243–249. (Eleventh)

Georgescu-Roegen, N. 1971. Entropy, Value and Development, in *The Entropy Law and the Economic Process*, Cambridge: Harvard University Press, pp. 276–292, 306–307. (Fifth)

Johnson, G. L. 1973. Review of The Entropy Law and the Economic Process by N. Georgescu-Roegen, *Journal of Economic Issues*, **VII**(3):492–499. (Seventh)

—— and G. E. Rossmiller. 1978. Improving Agricultural Decision Making, in

Agricultural Sector Planning, George E. Rossmiller, ed., East Lansing: Dept. of Agricultural Economics, Michigan State University, pp. 41–51. (Ninth)

Knight, F. H. 1946. *Risk, Uncertainty and Profit*, New York: Houghton Mifflin (originally published in 1921), pp. 205–208. (Sixth)

Parsons, K. H. 1958. The Value Problem in Agricultural Policy, in *Agricultural Adjustment Problems in a Growing Economy*, E. Heady et al., eds., Ames: Iowa State College Press, pp. 285–299. (Third)

——— 1949. The Logical Foundations of Economic Research, *Journal of Farm Economics*, November, pp. 656–686. (Fourth)

Randall, A. 1974. Information, Power, and Academic Responsibility, *American Journal of Agricultural Economics*, 56(2):227–234. (Twelfth)

Salter, L. 1948. Scientific Method and Social Science, in *A Critical Review of Research in Land Economics*, Minneapolis: University of Minnesota Press, pp. 68–69. (Second)

Whitaker, Edmund. 1940. *A History of Economic Ideas*, New York: Longmans Green, pp. 730–744. (First)

ADDITIONAL REFERENCES

Bell, Daniel, and Irving Kristol. 1981. *The Crisis in Economic Theory*, New York: Basic Books.

Blaug, Mark. 1980. *The Methodology of Economics*, Cambridge, UK: Cambridge University Press.

Boulding, Kenneth. 1981. *Evolutionary Economics*, Beverly Hills, CA: Sage Publications.

——— 1956. *The Image*, Ann Arbor: The University of Michigan Press.

Caldwell, Bruce. 1982. *Beyond Positivism: Economic Methodology in the Twentieth Century*, London: Allen and Unwin.

Commons, J. R. 1934. *Institutional Economics*, New York: Macmillan.

Eichner, Alfred. 1983. *Why Economics Is Not Yet a Science*, Armonk, NY: M. E. Sharpe.

Heilbroner, Robert L. 1969. *Economic Means and Social Ends*, Englewood Cliffs: Prentice-Hall, Inc.

Keynes, J. N. 1963. *The Scope and Method of Political Economy*, 4th ed., New York: Augustus M. Kelley, Bookseller, pp. 9–20.

McCloskey, Donald N. 1983. The Rhetoric of Economics, *Journal of Economic Literature* **XXI**(2):481–517.

Myrdal, G. 1944. *The American Dilemma*, New York: Harper.

——— 1969. *Objectivity in Social Research*, New York: Pantheon.

Nelson, Richard R. and Sidney G. Winter. 1982. *An Evolutionary Theory of Economic Change*, Cambridge, Belknap Press of Harvard University Press.

Robbins, Lionel. 1949. *An Essay on the Nature & Significance of Economic Science*, 2nd ed., London: Macmillan.

II

Research Case Studies

This part illustrates with case studies how the different philosophies considered in Part I have been important in doing problem-solving, subject-matter, and disciplinary research. Two case studies are considered under each of the three basic kinds of research. For disciplinary research, both positivistic research and research on values of known relevance are considered with little attention to disciplinary research of unknown relevance. For subject-matter research, the case studies illustrate research to acquire both value-free positivistic knowledge and knowledge of values. The problem-solving case studies illustrate both pragmatic and nonpragmatic approaches to decision making. For each of the case studies, attention is given to support and accountability, administration and conduct, review and evaluation, and durability and practical impact of results. These subjects are addressed more generally in Chapters 13–16 of Part III.

Chapter 10

Disciplinary Case Studies

In this chapter, two disciplinary case studies are considered—Wassily Leontief's research on input/output analysis and T. W. Schultz's research on human capital. Both of these outstanding researchers won the Nobel Prize in recognition for their research.

Leontief's citation read as follows [Swedish Journal of Economics, 1973]:

> The Royal Swedish Academy of Sciences has awarded Professor Wassily Leontief the 1973 Prize in Economic Science in memory of Alfred Nobel. Professor Leontief is awarded the prize "for the development of the input-output method and for its application to important economic problems."
>
> Professor Leontief is the sole and unchallenged creator of the input-output technique. This important innovation has given economic science an empirically useful method to highlight the general interdependence in the production system of a society. In particular, the method provides tools for a systematic analysis of the complicated inter-industry transactions in an economy.
>
> Professor Leontief outlined the input-output technique as early as the nineteen-thirties. A comprehensive version of the analysis was published in 1941 in the book *The Structure of American Economy 1919–1929*. A considerably extended version appeared ten years later.

Input-output analysis describes the interdependence in the production system as a network of deliveries between the various sectors of production. For every production sector, technical coefficients define the quantities of intermediary products which are required per unit produced of each commodity.

Final demands of products for consumption, investment and exports in the model are usually treated as determined by conditions outside the production system. The purpose of the analysis is then to find out how much production has to be increased in the various sectors of the economy to satisfy a given desired or planned increase in final demand for consumption, investment and exports. The increased production in each sector then has to cover not only the change in final demand but also the derived changes in demand for intermediary products in the various production sectors.

The input-output system has found extensive use especially in forecasting and planning, both in the short and in the long run. The wide usefulness of the input-output technique is indicated by the fact that it is used in forecasting and planning in quite different types of economic systems—decentralized market economies with mainly private enterprise as well as centrally planned economies dominated by public ownership.

The method has proved particularly effective in the analysis of sudden and large changes, as in the case of military mobilization or other far-reaching transformations of an economy. The method has also been applied in studies of how cost and price changes are transmitted through various sectors of an economy.

Schultz's citation read as follows [Scandinavian Journal of Economics, 1980]:

Theodore W. Schultz began as an agricultural economist. During the 1930s and 1940s, he published a series of studies on the crisis in American agriculture, and later took up agricultural issues in various developing countries throughout the world. His best known works from this period are *Agriculture in an Unstable Economy* . . . and *Production and Welfare of Agriculture* . . . His most important book was *Transforming Traditional Agriculture* . . . The main characteristic of Schultz's studies in agricultural economics is that he does not treat the agricultural economy in isolation, but as an integral part of the entire economy. Schultz's analytical interest has been focused on the imbalance between relative poverty and under-development in agriculture as compared with the higher productivity and higher income levels in industry and other urban economic activities. He applied this approach to industrialized countries such as the United States and to the many developing countries he has studied.

Schultz has received many of the impulses for his notable analysis of the importance of human resources for economic and social development from his studies of productivity problems in agriculture in the United States and the developing world.

Schultz's analysis of the development potential of agriculture is based on a disequilibrium approach. It is the gap between traditional production methods and the more effective methods now available which creates the conditions necessary for dynamic development. Using this approach, Schultz has presented detailed critiques of the developing countries' industrialization policies and their neglect of agriculture. Schultz was the first to systematize the analysis of how investments in education can affect productivity in agriculture as well as in the economy as a whole. Well aware of the limitations of the method, Schultz has as a first approximation defined and measured the size of educational capital as a sum of accumulated investments in education. A large proportion of the costs of these education investments consists of a loss of earnings from employment during periods of study. These therefore constitute a kind of alternative costs which can be taken into account in private and national contexts.

Schultz and his students have shown that for a long time, there has been a considerably higher yield on "human capital" than on physical capital in the American economy, and that this tension has resulted in much more rapid expansion of education investments than other investments.

Schultz has always kept close to economic reality in his work as an economic researcher and as an adviser in various capacities. He has shown great wisdom as an economist, with a striking ability to define developmental factors which model-building economists are inclined to neglect. The extent of his approach is also manifest in a number of other factors and contexts related to human resources (the human factor). Schultz has done research on subjects connected with health and disease as essential factors in economic development in the Third World, as well as on population issues in general. During his long research career, he has shown outstanding skill in asking the relevant questions, and has opened up many avenues of new research. Few economists have done so much to inspire colleagues and students to perform worthwhile research.

In this chapter, each of these two pieces of research is classified as to kind, examined for kind of knowledge generated, and analyzed for philosophic orientation. Attention is also given to how the research was administered and to the durability and practicality of its results.

The last section of the chapter advances some philosophical and methodological generalizations about disciplinary research. These generalizations are based on Part I as well as on these two case studies.

Chapter 11 deals with subject matter research and Chapter 12 with problem-solving research. Each ends with philosophical and methodological generalizations about the kinds of research considered. Chapters 13–16 provide generalizations about the administration of problem-solving, subject-matter and disciplinary research. Philosophical and methodological generalizations that cross the three kinds of research are found in Chapter 17.

WASSILY LEONTIEF'S RESEARCH ON
INPUT/OUTPUT RELATIONSHIPS

Leontief's input/output (I/O) research has two historical backgrounds—one long-term and a short-term one dealing with the influence of then-current problems and events on Leontief's thinking. Viewed in the long term, the roots of what Leontief did can be traced back in the history of economic thought to F. Quesnay's *Tableau Economique*, the work of Leon Walras, and the works of such mathematicians and economists as Gossen, Jevons, and Cournot.

The immediate factors influencing Leontief are probably more interesting than his long-term historical precursors. Leontief received his undergraduate education in economics at the University of Leningrad from 1921 to 1925. When he left Russia before he was 20 to begin a career in Germany and the West, he was concerned about what is known as the "method of balances" then used by Soviet planners. He sought a more systematic way of analyzing the relationships between the sectors and subsectors of a total economy to replace the haphazard, relatively unsystematic method of balances. His first work was published in Russian in 1925. His Ph.D. degree was from the University of Berlin in 1928. It dealt with circular economic flows and used elementary I/O concepts. His work and that of various German economists at the University of Kiel attracted the attention of the director of the National Bureau of Economic Research (NBER) in New York and led to an invitation to Leontief to join that agency. In turn, his work at the NBER on I/O relationships attracted the attention of the economics faculty at Harvard.

In looking at the history of Leontief's research on I/O analysis, it is important to stress that it had an extremely practical origin—dissatisfaction with the method of balances.

Leontief's Research Can Be Classified as Relevant Disciplinary

Though the practical need for Leontief's research was clear, his research was highly disciplinary in nature and is best classified as relevant disciplinary research. It is highly specialized within economics. Leontief focused on the technical and monetary flows within an economy without devoting specific attention to the four prime movers of economic development: capital accumulation, the generation of technological advance, the restructuring of institutions, and investments in human capital to improve the quality of the human agent. A planner in possession of a Leontief I/O table and a complete analysis of that table still has only one specialized kind of knowledge from economics to use in solving individual planning problems. If a particular planning problem involves technological advance, institutional change, or human development, the planner in command of Leontief's approach still has to consult with disciplinarians or subject-matter researchers dealing with such changes before successfully solving the problem. Current system science analyses of economies recognize this and use I/O components as parts of multidisciplinary, subject-matter, or problem-solving models emphasizing technical, institutional, and human change components in a manner consistent with the subject matter being investigated. Leontief's work on I/O analysis was very disciplinary and extremely relevant but could hardly be classified as either subject-matter or problem-solving research in the sense in which these two terms are used in this book.

The relevance of Leontief's work was quickly recognized in the United States and abroad. In addition to the governments of central planned economies, users have included the governments of France, Japan, and many other countries. Use of I/O in the United States has been somewhat sporadic depending on the administration in power, its needs, and its attitude toward planning and public administration.

Kinds of Knowledge Sought

An I/O analysis is based on information about monetary values (quantities multiplied by fixed prices) of inputs and products moving between the various subsectors of the economy. It also involves normative information (expressed as monetary *values*) about payments for the contributions of governmental and productive factors as well as the final demands of the users of goods and services generated by the economy. Finally, these data generate the gross national product, which is also expressed as a monetary value. An I/O analysis is useful to a person interested in maximizing GNP; thus, it helps provide knowledge of use in reaching prescriptions.

Philosophic Orientation

Despite the fact that an I/O analysis deals objectively with descriptive knowledge of monetary values as well as with value-free positive information, I/O work is properly regarded as positivistic. Recall from Chapters 4 and 7 that knowledge about who values what is acceptable knowledge to positivists. Knowledge of monetary values is normative, as that word is used in this book, even if produced by positivistic methods and is acceptable to positivists. We simply have here an example of positivistic research on behavioral values and a demonstration that behavioral knowledge of values is producible by logically positivistic methods and is acceptable to positivists.

The methods of positivism were used by Leontief in researching value as well as value-free positive questions important in conducting an I/O analysis. Fundamentally, he combined logic with observation to produce both value-free positivistic and value knowledge. The question did not arise as to whether there is a reality corresponding to the behavioral values Leontief described. The only reality involved was the reality of the monetary values established behaviorally in the economies being researched. Leontief and his colleagues used positivistic methods in assembling both positivistic information on the flows of physical commodities and services within the economy and in measuring monetary values in the same economy.

Financial Support and Accountability

Leontief's research on I/O analysis received financial support from Harvard University. It was also supported indirectly by a large amount of funding for closely related but more applied projects in governments. These projects drew heavily on his results and, in turn, contributed important feedback to his basic disciplinary research work.

In his early work at the University of Kiel, Leontief undoubtedly benefitted from the faculty and other resources of that university in producing his Ph.D. dissertation. His first professional article was written in Germany, translated into Russian and published in the Soviet Union, and translated later into English. It was at the University of Kiel that Leontief's work came to the attention of administrators from the NBER. Wesley Mitchell of the NBER invited Leontief to the Bureau, from which he was recruited to Harvard University to lecture on international trade. Haldor Fisher et al., from Battelle Institute, report [1973] that Leontief imposed the condition when he joined Harvard that his research work on I/O relationships be supported, and that the Harvard economics faculty investigated the concept and found it "completely impractical but" granted funds "with the understanding that Leontief would report his failure when the money had been spent."

His book on I/O analysis published by Harvard University Press was not a financial success. Though the Harvard Press declined to reprint it, Oxford University Press saw an opportunity and republished it [1966].

In 1941, the U.S. Bureau of Labor Statistics (BLS) was given responsibility for studying the impact of military demobilization on the U.S. economy. BLS leaders knew of Leontief's promising work. After a BLS team visited Harvard, it was decided to use I/O analysis to study the future demobilization of the U.S. economy. In 1945, the results of a cooperative BLS/Harvard effort to develop an I/O table for the United States for 1939 were published. Also, an impromptu German tableau was used to guide the efforts of the Allies in disrupting the German economy during World War II. The U.S. Office of War Mobilization and Reconversion also used the U.S. I/O analysis. Resources and financial support for I/O analysis research also came from the National Security Resources Board and from the U.S. Air Force Project SCOOP.

I/O analysis work in the federal government helped establish many important linkages throughout the government that made it possible to assemble data from a large number of federal agencies for an I/O table for the U.S. There was also a mobilization project that drew heavily on Leontief's I/O research results. In 1953, the Eisenhower administration reviewed the military projects in this area and greatly reduced funding for Leontief's work. In a sense, I/O analysis went underground or returned to an emphasis on disciplinary basics at Harvard University. An important exception was in the Office of Business Economics in the Department of Commerce, where the National Accounts

Review Committee (NARC) was concerned about the practical implications of the relationship between I/O analysis and national accounting. By 1964, the national 1958 I/O table was produced and published.

Throughout the period of varying governmental emphasis on I/O analysis, the Harvard Economic Research Project and Leontief provided a stabilizing influence to illustrate the dependence of society on basic disciplinary research and researchers in universities. Leontief and his colleagues at Harvard specialized in one aspect of disciplinary economic research—I/O analysis. Harvard University and Leontief, each with their own strengths and reputations, were able to provide the financial support needed for this on-going basic disciplinary research project. The subject-matter and problem-solving research in government that used I/O analysis experienced wide fluctuations in financial support.

Conduct and Administration

Leontief's conduct of his I/O research project was that of an ideal, disciplinary, intellectual leader. He and his close associates at Harvard specialized on one aspect of disciplinary economic research—I/O analysis—in which they could reap the benefits of specialization. He cooperated to make the results of his basic disciplinary research available to governmental agencies to use them for subject-matter and problem-solving research. In turn, their subject-matter and problem-solving research provided valuable feedback and substantial resources to carry out the practical, more detailed development of I/O concepts and techniques. "Discipline" from his disciplinary peers in economics helped Leontief administer his own basic research.

From the above, the administrative pattern Leontief followed in conducting his research on I/O analysis seems clear. He was a disciplinarian specializing in an undeveloped sub-part of economics—I/O analysis. He did not have a large administrative structure at Harvard University. He relied on his own efforts and those of closely associated colleagues and students. Support was drawn from his university and from the Rockefeller Foundation via traditional university channels.

Review and Evaluation

Leontief's research and that of his closely associated colleagues and students at Harvard University was under almost continuous disciplinary review and evaluation. The process that went on at Harvard University started much earlier with the publication of his first input/output article in Germany and its republication in the Soviet Union and elsewhere. His work was always "reviewed and evaluated" by himself to determine its practical relevance. The most significant evaluation of Leontief's I/O research was, of course, the 1973 Nobel Prize in Economics.

Durability and Practical Importance

The durability of Leontief's research on I/O analysis is attested to by its disciplinary and practical importance over almost six decades and by an outlook that indicates I/O analysis will be important in economics and in government and business for the foreseeable future. As is usually true for disciplinary research results, the product of his I/O analysis research has proven durable. Virtually all major graduate programs in economics teach I/O analysis.

The practical applications of I/O analysis came slowly and unevenly. J. M. Keynes' important contribution to macroeconomics was a strong competitor during the 1930s and 1940s. Much stress was placed on the work of Keynes, so Leontief's I/O analysis work may have been neglected in its earlier phases. However, as I/O analysis established its close relationship with national accounting research and was able to draw more and more on the efficiency of modern computers, I/O analysis became relatively stronger and found more and more important applications.

It is instructive to note that the results of applied I/O work of a subject-matter or problem-solving nature have lacked the durability of the results of basic disciplinary work on I/O analysis. I/O tables for countries go out of date and must be redone. Problem-solving research results based on I/O analysis are time, place, and problem-specific. Even subject-matter research, with its lesser time specificity than problem-solving research, is typically more ephemeral than the results of Leontief's basic disciplinary research on I/O.

It is also instructive to note that I/O analysis is a very specialized part of economics, while problem-solving and subject-matter research are multi-disciplinary and, hence, broader. So, it should not be surprising that some users of I/O analysis have been disappointed. This has occurred when they have made the mistake of concluding that real-world problems can be solved with a specialized, highly relevant disciplinary technique—I/O analysis—instead of realizing that most real-world problems and most subject-matter research are multidisciplinary in nature. Subject-matter and problem-solving researchers trying to model the processes of development realize sooner or later that the four prime movers of economic development are capital accumulation, technological advance, institutional improvements, and improvements in the human agent. I/O analysis, a specialized economics technique that analyses commodity, service, and financial flows, should not be expected to be of much help in solving specific developmental problems. In this sense, I/O analysis is always in danger of being misused. Instead of being used as a technique to interrelate the different subsectors of an economy, there is the danger of it being used in solving development and other problems in a way that precludes multidisciplinary work on how to generate, implement, and use capital accumulation and generate technical, institutional and human change.

T. W. SCHULTZ'S RESEARCH ON HUMAN CAPITAL

Schultz's research program originated out of his dissatisfaction with attempts to explain changes in the output of U.S. agriculture in terms of changes in the amounts of land, capital, and labor utilized. It was clear that there were increases in output not associated with changes in the use of land, conventionally conceived physical capital, and a standardized quality of labor [1956, 1958]. The attempt to unravel this empirical puzzle in U.S. agriculture led him into a consideration of technological advance through agricultural research, agricultural extension work, vocational agricultural training, and general education. From 1952 to 1982, Schultz, his graduate students, and younger colleagues, pursued the answer to this puzzle.

An Example of Relevant Disciplinary Research

Schultz's research on human capital at the University of Chicago can be regarded as *relevant disciplinary research*. It was relevant (in its origin) to the problems of generating increased agricultural productivity faced by many public decision makers in many parts of the world. While the research eventually went far beyond agriculture, it continued to demonstrate its relevance for understanding and bringing about increased productivity in the whole of society. The relevance of Schultz's work in this area was recognized when he was named a co-recipient of the Nobel Prize for Economics in 1979.

At first blush, Schultz's research on technological and institutional change and, later, on human capital appears to be multidisciplinary. After all, it is concerned with changes studied in other disciplines and commonly taken as fixed or given in static economic analyses. However, his interest was in the changes induced by incentives to create new technology, to develop new institutions, and to make investments to improve the quality of the human element. Time and again, the powerful tools of economics were used to explain why it is advantageous for individuals, businesses, and governments to use resources to create new technologies, to produce the goods and equipment embodying these new technologies, to use those goods and equipment, to change institutions, and to invest in the education and on-the-job training required to handle new technologies and operate in changing environments. Eventually, the interests of Schultz, his colleagues, and his students focused on entrepreneurship and its important role in adjusting to the disequilibria created by technological advance, new and improved institutional arrangements, and larger quantities of highly skilled labor.

Schultz's research on human capital evolved, transformed itself repeatedly, and changed in a way that makes it difficult to be explicit about objectives. Undoubtedly, Schultz as an economist was motivated to demonstrate the usefulness of economic analysis. He also has a strong sense of curiosity. Those who know him realize he enjoyed putting together the various pieces of the puzzle of understanding the increased productivity of modern societies. In turn, the general objective of understanding the origin of improved productive capacity became more specific. A subobjective became that of understanding the economics of technological change, first in agriculture, then in society as a whole. Another intermediate subobjective was to understand something about the economics of institutional change, though less attention was paid to this than to the economics of technological change.

It also became evident that both technological and institutional change occur as the result of the activities of highly trained, educated people. At first, leaders such as Henry Ford and Thomas Edison made advances through "inventions." However, as technology became more advanced, the personal genius, hard work, and creativity of such men had to be supplemented by highly technical education in the biological and physical sciences. Thus, while technological advance is crucial for improvement in productive capacity, it became apparent to Schultz that education and improvements in the people who create advanced technological changes are even more fundamental. Similarly, while improvements in policies and the institutional structures that govern a society are important, improvements in the people who create the new institutions and operate within them are even more fundamental. Schultz, his colleagues, and his students were driven sequentially to concentrate on change in the human element—on investment in the productive capacity of human beings and on the economizing processes that make governments, businesses, and individuals invest in human beings.

Kinds of Knowledge Sought

In retrospect, Schultz's research program on human capital sought primarily value-free positive and value knowledge. Within these two kinds of knowledge, the research program concentrated on knowledge of interest to economists. Positivistic knowledge was sought about the quantities and natures of resources used first in agricultural, then in all forms of production. Positivistic knowledge was sought concerning the outcomes of productive processes. While production can best be defined in terms of the creation of value (and was so defined in earlier literature of economics as the creation of time, form, and place utility), the goods and services that have time, form, and place utility can also be described in physical, positivistic terms as amounting to so many pounds or tons of this or that commodity and so many hours or units of this or that service.

Value knowledge obtained in the project included information about both monetary and nonmonetary values. Data on nonmonetary values are often scarce as such knowledge is not easily quantified. In many instances, the work tended to establish (1) that values were assigned to an institutional change or to the results of investments in the human agent, and (2) that maximizing parents, students, and educational agencies offset these values against the costs (nonmonetary and monetary) involved in attaining them. The knowledge of values (whether monetary or nonmonetary) was sometimes about values in exchange as public, business, and individual decision makers trade off one value against another in deciding what to do. In other instances, the concern was with intrinsic values, as when the total value to society of a technological advance was under consideration.

Schultz's research was classified at the beginning of this case study as relevant disciplinary because it produced knowledge of interest to economists and of importance to the public, businesses, and individuals making decisions about human capital and the roles it plays in generating technological advances and institutional improvements. By its nature, economics is concerned with prescriptive knowledge as defined in Chapter 2. Broadly speaking, economists use prescriptive knowledge (1) to predict or explain the behavior of producers, consumers, resource owners, and investors, and (2) as a basis for recommendations to decision makers. In Schultz's research program, the prescriptive knowledge generated has been used primarily to explain or predict the behavior of public, business, and individual decision makers about investments in human capital. These predictions and explanations have also been important in formulating explicit and implicit recommendations to private and public decision makers.

Philosophic Orientation

For the most part, the work done under this research program was both theoretical and empirical. The theory (logic) of economics was used to structure empirical work. While Schultz's work was relatively quantitative, much of it cannot be termed econometric. Where the paucity of data precluded econometric estimation of the parameters of the structural equations, he relied on cross-tabular analyses and examination of time-series data to show the importance of independent variables and something about the magnitude of their possible influences on dependent variables. In some instances, however, quite rigorous econometric analyses were carried out.

Work on the project reveals the general procedure of using primitive, undefined, experiential terms to convert abstract, analytical, or theoretical statements into contingent synthetic statements. While this general procedure has been formalized by philosophers trying to understand the success of biological and physical scientists in generating value-free positivistic knowledge, it has also been used extensively by economists and econometricians to deal with knowledge of values (particularly monetary values) as well as value-free knowledge. Schultz's research is no exception. This general procedure was used in working with monetary and nonmonetary values in a rather eclectic manner.

Despite Schultz's Ph.D. from the University of Wisconsin where pragmatic institutional economics was stressed, his research work on human capital has not been particularly pragmatic. The focus has been on the use of neoclassical theory to explain and predict the behavior of public, business, and private decision makers. He concentrates on the values gained and sacrificed in making decisions to improve human beings through investments in their productive capacity, with little attention to interdependence between value-free and value facts.

As little has been written by participants in his research program on methodological or philosophic issues, their underlying methodological and philosophical commitments have to be inferred from what they have done. It can be inferred that the participants were thorough-going logical positivists who regarded the information they generated on values as behavioral and not as measuring values as characteristics of the real world. On the other hand, one can hypothesize that the researchers were simply eclectic and did what they were able to do with the data, techniques and methods at their disposal. In any event, they have demonstrated an ability to work objectively with both value-free positivistic knowledge and knowledge of values, whether monetary or nonmonetary.

Research Projects Require Financial Support and Accountability, Administration and Conduct, and Review and Evaluation

These topics, as well as the durability and practical importance of Schultz's results, are examined next.

Financial Support and Accountability   The patterns of financial support and accountability for Schultz's research follow those typical for disciplinary research. As a former head of a complex department at Iowa State College, as Chairman of the Department of Economics at the University of Chicago, and as a highly productive researcher, Schultz had earned the respect of administrators of research funds in foundations and public agencies. He received transitory (soft money) funding with few strings attached from a number of agencies including the Rockefeller Foundation. His salary and those of his closely associated colleagues, plus some operating expenses, were often covered with "hard money" funding, first from Iowa State College, then from the University of Chicago. Soft money was often used to reinforce his own capable research leadership with appointments of graduate students and junior staff for short periods of time to work on subjects of interest to him.

The funding arrangements were typical of those that work well to fund capable disciplinarians working at the disciplinary end of the research spectrum rather than the problem-solving end. The pattern is for a university to commit an adequate salary and research funds from hard money funds to a capable person who, in turn, secures additional soft money funding for students and young colleagues. Professor Schultz, who was certainly such a man, exercised intellectual leadership and subjected a program of disciplinary research to the indirect administration and accountability of "discipline" from the discipline of economics. Few strings in the form of demands for direct financial accountability were attached to either his soft or hard money funding.

However, an interesting situation arose from a National Institutes of Health (NIH) grant received by Schultz. The grant was from funds to study mental health. At least some investments in mental health can be viewed legitimately as investments in human capital; thus these funds were used by Schultz to research investments in human capital. For a decade, NIH administrators were impressed with the productivity and relevance of the research being done. However, at the end of the tenth year, NIH finance officers raised questions as to whether the research was oriented enough to mental health problems to lead to their solution. As this question was pressed further, it was decided that the research being done at the University of Chicago was not sufficiently focused on mental health problems to justify continued financing. Reciprocally, Schultz was not inclined to divert his disciplinary efforts to efforts to solve more specific mental health problems.

The situation nicely illustrates the difference in being accountable to a discipline and to those who support disciplinary work in contrast to being accountable for problem-oriented work to those who provide financial support for such work. While Nobel Prize quality research was being done, it was relevant disciplinary research and not closely enough oriented to research on the mental health problems the National Institutes of Health wanted to finance. The results Schultz and his colleagues were producing were relevant disciplinary but were not focused closely enough on solving mental health problems or even on subject-matter knowledge important in solving mental health problems.

Administration and Conduct The administration and conduct of this research program typifies that of many excellent disciplinary research efforts. The original puzzle of explaining sources of increased productivity was pursued in a scholarly manner guided more by curiosity and a desire to know than by administrators and organization charts. "Disciplinary discipline" exercised in workshops, conferences, presentations, and critiquing of papers was far more important than administrative directives from Schultz, his University of Chicago administrators, or administrators in the soft money funding agencies.

Review and Evaluation Few research projects and programs are reviewed and evaluated as continuously by disciplinary peers as Schultz's research on human capital (including the earlier research out of which his research on human capital emerged). His bibliography and those of his colleagues reveal a continuous stream of scholarly and popular articles that exposed hypotheses, theories, and empirical results to criticism by scholars and practitioners alike. Schultz depended on these criticisms to correct errors and to supplement his own leadership. Important examples include his "Reflections on Agricultural Production, Output and Supply" [1956], "Output-Input Relationships Revisited" [1958], "Investment in Man: An Economist's View" [1959], "Capital Formation by Education" [1960], "Education and Economic Growth" [1961], and "Reflections on Investments in Man" [1962]. Further, publication did not stop with his definitive book, *Investment in Human Capital: The Role of Education and Research* [1971].

Research proposals as well as projects and their results are often reviewed and evaluated. Review of research proposals is customary and often mandatory in connection with the funding of projects, especially at the problem-solving end of the spectrum. Proposals for research programs are less likely to be reviewed in part because the programs tend to evolve as the projects develop. Soft money support for Schultz's program was sometimes based on faith that he would develop a worthwhile program as much as on detailed knowledge of the projects being funded.

Project proposals, research results, and publications were reviewed and evaluated by peers within the economics department, from the remainder of the University of Chicago, by invited conferees, and by disciplinary peers in the disciplines concerned with human capital. These reviews and evaluations were at least as crucial for the researchers as for the project funders.

Schultz's Presidential Address to the American Economics Association entitled "Investment in Human Capital" [1961] has been reprinted in at least 20 books. 3,000 reprints have been distributed and its contents are widely quoted. This and other publications by Schultz and his co-workers have received favorable peer-group recognition on many occasions, the most prestigious being the Francis Walker Prize of the American Economics Association given every five years to the economist deemed to have made the most important contribution to economics, and his sharing of the Nobel Prize in Economics with Arthur Lewis. Also, widespread approval of his research came from the philanthropic foundations of the United States, the National Science Foundation, and the U.S. Academy of Sciences.

Durability and Practical Importance   Schultz's research on human capital and related topics over a 25–30 year period has proven both durable and of practical significance. The length of the research program attests to the durability of its results. Research administrators and educators around the world have accepted the results of the program and have used them repeatedly to improve research and educational programs. The practical relevance and great importance of the results are widely recognized.

PHILOSOPHICAL AND METHODOLOGICAL
GENERALIZATIONS ABOUT DISCIPLINARY RESEARCH

These two case studies and the material in the first nine chapters of this book provide a basis for some generalizations about disciplinary research. These generalizations and similar ones about subject-matter and problem-solving research at the ends of Chapters 11 and 12 provide the basis for philosophic and methodological generalizations on all three kinds of research in Chapter 17. Chapters 13–16 deal with the conduct, administration, evaluation, and durability of research and also draw on the case studies in this chapter and two each in Chapters 11 and 12.

The tendency to specialize and the possibility of specializing within disciplinary research is nicely illustrated by these two case studies. Leontief specialized in I/O relationships and Schultz specialized, eventually, in improvements in the human agent or human capital investments. This permitted them to abstract from many of the other complexities of economics and from the complexities in other disciplines that are important in using the research results they produced yet were not essential for their disciplinary results.

Another generalization is that disciplinary research progress can be stimulated by disciplinary researchers coming into contact with practical problems. Leontief was stimulated by the "method of balances and its shortcomings" used in planning centrally controlled socialist economies. Schultz was stimulated by the puzzle of explaining why increases in agricultural output were not directly related over time to increases in the amounts of land, labor, and physical capital employed. Practical problems were crucial in stimulating both researchers.

As the reader progresses through the case studies of Chapters 10–12, it will become clear that actual pieces of research seldom fall neatly into the three broad research categories distinguished in this book. This results from the gray areas between the classes of research we have defined and the mixed nature of many research efforts. It is precisely because of these penumbra and mixes that it is crucial to keep in mind the important differences between the three kinds of research. As projects shade into one kind of research from another, researchers must be aware of the implications for appropriate philosophic orientations, kind of information sought and, especially, for financial and political support, accountability, administrative needs, the relevance of different peer groups, and for practicality versus durability

Philosophically, these two extraordinarily good disciplinary researchers were more eclectic than their training would lead one to expect. Leontief could be expected to have a positivistic orientation and T. W. Schultz a pragmatic insitutional orientation from his Ph.D. at Wisconsin. Leontief worked with value and value-free positivistic data, and objectively handled both. Schultz also worked with both without becoming enmeshed in the complexities of a pragmatic approach that would have prevented him from specializing on human capital and bringing the powerful tools of neoclassical theory to bear on his specialized task. This should not be taken to imply that either Leontief or Schultz would not have broadened their view to consider the multidisciplinary complexities encountered in using their contributions to economics to solve real-world problems.

Financially, both research efforts were modest. Probably the largest source of financial support was their salaries and the overhead their universities incurred to keep two such competent people on their faculties. Both researchers were able to attract outside financial support. Both, in turn, were able to separate their personal research on their specialized disciplinary topics from the problem-solving and subject-matter objectives of outside donors. Leontief left the subject-matter and problem-solving work largely to government agencies whom he provided with the results of his disciplinary research. Schultz drew on the experiences of operating agencies to estimate the consequences of making investments in human agents but did not become deeply involved as a consultant or as a problem-solving or subject-matter researcher in the affairs of these agencies. He utilized data from the experiences of the agencies but did not do problem-solving and subject-matter research for them. He has, however, lectured them on the errors in their ways. In at least one instance noted above, Schultz gave up outside financing because his soft money source wanted research more germane to the problems it had to address.

Accountability in both instances was largely to peers in economics. Leontief left accountability for problem-solving and subject-matter research expenditures to the government agencies employing I/O analyses, while making his own disciplinary research accountable to his disciplinary peers. The same was true for Schultz. Both researchers actively sought criticisms and evaluations from what they regarded as valuable, competent peers. In one or two instances, Leontief's work received evaluations that later proved inaccurate. I refer to the evaluation of the committee of the economics faculty at Harvard University, which found the I/O research impractical and granted resources to Leontief to pursue it on the condition that he would report his "failure" when the resources were used up. Also, he encountered an adverse evaluation when Harvard University Press elected not to reprint his 1936 book. Schultz also ran into such adverse evaluations and criticisms but, like Leontief, felt confident that his efforts were productive.

Both researchers conducted their research in an academic manner consistent with the disciplinary nature of what they were doing. Both were individualistic. Both used relatively small resources to support their students and close associates. Neither employed a top-down type of line administration in conducting their research. Both used the "discipline" of their discipline as an administrative tool and let evolution of intellectual processes guide their work and the work of those with whom they were closely associated.

Though the relationships of these two pieces of relevant disciplinary research to problem-solving and subject-matter research were different, both are differentiable from subject-matter and problem-solving research. Leontief drew on a practical problem for the definition of his disciplinary research. He also made the results of his disciplinary research available to users who faced practical problems in both governments and private business. By contrast. Schultz saw a disciplinary puzzle of practical consequences in the data on the performance of the agricultural economy, then of other parts of the overall economy. In researching his disciplinary puzzle, Schultz used the data indicating the consequences of investments in the human agent to develop his disciplinary theories and to establish their empirical importance.

Schultz was less of a consultant to agencies using his theory than he was a user of their experiences. When it came to consulting, Schultz more often went directly to the practical policy consequences of his research than Leontief. Leontief had generated a technique for analysis, whereas Schultz generated theories and data indicating how to generate development by investing in the human agent. Schultz was prepared to do direct consulting on solutions of problems for which his research results were relevant. Leontief was prepared to consult with researchers on how to research problems encountered by the administrators of either controlled economies or of portions of economies under the control of government administrators.

Both pieces of research have proven durable in accordance with our earlier analysis of the three types of research. Also in accord with our earlier analysis, the subject-matter and problem-solving applications of Leontief's I/O analysis have not proven to be very durable. I/O matrices are specific to time and place. When time passes or when one moves from one country to another, I/O tableaus have to be redone. The applications are ephemeral but the basic technique Leontief pioneered is durable. Similarly, the theory of human capital investments developed by Schultz is durable, but when this theory is used to solve problems of development, the solutions themselves are as ephemeral as the problems solved.

A final generalization is the distinction between disciplinary research of known and unknown relevance. Both case studies of disciplinary research in this chapter are of known relevance. Both researchers knew early in their programs that what they were doing was of practical importance even though they were making basic advances in the discipline of economics. While disciplinary researchers sometimes defend work of dubious relevance as important for the development of the discipline, it is difficult to find examples of disciplinary research in economics that were of unknown relevance when done. This is not to say that such research has not been done. Discussions about the philosophy of science sometimes stress that disciplinary research of unknown relevance is of "long-term disciplinary value" if it fills in missing logic or missing data for a discipline such as economics, chemistry, or physics. While it is hard to counter this argument in principal and while this book makes a place for disciplinary research of unknown relevance, I have found it difficult to locate clear-cut, illustrative case studies of it.

ADDITIONAL REFERENCES

Fisher, W. H., C. H. Chelton and G. C. Stacey. 1973. Interactions of Science and Technology in the Innovative Process: Some Case Studies; National Science Foundation Contract NSF-C667, Final Report on Input-Output Analysis; Battelle Columbus Laboratories, Columbus, Ohio.

Leontief, Wassily. 1966. *Input-Output Economics*, Oxford: Oxford University Press, Inc.

Scandinavian Journal of Economics. 1980. The Nobel Memorial Prize in Economics 1979: The Official Announcement of the Royal Academy of Sciences, 82(1):59–61.

Schultz, T. W. 1956. Reflections on Agricultural Production, Output and Supply, *Journal of Farm Economics* 38:746–762.

––––– 1958. Output-Input Relationships Revisited, *Journal of Farm Economics*, 40:924–932.

––––– 1959. Investment in Man: An Economist's View, in *Proceedings and Debates* of the 86th Congress, 1st Session, No. 169, Vol. 106, October 5.

––––– 1960. Capital Formation by Education, *The Journal of Political Economy*, LXVII(6):571–583.

––––– 1961. Investment in Human Capital, *American Economic Review*, 51:1–17. (American Economic Association Presidential Address; reprinted at least twenty times, and translated into Slovak, Spanish, Portuguese, Hungarian, Italian, French, Japanese.)

––––– 1962. Reflections on Investment in Man, *Journal of Political Economy*, 70(5):1–8, Part II.

––––– 1971. *Investment in Human Capital: The Role of Education and Research*, New York: Free Press (Translated in Portuguese.)

Swedish Journal of Economics. 1973. The Nobel Memorial Prize in Economics 1973: The Official Announcement of the Royal Academy of Sciences, 75(4):428–429.

Chapter 11

Subject-Matter
Case Studies

In this chapter, two subject-matter case studies are presented: Karl Fox's research on social indicators and the World Food and Nutrition Study that was the product of a large, complex multidisciplinary committee project. In the two sections dealing with these case studies, each is classified by kind of research. Attention is also given to the kinds of knowledge generated and to the philosophic orientations that guided the methods employed. Financing, accountability, review and evaluation, administration, and conduct of the research are also considered. Attention is given to the durability and the practicality of the results of the two studies. The last section of the chapter presents some philosophical and methodological generalizations about subject-matter research based on Part I of this book and these two case studies.

KARL FOX'S RESEARCH ON SOCIAL INDICATORS

While the research considered in this case study was supported largely by the National Science Foundation under grant GS-2363 to Iowa State University, it did not materialize out of the need of NSF project managers and Iowa State University for the results. Instead, it originated in the early and continuing experiences of Karl Fox and his concern about the importance of developing measures of the performance of societies.

In the preface of his book, *Social Indicators and Social Theory: Elements of an Operational System* [1974], Fox describes several aspects of his training, an experience that stimulated his interest in this subject. In a personal communication, Fox also stresses two earlier influences. The first was a strong interest in mathematics (his original choice as an undergraduate major) and its applications to physics—the combination of abstract theory and relatively precise measurement of relationships between variables (hopefully, causal relationships or "laws") appealed to him. The second was a broad but somewhat desultory interest in the social sciences, facilitated by the presence in his home of the *Encyclopaedia of the Social Sciences*. Fox scanned the individual volumes as they appeared and used specific articles as references in his high school and college social science courses.

He received an M.A. in sociology in 1938, but his attempts to estimate substantive or causal relationships explaining differences in the crude death rates of population subgroups convinced him that his research objectives were 35 years ahead of the available data. His M.A. thesis was entitled *A Critique of Mortality Statistics*. As a graduate student in economics at Berkeley (1938-1942) he was strongly influenced by the now-classic works in applied econometrics that were then appearing, most notably Henry Schultz's *The Theory and Measurement of Demand* [1938] and Jan Tinbergen's *Statistical Testing of Business Cycle Theories* [1939]. He particularly admired the integration of theory, statistical methods, and data achieved by these men, and perceived a similar integration in Mordecai Ezekiel's *Methods of Correlation Analysis* [1930, 1941] and in the tradition of statistical demand analysis pioneered by Ezekiel, Waugh, and others mostly in the U.S. Bureau of Agricultural Economics (BAE).

Fox spent 1944-1954 in the BAE working in this tradition. He was influenced by Frederick V. Waugh in the direction of using advanced economic and statistical theory in basic research, and by O. V. Wells in the direction of making and/or coordinating fast-moving analyses of specific problems faced by USDA administrators. His work for Wells strengthened his conviction about the importance of accurate, prompt, and conceptually appropriate measures of economic and social performance for the use of public and private decision makers. The BAE phase of Fox's career is reflected in his book, *Econometric Analysis for Public Policy* [1958], and his coauthorship of Ezekiel and Fox, *Methods of Correlation and Regression Analysis: Third Edition* [1959].

His move to Iowa State University in 1955 to head its Department of Economics and Sociology brought an abrupt change in his research activities. The new themes were attempts to specify the objective functions of policy makers, attempts to measure and assign values to the outputs of universities, and attempts to combine monetary and nonmonetary measures of community development and rural social change.

Jan Tinbergen's [1952] *On the Theory of Economic Policy* presents a hypothetical president or prime minister with a model of the national economy, showing the expected effects of available policy instruments on potential targets (unemployment, rate of inflation, and budget deficit). The model was built and analyzed with the methods of the logical positivists. It generated behavioral knowledge about monetary values—about who values what and how much— without implying that those values correspond with characteristics of a natural real world. Policy makers were then responsible for (1) generating prescriptions to solve problems after determining the proper trade-offs between the alternative values, and (2) steering the economy in the prescribed direction. The prescriptions are subject to the positive constraints (input/output relations and others) inherent in the model.

Fox viewed the allocation of resources by university administrators with a similar perspective: they were transferring resources between disciplines, functions, and levels of instruction *as if* they knew not only the (positive) production functions of the university but also the costs of its inputs and values of its various outputs. If certain outputs (for example, the output of students graduating from different curricula) could be assigned monetary values, the opportunity costs of resources transferred from one curriculum to another or from teaching to research could also be estimated. Fox believed that explicit recognition and discussion of such opportunity costs by university administrators would lead to improved resource allocation and accountability.

As interest in community development increased, Fox saw a logical need for defining and measuring all the outputs of complete communities and assigning market and/or nonmonetary values to them as a basis for measuring changes in the well-being of community residents.

In all three areas, Fox's contributions were mainly conceptual and illustrative rather than fully empirical. Most of them were reported in Fox, Sengupta, and Thorbecke, *The Theory of Quantitative Economic Policy* [1973]; Fox, ed. *Economic Analysis for Educational Planning: Resource Allocation in Nonmarket Systems* [1972]; and a series of papers beginning with "The Concept of Community Development" in 1961.

Fox's service on the Board of Directors of the Social Science Research Council from 1963 to 1967 motivated him to read widely in social sciences other than economics. The Board's chairman, Herbert Simon (later a Nobel Laureate), became something of a role model for Fox in this respect. Publication of the new *International Encyclopedia of the Social Sciences* in 1968 greatly facilitated Fox's program of self-education. By October 1968 he had written a chapter entitled "Operations Research and Complex Social Systems" containing many of the concepts he later developed at length in *Social Indicators and Social*

Theory. The chapter cited appears in Sengupta and Fox, *Economic Analysis and Operations Research* [1969]; the preface was dated October 9, 1968.

The social indicators movement, led mainly by sociologists, began to gather momentum in the mid-1960s. Fox read some of its major publications, including Bauer, ed. *Social Indicators* [1966] and the three volumes of hearings conducted by Senator Mondale on his proposed "Full Opportunity and Social Accounting Act of 1967," but did not identify himself with the movement in any way. His decision to write *Social Indicators and Social Theory* was not made until the winter of 1972–1973.

Certain other aspects of Fox's experience should be noted. Until 1960, nearly all his research was done within disciplinary boundaries and in accordance with disciplinary standards. He was elected a Fellow of the Econometric Society in 1959, the American Statistical Association in 1961, and the American Agricultural Economics Association in 1972. The depth of his logically positivistic interest in what he calls "the vertical integration of theory, methods, and data" within individual disciplines is reflected in his authorship or coauthorship of one book on applied regression analysis and two on economic statistics: Ezekiel and Fox, *Methods of Correlation and Regression Analysis* [1959], Fox, *Intermediate Economic Statistics* [1968], and Merrill and Fox, *Introduction to Economic Statistics* [1970]. His interests in the 1960s led him into interdisciplinary or subject-matter fields (operations research, regional science, educational administration). Within those fields he was most strongly influenced by people who had also met standards of excellence in individual disciplines—in his preface he mentions Jati K. Sengupta, Brian J. L. Berry, William L. Garrison, Walter Isard, Charles L. Leven, and Charles M. Tiebout.

Kind of Research

Fox's research on social indicators can be classified as *subject-matter research.* His work goes too far beyond economics into the other social sciences to be classified as *disciplinary.* On the other hand, it is too basic and fundamental to be classified as *problem-solving research* and it certainly does not address the problems of any single public or private decision-making unit. Clearly, Fox was trying to produce new multidisciplinary theoretical and, to a lesser extent, empirical knowledge about the performance of society. He did this in the belief that such knowledge would be more useful to decision makers than the knowledge then at their disposal.

A New Discipline or Empire Building?

It might be hypothesized that Fox tried to integrate contributions from a number of social science disciplines into a new discipline the way bio/physical investigators integrated contributions from chemistry and biology into a new discipline called biochemistry. An alternative to the new-discipline hypothesis is that he was an empire-building economist trying to annex territory from a number of other social sciences. Neither hypothesis seems tenable. Fox's research seems best interpreted as a multidisciplinary, subject-matter attempt to draw together theories and empirical knowledge from a number of disciplines to provide information to appraise the performance of a society.

Kinds of Knowledge Sought

Fox's primary emphasis was on how to use experiential data and theoretical constructs to produce quantified value propositions about the performance of a society. This statement needs elaboration. Fox was interested primarily in developing a means of inferring values attached to different activities on the basis of the amounts of time people allocate to them. His interest was in nonmonetary as well as monetary values. However, because monetary values are traded off against nonmonetary values, Fox elected to use money as a "common denominator" between nonmonentary and monetary values. In effect, he monetized nonmonetary values to obtain a single measure of the overall performance of a society.

Note that Fox's interest in social indicators has been primarily in values "in exchange." He has not tried to determine the *total intrinsic* value of the various activities between which people allocate their time. Instead, he has proposed a method of measuring the value people assign to *marginal amounts* of time required to engage in marginal increments of one activity in terms of what has been given up by not using that time to engage in another activity. The convenient common denominator turned out to be monetary *values in exchange.* He estimates the amount of value people assign to marginal increments of activities without concluding that those marginal increments really have that value.

Just as Fox has not raised questions about whether the given activity really has value as opposed to concluding that people merely assign the exchange values inferred from the time they allocate to different activities, he does not even question whether people make valuational mistakes and, hence, misallocate their time in view of their own perceptions of value. For example, Fox's approach would not raise questions as to the fairness of earning differentials between white and black or male and female workers or the relative amounts of time spent on housework by husbands and wives. If the value systems, laws, institutional arrangements, and allocations of rights and privileges in the society changed in such a way as to narrow these differentials, Fox's system would record the altered "values in exchange" without evaluative comment. Moreover, time spent by activists trying to reduce inequalities would be credited with the same (exchange) value as time spent by reactionaries trying to increase the same inequalities.

It should also be pointed out that the values in exchange Fox measures are conditioned by the distribution of the ownership of resources in a society. If such distributions change, the social indicators Fox generates would change. More importantly, their *meanings* as well as their magnitudes would change. Thus, Fox's "*social*" indicators must have very limited value in measuring the social consequences of large-scale reforms in education, political processes, the ownership of land and capital (human as well as physical), participatory rights, military and police protection, and social rights. In the preface to his *Social Indicators and Social Theory,* Fox wisely indicated that it is unclear whether concepts pertaining to social indicators from different disciplines and specialties *should* be formally integrated or that the variables themselves would be worth the cost of measurement. He further indicated that he felt his work would be useful even if it led other research workers to conclude that some of his suggestions should *not* be implemented. He had pointed out earlier that social indicators have to be numerical, practical, and operational. It seems fair to conclude that Fox feels the social indicator he has devised is more operational, practical, and as numerical as gross national product (the indicator it would supersede) even if his work is subject to the kind of criticisms presented above.

Philosophic Orientation

Fox's philosophic orientation is best interpreted as logically positivistic because he can be viewed as combining abstract logical reasoning with experiential information to produce synthetic knowledge in the manner generally prescribed by students of logical positivism. In this sense, his methods are those of the positivists and his behavioral measures of values are acceptable to them. This is extremely interesting as he proposes to produce propositions about the goodness or badness of the performance of society—albeit behavioral ones.

It is important to recall from Chapters 3, 4, and 7 that the methods of logical positivism do not preclude research on behavioral values, which is what Fox proposes to measure. Logical positivism, which regards the values people hold to be emotive and unobjective, does not preclude the attainment of objective knowledge about what values they actually hold. Fox uses the *experiences* of people in allocating their time in the pursuit of alternative *experienced* or *experienceable* goods and the avoidance of alternative *experienced* or *experienceable* bads in a linear programming *analysis* to infer the shadow *values* of time allotted to various activities. In effect, he uses undefined value terms along with the *logic* of linear programming to derive *synthetic* knowledge of values. He practices a form of "positivistic normativism." The knowledge of values he proposes to generate is subjectable to the tests of coherence, correspondence, and clarity (lack of ambiguity.)

Discussion of using such tests is found in the previous section of this chapter. In that section, logic tells us that the derived social indicators are measures of the exchange value people attach to conditions, situations, and things rather than the real value of the condition, situation, or thing, but then all descriptive knowledge (value-free or about values) consists of perceptions of reality we have "faith" correspond to reality. Nonetheless, Fox's social indicators would be of limited value in measuring the consequences of major reform in the ownership of income-producing rights and privileges as his indicators should only be regarded as measuring exchange or extrinsic (not intrinsic) values.

There is little evidence of pragmatic guidance in Fox's work. While he sought an "operational way" of producing social indicator data, this is hardly pragmatism as defined earlier in this book. The subobjective of finding an operational way does not mean that the truths of the measures of value he seeks are treated as interdependent with the truth of value-free propositions. Even to insist that an indicator be operational is not quite the same as insisting that a social indicator pass the test of workability when used to solve practical problems of, say, land or educational reform to improve a society.

Administration

Administration of the project involved obtaining financing and accounting for it as well as the conduct and administration of the work. The research accomplished was also subjected to review and evaluation. Under this general rubric of administration, attention is also given to the durability and practical impact of research results.

Financial Support and Accountability   As noted above, the research project under investigation here has historical roots going back to work done before Karl Fox was born. It also has historical and current financial roots in other projects. Fox's earlier NSF work (1962–1971) with Thorbecke in the economic program of NSF attracted favorable comments from reviewers. This work involved applications of Tinbergen's quantitative policy analysis techniques to national and regional economic models, universities, communities, and functional economic areas. In 1971, Thorbecke and Fox separated their work. The main financial support for Karl Fox's work on social indicators came under National Science Foundation (NSF) grant GS-2363 to Iowa State University. James Blackman was responsible at NSF for the administration of the grant.

The grant proposal was entitled "Conceptual and Quantitative Research on the Higher Education Sector and Its Components: With Emphasis on Optimization Techniques, Econometric and Policy Models, Consistent Measures of Economic and Noneconomic Outputs and the Relationship of Sector Components to the Structure of the Surrounding Society." Funding of $89,786 was requested for two years work starting in September 1971, only part of which was to go to social indicator research according to the title of the proposal.

Fox had a good disciplinary track record, while Blackman had faith that disciplinary research in social sciences was valuable. Note that the stress on social indicators emerged out of the conduct of the project, having been only hinted at originally.

Fox left administrative work at Iowa State University in February 1972 but retained his research and teaching position as distinguished professor in sciences and humanities and professor of economics.

Fox also left Iowa State University in 1972 to spend 14 months at Berkeley. The NSF approved the transfer of his working location to Berkeley because some of the most advanced research on the higher education sector was being conducted there under the supervision of Frederick E. Balderston, Charles J. Hitch, and Clark Kerr. While at Berkeley, Fox reports that he read the entire *International Encyclopedia of Social Sciences* except for the articles on economics and quantitative methods, fields in which he was already well-informed.

Conduct and Administration   As increasing stress was placed on social indicators, it became clear to Fox that he would be drawing on theory and empirical information from a large number of other disciplines. He sought advice and references from faculty members at Berkeley in several fields, but for the most part he drew directly on the published literature. He had no graduate assistants but he did hire a "runner" to track down references scattered among the specialized libraries on the Berkeley campus.

Fox's use of time budgets to estimate the values of activities engaged in by people was, of course, related to the work done by T. W. Schultz on human capital. However, there was no close interaction between Fox and either Schultz or Gary Becker, who worked closely with Schultz at Chicago. Fox had encountered human capital theory concepts in reading Alfred Marshall, but did not draw heavily on the then-current Chicago work other than Becker's research on time allocation, which was influential as it both suggested and confirmed Fox's approach. There is no evidence of a lack of congeniality between Fox and the Chicago group, but there was a conviction on Fox's part that his mathematical technique for deriving social indicators from time budgets had merit quite apart from the "investigation" of the economics of investing in human capital.

Fox was something of a loner, preferring to stay away from crowded research areas. He drew heavily on Roger Barker's ideas concerning ecological psychology as well as Barker's work with the National Council of Churches on changes in a small community, without becoming closely involved with him. Other people whose work contributed to Fox's thinking included Bertram Gross, Richard L. Meier, Henry A. Murray, Erik Erikson, Eric Berne, Talcott Parsons, Wilder Penfield, Hadley Cantril, Philip Converse, John P. Robinson, Nestor Terleckyj, Paul van Moeseke, Richard Stone, Herbert Simon, Peter M. Blau, Otis Dudley Duncan, Thomas H. Holmes, Richard Rahe, Bob R. Holdren, Victor E. Smith, Henri Theil, C. J. Galpin, and Frederick V. Waugh.

As late as 1972, Fox debated the merits of writing a book on social theory and indicators versus a book on higher education under his NSF grant. Early in 1973 he decided to place his emphasis on social indicators despite the prominence of the higher education sector in the title of his NSF grant. This shift in emphasis was in accordance with NSF 73-12 (pp. 24–25) *Grants For Scientific Research*, which states:

> The Foundation believes that the principal investigator, operating within the established policies of the grantee institution, should feel free to pursue interesting and important leads which may arise during the conduct of the research. The principal investigator may discontinue or materially modify unpromising lines of inquiry, without jeopardizing continuation of support for the remainder of the grant period, when it appears from a scientific standpoint that the inquiry as originally envisaged will no longer be fruitful or that a related line of inquiry will be more promising. However, when such modification would result in a major deviation from original research objectives, prior approval by the Foundation must be obtained.

The pattern that emerges from Fox's conduct and administration of the project is an exemplary academic one that seems more appropriate to the disciplinary end than to the problem-solving end of the spectrum running from problem-solving to disciplinary research. The work, like much disciplinary work in economics, was mainly that of one person. Though the work is multidisciplinary, it attempts to integrate concepts and propositions from the different disciplines into a coherent entity.

Although Fox emphasized "social indicators" in the title of his book, his conceptual framework is that of "social accounts." Fox credits Bertram Gross [1966] with the first (and classic) statement of the need and prospects for social system *accounts* and notes that Senator Mondale's bill was entitled "The Full Opportunity and Social *Accounting* Act of 1967." However, it appeared to Fox by 1973 that no one was seriously trying to implement social accounts on the comprehensive scale envisaged by Gross. An accounting framework imposes severe rigor: units of measurement must be defined, double-counting must be avoided, money (or time, energy, or materials) must be completely "accounted for," and outputs must be attributed to inputs. Fox believed that the transition from "economic indicators" in the 1920s to "national economic accounts" in the 1930s had greatly improved our ability to measure economic performance, and that a transition from "indicators" to "accounts" in major segments of the loosely-structured social indicators field could lead to similar advances in our ability to measure the performance of the social system as a whole.

Blackman, at NSF, treated the project as if it were disciplinary—he allowed Fox great latitude both in shifting direction with "changes in intellectual winds" and even in changing his place of work. Fox developed his program of work with minimal attention to the problems decision makers have to solve. By the end of the project, the objective had become one of developing better measures of social welfare of importance in several disciplines, particularly economics. Disciplinary progress was attempted for several disciplines, yet overall there was the knowledge that such measures would prove highly important to a substantial body of public decision makers concerned with improving the performance of various societies and social groups.

WORLD FOOD AND NUTRITION STUDY (WFNS)

This study [National Research Council, 1977b] resulted from a request President Ford made to the U.S. National Academy of Science (NAS). NAS was requested to produce the WFNS and include recommendations in it as to how U.S. research on food, agriculture, and nutrition could be organized and supported to solve problems involving food and nutrition around the world. The WFNS produced tentative recommendations (almost prescriptions) on what research should be supported and with how much budget.

The need for the study grew out of the food shortages that materialized temporarily in the early 1970s as the result of poor weather and the disappearance of U.S., Canadian, Australian, and European grain reserves. Those reserves had disappeared in part as a result of the tendency of both the developed and less developed worlds to expand grain consumption by using world grain reserves as a means of keeping food prices low. Low food prices, in turn, also depressed food production in the less developed world. However, U.S., Canadian, Australian, and European grain producers had received price supports and subsidies, which made it possible for them to maintain and expand grain production to generate "surpluses," which were often used to keep food prices low. When those reserves were used up, Presidents Carter and Ford and others became concerned about the need to increase food (grain) production abroad and in the U.S. to improve the nutritional level of the underfed around the world.

Kind of Research

Note that the effort was named the World Food and Nutrition *Study*, not the World Food and Nutrition *Research Project*. Thus, there seems to have been some question as to whether it was a research effort. In this chapter, however, it is treated as subject-matter research and not as disciplinary or problem-solving research.

The WFNS had prescriptive objectives—to recommend how U.S. research capacity could best be used to address world food and nutrition problems. Such a practical prescriptive objective indicates that it was a problem-solving research effort, which may explain why it was regarded by some disciplinary positivistic scientists as a study rather than as research. Some purists among positivistic disciplinary scientists do not regard problem-solving activities as scientific research.

Because the the WFNS was to recommend how U.S. research capacity could be used to alleviate problems involving food and nutrition around the world, the requested research (study) appears at first blush to be problem-solving in nature as it (1) was supposed to generate recommendations (prescriptions) about how the U.S. could best use its research capacity, and (2) was also conceived as multidisciplinary.

However, two difficulties are involved in classifying the WFNS as problem solving. First, it was understood that the WFNS would produce *recommendations* to the President of the United States to use in dealing with his administrative agencies and with the Congress in reaching *their* solutions to food and nutrition problems. Thus, it was clear that the recommendations were to be treated more as tentative intermediate inputs into decision processes than as actual solutions to problems. In turn, this indicates that the research was more subject-matter than problem-solving in nature. Everyone who understood the process realized, at least implicitly, that the recommendations would be tempered with political and strategic information in Presidential decision-making processes concerning what the *United States should do* to bring its research capacity to bear on the solutions of world food and nutrition problems. As soon as this is seen, it is realized that this study assembled and generated a multidisciplinary body of information, sometimes *semiprescriptive* but always intermediate in nature on a subject of importance to a set of decision makers in the U.S. government trying to solve a set of problems. Viewed in this manner, the effort is a *subject-matter* not a problem-solving research effort.

The subject-matter interpretation is further strengthened when one realizes that the study was commissioned by Republican President Ford, with the results being delivered to Democratic President Carter. Such a change meant that there was little reason to expect that the recommendations of a study commissioned by one president would be accepted as prescriptive by another. The most that could be hoped for was that the results of the study would be used in the decision-making processes of President Carter's administration.

Kinds of Knowledge

The WFNS assembled and, in some instances, developed value-free *positivistic* knowledge from the biological and technical disciplines concerned with food production and nutrition.

The WFNS also assembled and, perhaps, generated some knowledge of the values associated with food and nutrition status. There were difficulties with this because of the dominance of philosophical positivism among the biological and technical scientists who tended to control the exercise. There was a tendency to regard objective generation of knowledge about real values as impossible. Even behavioral knowledge about market or exchange values was often regarded as unreliable by biological and physical scientists, who are relatively uninformed about market economies and values in exchange. In many instances, intuitive feelings and arbitrary assumptions about the *intrinsic* values as contrasted to the exchange values of food and various nutritional conditions were used to the neglect of efforts to generate *objective* knowledge of values on the basis of logic and experience, as objectivity is defined in this book.

The WFNS did develop recommendations (prescriptive knowledge). However, these prescriptions did not emerge in an objective manner out of maximization calculations based on objective knowledge and the use of stated decision rules in which the roles of power were explicitly considered. Instead, they emerged out of semipolitical negotiations among WFNS committees and members (1) often employing arbitrary knowledge of values and somewhat less arbitrary, more objective value-free knowledge, (2) pursuing vested disciplinary and subject-matter objectives more than the values relevant for solving real-world problems involving food and nutrition, and (3) using the power of their prestige and authority in NSF and NAS circles in an unstated way to influence recommendations and budget priorities. In short, prescriptions were generated in a process that seemed more arbitrary than objective. The bureaucratic objectives of disciplinary and subject-matter administrative units seem to have been assigned more value than the values "actually important" to decision makers facing food production and nutrition problems.

Philosophic Orientation

The WFNS had a mixed philosophic orientation. It was conducted by the NAS with funding from the NSF. These organizations are populated with many scientists of positivistic persuasions who tend to accept positivism as *the* philosophy of science rather than as *a* philosophy of science. In addition, even the economist directing the exercise, Joel Bernstein, had come under the influence of Milton Friedman's "positivism" while receiving his Ph.D. training at the University of Chicago. In a similar vein, Charles French, the codirector, had a positivistic orientation growing out of his earlier role as chairman of the Department of Agricultural Economics in Purdue University's College of Agriculture. Like most colleges of agriculture, Purdue tends to be controlled by positivistic biological and physical scientists.

Though the WFNS was multidisciplinary and included a number of social scientists among its subcommittee members, several of the social scientists on the sub-committee were also positivistically oriented. For the most part, the social scientists were selected from social scientists who got along fairly well with the positivistic leadership of NAS or NSF or who had gotten along fairly well with the positivistic social scientists directing the project. Thus, as a group, the social scientists were not well-equipped philosophically to offset the dominance of their positivistic fellow members.

In the study, inadequate attention was paid to values in exchange as determined in market processes. Many of the biological and physical scientists regarded market prices as suspect, rather than as the consequences of a significant amount of knowledge of intrinsic values used by producers and consumers in trading with each other subject to the constraints of the real incomes they possess as a consequence of their income-earning rights. Nutritionists, for instance, think about the intrinsic values of food rather than of its exchange value in markets. While the nutritionists have considerable objective knowledge about the intrinsic value of different kinds of food, the positivistic presupposition that there are no normative experiences to use in developing objective knowledge of goodness and badness (values) as real characteristics of an objective world seemed to provide others with a perverse justification for (1) accepting arbitrary propositions about intrinsic values, and (2) ignoring the behavioral exchange values revealed by the operation of markets.

Social scientists who attempted to work with intrinsic values and with values in exchange (market prices) in an objective way were overridden, particularly when attention to such values made those scientists less decisive than those who reached recommendations on the basis of unquestioned and often unstated arbitrary values. A common complaint about the social scientists was that they were unable to come up with definite prescriptions about what "ought to be done." Unfortunately, many WFNS prescriptions were generated by positivists rather than by people prepared to work objectively with values and decision rules to arrive at prescriptive knowledge about what the research priorities ought to be.

If the above sounds too severe, note that the WFNS recommended that 99.7% of the U.S. research budget go in support of biological and technical research. This incongruous recommendation flies in the face of knowledge that the four prime movers of increased productive capacity are advances in capital accumulation, technology, improvements in institutions and policies, and investments in human beings. Technical advance alone is not enough. The world provides numerous instances where excellent technological advances have been cancelled out by inappropriate institutions, unwise policies, and lack of ability to generate and use the inputs carrying the technological advance.

While there is a great need for improvements in biological and physical technologies to produce food and improve nutrition, the need is not so great that 99.7% of a recommended research budget should go to that end, with only three tenths of one percent to the improvement of institutions, policies, and the human agent. Three tenths of one percent for the social sciences would leave most of the world's institutional, policy, and human constraints on production and utilization unattended, unresearched, and either still in place or changed through failure, chaos, and revolution.

Financial Support

The WFNS was supported financially with funds from the NSF and the resources of many contributing universities and agencies. The President asked the NAS to administer the project and directed the NSF to make financial resources available to the Academy. The NAS is so prestigious that most universities and public research agencies happily contribute the services of their personnel. In addition to the prestige that comes to a university or research agency when its personnel serve on NAS committees, there is the hope that it will lead to additional research support. These considerations raise questions about the objectivity of the exercise.

Accountability

Perhaps because the WFNS was not regarded as research—at least not in the sense of being disciplinary research—its output was not subjected to external peer review or even review by the decision makers to whom it was making recommendations. However, there was substantial internal review of supporting value-free knowledge, knowledge of values, and the prescriptions themselves. Unfortunately, internal review was not adequate because study members held specialized philosophic orientations and felt loyalty to their disciplines and subject areas. As a result, the internal reviews tended to endorse the results attained—correct or incorrect.

Financial accountability of the WFNS to NSF was tight as the NAS is strictly accountable for NSF funds to the federal government. On the other hand, financial accountability for university and institute people who serve on NAS's WFNS committees had to be rather loose to permit the volunteering of such large amounts of highly paid scientific expertise.

Conduct

The WFNS was supervised and administered out of the offices of the NAS by a project director and associate director. There was an overall steering committee, chaired by Harrison Brown, that included high-level administrators from foundations, universities, private businesses, consuls, research institutes, and experiment stations. Joel Bernstein, a former administrator from the Agency for International Development, served as study director. There were 14 study teams [National Research Council, 1977a], dealing with (1) crop productivity, (2) animal productivity, (3) aquatic food sources, (4) agricultural resources, (5) weather and climate, (6) food availability to consumers, (7) rural institutions, policies, and social science research, (8) information systems, (9) nutrition, (10) interdependencies, (11) new approaches to increasing food supplies, (12) new approaches to the alleviation of hunger, and (14) agricultural research organization.

Study Team 13 was responsible for the priority ranking of research efforts. Its members included:

Emery N. Castle (Chairman), Resources for the Future, Inc.
Aaron M. Altshul, Georgetown University Medical School
Chester B. Baker, University of Illinois
Lawrence Bogorad, Harvard University
Harold E. Calbert, University of Wisconsin
Gerald A. Carlson, North Carolina State University
Robert F. Chandler, Templeton, Massachusetts
Lehman B. Fletcher, Iowa State University
D. Mark Hegsted, Harvard School of Public Health
Keith A. Huston, University of Minnesota
John D. Isaacs, Scripps Institution of Oceanography
James H. Jensen, Green Valley, Arizona
Herbert W. Johnson, University of Minnesota
Robert L. Metcalf, University of Illinois
Harold F. Robinson, Western Carolina University
Lauren Soth, West Des Moines, Iowa
Carl E. Taylor, Johns Hopkins University

As No. 13's report was not widely reviewed or printed, it is difficult to submit it to ex post scrutiny.

Each study team was "to identify outstanding areas of research and development required to help meet world food and nutrition needs." It was also to develop recommendations about important research that should be conducted. These recommendations were to be "reconciled" by Study Team 13, which was to establish priorities for the recommendations in the final report.

Study Team 13 assessed and ranked more than 100 research areas provided by the subject-matter study teams. This phase involved several steps:

- Study Team 13 and the Steering Committee staff discussed the scope, purpose, organization, and methods of the World Food and Nutrition Study and the process proposed for the study team's work.
- A staff group, including the lead analyst of Study Team 13, highlighted and annotated the full set of research priorities provided in profile form by the study teams. This procedure facilitated identifying the answers to the standard questions bearing on the selection of research priorities.
- The members of Study Team 13 then studied at length the annotated profiles and overview comments of the 12 study teams. They also met with each study team chairman, who highlighted his team's report and responded to questions.
- Next, each member of Study Team 13, without consulting with the others, ranked each research area from 0 to 10 according to four criteria: (1) probability of success, (2) global effect on hunger and malnutrition if the research succeeds, (3) cost and feasibility of doing the proposed research, and (4) overall priority, based on judgments about the first three criteria. Research areas were ranked according to these four criteria for two time periods: 15 years after the research effort

is accelerated, and beyond 15 years. The key considerations for the overall priority rating were probability of success and effect. Feasibility moderated the decisions on how to do recommended research. Each member of Study Team 13 was requested to comment on all high or low ratings (8 to 10, 1 to 3). Each member also was invited to comment on any other point that he felt useful, such as interrelationships of priority areas, nature or appropriateness of assumptions or gaps in needed analysis.

• The lead analyst of Study Team 13 and the Steering Committee staff summarized the rating sheets in three tables. The first table provided the average of Study Team 13's ratings on the eight criteria for each research area. The second table showed, for estimated effects in both less than and more than 15 years, the distribution of low, medium, and high *overall* ratings for each area, the ranking of the area's average overall rating, and assignment of the research area to one of five priority categories based on the contents of the rating sheets and supplemental information in the profiles.

Those categories were:

A . High chance of successful research; very strong worldwide effect if research succeeds.
B . High chance of successful research; strong effect largely for specific geographic (political or ecological) zones or population groups.
C . Success of research relatively uncertain (more risky than A, B, or D, but chances still good); very strong worldwide effect if research succeeds.
D . High chance of successful research; relatively moderate effect if research succeeds (i.e., prospect of substantial global effect at low risk, though total effect of successful research well below A or C; effect could be more or less than B, but more diffused).
E . Lesser expectations than A to D.

The third table was an interpretative summary of the comments provided by the members of Study Team 13 on their rating sheets.

• Study Team 13 met to discuss the foregoing materials, especially research items on which there were highly divergent views, problems in dealing with uneven levels of scope and presentation among the research profiles, and difficulties in reaching conclusions in some subject areas on the basis of the materials at hand. During this period and also prior to the first ratings some items were combined into more comparable units.
• Study team members then provided a second round of individual ratings of a consolidated list of 76 research items. The ratings were confined to the overall priority of each research area, for effects in both the shorter and longer time periods. For this process, the study team members used their previous rating sheets, the research profiles, and the materials from the first two steps.
• Study Team 13 then prepared its report for the Steering Committee. It began by considering a list of all research items with an average rating in the second round above 6.0 in the short run and 7.0 in the long run. A list of items previously rated high, but not so high in the second rating, also was considered. The study team then discussed those items that ranked high and those areas in which there

was concern that major omission or error might occur. Several items were added to the top priority list primarily to broaden and complete research areas. In addition, three areas of concern were identified that had no items in the top category, due to the study team's difficulties in dealing with the materials they received in the limited time available to them. The report identified 31 top priority and near top priority research areas for either short-run or long-run effect or both. The report also called attention to the need to develop priority research needs more adequately in three broad subject areas that Study Team 13 felt had been handled inadequately.

Durability

As a subject-matter research effort, the WFNS should not be expected to be very durable. Ordinarily, the durability of subject-matter research falls between ephemeral problem-solving research and very durable disciplinary research. Even before the WFNS was delivered to President Carter, he had established a competitive Presidential Commission on World Hunger (CWH) with broader objectives than those of the WFNS. The CWH was to examine what the U.S. could do to alleviate world hunger, so it partially duplicated the WFNS.

It is difficult to judge the durability of the WFNS; it did have some effect on the conclusions of the CWH. The CWH members included not only scientists but also congressional, religious, and business leaders. Especially in attempts to publicize the results of the CWH, the biological, technical, and positivistic conclusions drawn by WFNS carry through to the output of the CWH.

There is more evidence that the results of the WFNS have been rather durable—perhaps even more than they should have been. As the Reagan administration attempted to restrain the growth of federal expenditures while expanding the military budget, it curtailed research expenditures rather heavily. Probably no phase of federally supported research has been more drastically curtailed than social science research on institutional policy and human investment issues. This curtailment is consistent with the pattern of recommendations that grew out of the WFNS. While I know of no direct connection between the two, NSF has greatly curtailed its support of social science research and the Reagan administration's support of social science research has been less than enthusiastic.

PHILOSOPHIC AND METHODOLOGICAL
GENERALIZATIONS ABOUT SUBJECT-MATTER RESEARCH

The two subject-matter research case studies considered in this chapter are quite different. Fox's study on social indicators is near the border between disciplinary and subject-matter research, whereas the WFNS is near the border with problem-solving research. Fox's research is classified as subject-matter research mainly because it involves more than one discipline; however, it does not include the biological and physical sciences, only the social sciences. The WFNS, on the other hand, was revealed to be a subject-matter study rather than "really" prescriptive and problem-solving as its recommendations were merely advisory.

At the two extremes of subject matter research where these two pieces of research fall, it is clear that it is difficult to differentiate them from the adjacent categories. Fox's research tends to fall in the penumbra between disciplinary and subject matter research whereas the WFNS tends to fall in the penumbra between subject-matter and problem-solving research. Knowing and understanding this about the two case studies is helpful in understanding their philosophic orientations, the kinds of information sought, financing, accountability problems, evaluation, practicality, and durability as these vary across the range of projects from the purely disciplinary to efforts designed to solve a specific problem.

Both studies show that subject-matter research may encounter a direct need for objective investigation of the values. Fox investigated behavioral values in exchange, including the trade-offs between monetary and nonmonetary values. Because he addresses exchange values, empirical conclusions based on his approach would be conditioned by the distribution of the ownership of rights and privileges within a society investigated. Further, because he proposed to deal with values in exchange as expressed by people, his procedures cannot produce conclusions about what really does have value whether or not the people involved hold that it does. The WFNS can be seriously criticized for the way it dealt with values. It did not objectively investigate either intrinsic or exchange values. Values in exchange, which are generated in the market place, were mostly rejected or viewed with suspicion by the biological and physical scientists who dominated the exercise. However, intrinsic values were not usually investigated objectively; instead, various things, situations, or conditions were often assumed to have value. To the extent that such value propositions were based on the logic and experiences of WFNS participants, this did not cause difficulties. Difficulty arose in the WFNS, however, when vested institutional, disciplinary, and subject-matter interests began to influence the selection of value propositions and, hence, the setting of research priorities and budget recommendations.

The WFNS encountered the constraints of positivism on attempts to objectively research value questions. These constraints opened the door to arbitrary value assumptions and the pursuit of vested interests. Who can raise questions on objectivity about value assumptions and the pursuit of vested interests when the underlying philosophy indicates there is nothing objective to be known about values?

As to financing, the WFNS was set up by President Ford, who insured that the NSF would make funds available to the NAS to conduct the study.

In turn, the NAS used its prestige to get U.S. universities, research agencies, and individuals to contribute substantial amounts of time to the project. Fox's research, on the other hand, was supported mainly by Iowa State University and the NSF.

Financial accountability was direct in both projects. Academy, university, and/or NSF accounting procedures had to be conformed to in both studies. Probably the loosest accounting in both projects was for the monetary value of the time university and other personnel "contributed" to the WFNS effort. Perhaps this is related to the pursuit in the WFNS of vested disciplinary and subject-matter interests. The administrators of the organizations that contributed the services of their reputable scientists to this effort probably hoped for more than a general improvement in the functioning of the U.S. system for handling food and nutrition research—i.e., it is likely they hoped for greater support for research programs of interest to them.

Review and evaluation procedures were quite different in the two projects. Fox conducted his project in an academic, discipline-like manner despite the fact that he worked across several social sciences. His proposal went through the regular review procedures of NSF—results were produced and written up in a book-length manuscript, copies of which were sent for comment to NSF, to several of Fox's colleagues in different disciplines, and to two scientific publishers. The publishers subjected it to peer review by two sociologists and a political scientist who were widely acquainted with the literature on social indicators. One publisher accepted the manuscript subject to the excision of certain chapters the reviewer thought were beyond the proper scope of social indicators; the other accepted it enthusiastically and without revision. Social scientists from at least three disciplines were involved in the review and evaluation process, and none of them had a vested interest in the project.

By contrast, the WFNS was largely reviewed internally. This seemed reasonable since there were participants from many disciplines. The difficulty for the WFNS arose because of positivistic dominance within the study and pursuit of vested institutional, subject-matter, and disciplinary interests, which apparently detracted significantly from the objectivity of the reviews and evaluations. Objectivity is encouraged by both external and internal review.

It is difficult at this point to judge the durability of the two projects. Clearly, Fox made a distinguished multidisciplinary contribution to subject-matter research involving the social sciences. However, his research has yet to be used by any significant government agency or problem-solving entity. There are a number of indications, though, that Fox's research is having considerable influence on the thinking of other research workers in the fields of social indicators and social system accounts. The NSF increased its support for Fox's research (under grant SOC 74-3996) from approximately $120,000 in 1974 to nearly $400,000 in 1976 (under grant SOC 76-20084). Within NSF, Murray Aborn, Program Director for Social Indicators and Special Projects, assumed responsibility for reviewing Fox's research proposals and funded the resulting projects under the short title, "Measurement and Valuation of Social System Outcomes."

By implication, Fox's 1974 book was well-received, and his subsequent research proposals were regarded as worthy of NSF support by peer reviewers from a number of social sciences. The breadth of *potential* interest in his results is suggested by his publication of an article "Social Accounts for Urban-Centered Regions" (with Syamal K. Ghosh) in the *International Regional Science Review* [1980]; a long chapter (with Syamal K. Ghosh), "A Behavior Setting Approach to Social Accounts Combining Concepts and Data from Ecological Psychology, Economics, and Studies of Time Use," in F. Thomas Juster and Kenneth C. Land, eds., *Social Accounting Systems: Essays on the State of the Art*, New York: Academic Press [1981]; and an article entitled "The Eco-Behavioral View of Human Societies and its Implications for Systems Science" in the *International Journal of Systems Sciences* [1983]. Fox also had book-length manuscripts in progress as of April 1983.

In the case of the WFNS, results were submitted to a different president than the one who commissioned it [National Research Council, 1977a and 1977b]. There is little evidence that this study had a direct impact on the decisions of President Carter and his administration. There is evidence, however, that it had an impact on some members of the CWH, and one can speculate as to whether the WFNS's low priorities for social science research have had anything to do with the cuts in social science research that have occurred since then in the NSF. There is evidence to the contrary that social science research in the Department of Agriculture has not been cut as severely as social science in NSF and in the rest of the Reagan administration.

ADDITIONAL REFERENCES

Bauer, Raymond A., ed. 1966. *Social Indicators,* Cambridge, MA: M.I.T. Press.

Ezekiel, Mordecai. 1930. *Methods of Correlation Analysis.* New York: Wiley, 2nd revised ed., 1941.

—— and K. Fox. 1959. *Methods of Corellation and Regression Analysis*, 3rd ed., New York: Wiley.

Fox, Karl A. 1958. *Econometric Analysis for Public Policy*, Ames: Iowa State University Press.

—— 1968. *Intermediate Economic Statistics*, New York: Wiley.

—— ed. 1972. *Economic Analysis for Educational Planning: Resource Allocation in Nonmarket Systems*, Baltimore: Johns Hopkins University Press.

—— 1974. *Social Indicators and Social Theory.* New York: Wiley.

—— 1983. The Eco-Behavioral View of Human Societies and Its Implications for Systems Science, *International Journal of Systems Science*, **14**(8):895–914.

—— J. K. Sengupta, and Erik Thorbecke. 1973. *The Theory of Quantitative Economic*

Policy: With Applications to Economic Growth, Stabilization and Planning, Amsterdam: North-Holland, and New York: American Elsevier, 1st ed., 1966.

—— and S. K. Ghosh. 1980. Social Accounts for Urban-Centered Regions, International Regional Science Review, 5(1):33-50.

—— 1981. A Behavior Setting Approach to Social Accounts Combining Concepts and Data from Ecological Psychology, Economics, and Studies of Time Use, in Social Accounting Systems: Essays on the State of the Art, F. Thomas Juster and Kenneth C. Land, eds., New York: Academic Press.

Gross, Bertram M. 1966. The State of the Nation: Social Systems Accounting, Ch. 3, pp. 154-271, in Raymond A. Bauer, ed., Social Indicators, Cambridge, MA: M.I.T. Press.

Merrill, William C. and Karl A. Fox. 1970. Introduction to Economic Statistics, New York: Wiley.

National Research Council. 1977a. Supporting Papers: World Food and Nutrition Study, Volumes I through V, Washington, DC: National Academy of Sciences.

—— 1977b. World Food and Nutrition Study, Washington, DC: National Academy of Sciences.

Presidential Commission on World Hunger. 1980. Overcoming World Hunger: The Challenge Ahead, Washington, DC: Report of the Presidential Commission on World Hunger, U.S. Government Printing Office, No. 041-002-00015-8.

Schultz, Henry. 1938. The Theory and Measurement of Demand, Chicago: University of Chicago Press.

Sengupta, J. K. and K. A. Fox. 1969. Economic Analysis and Operations Research: Optimization Techniques in Quantitative Economic Models, Amsterdam: North–Holland.

Tinbergen, Jan. 1939. Statistical Testing of Business Cycle Theories: Volume I. A Method and Its Application to Investment Activity: Volume II. Business Cycles in the United States of America, 1919-1932, Geneva: League of Nations Economic Intelligence Service.

—— 1952. On the Theory of Economic Policy, Amsterdam: North-Holland.

Chapter 12

Problem-Solving
Case Studies

Two problem-solving case studies are considered in this chapter. The first is eclectic and easily identified as problem-solving research. The second is adversarial and dialectic and less clearly classified as research even if obviously problem-solving in nature.

The Michigan Pickle Study is clearly a case of problem-solving research. The other study has to do with the activities of the Michigan Public Service Commission as it handled an application from Consumers Power Company for an interim rate increase. Though the rate-increase case study was much more adversarial and dialectic, the Michigan Pickle Study was not free of adversarial activities. Both studies deal with specific problems of establishing publicly controlled prices or rates by public agencies.

After describing each case the chapter classifies the two research efforts as to kind, examines them for the kinds of knowledge generated, then analyzing them for their philosophic orientations. Attention is also given to how the two activities were administered. Administrative processes examined involve financing and accountability, conduct, and review and evaluation. Some attention is also given to the durability and practicality of the results.

The last section of the chapter summarizes the implications of the two case studies for problem-solving research, the generalizations being based on the chapters in Part I and on the two case studies examined here. Chapters 10 and 11 dealt with disciplinary and subject-matter research. Those two chapters, along with this chapter, provide information to be used in reaching generalizations in the chapters of Part III that deal with research administration and, in the case of Chapter 17, with overall generalizations concerning all three kinds of research—disciplinary, subject-matter, and problem solving.

THE MICHIGAN PICKLE STUDY

This is a clear-cut example of problem-solving research conducted by the Department of Agricultural Economics at the Michigan Agricultural Experiment Station [Stuckman, 1959; Johnson and Zerby, 1973].

In 1957, several groups became concerned about the relatively low earnings of Mexican Nationals being brought to Michigan to pick pickles. These groups included the U.S. Department of State (USDS), which had responsibility under Public law 78 for negotiating with the Mexican goverment on matters concerning employment of Mexican Nationals in the United States; the U.S. Department of Labor (USDL), whose interest in the earnings of Mexican Nationals grew out of the pressure exerted on it by labor unions who wanted to avoid competition for domestic employment; and the pickle processors, who wanted to preserve the ability of farmers to deliver pickles. Pickle producers also had a keen interest in wage rates paid to Mexican Nationals. Last, and probably least in terms of power to influence the situation, was the Mexican National himself.

As a result of pressure from these various groups, representatives of the National Pickle Packers Association (NPPA) and the National Pickle Growers Association (NPGA) produced a formula for paying Mexican Nationals for picking the 1958 crop. It was generally recognized in designing this formula that earnings for Mexican Nationals were low on fields with poor yields. The new formula provided that Mexican Nationals who worked in fields producing more than 120 bushels per acre would be paid one-half the value of the crop. The proportion of the value of the crop going to the Mexican Nationals who picked in fields yielding less than 120 bushels was increased.

The Department of Agricultural Economics at Michigan State University (MSU) was asked by the NPPA and NPGA in the spring of 1958 to evaluate the operation of the new formula in the summer of 1958. Objective evaluation was sought in view of tensions resulting from the problem.

Research Objectives and Accomplishments

In the correspondence involved in setting up the project, the head of the Agricultural Economics Department wrote:

It was my understanding that during the summer of 1958, we would try to accomplish two things: (1) the evaluation of hourly earnings of laborers picking pickles
in the State of Michigan, and (2) the evaluation of the formula which the USDL
has agreed to allow the pickle industry to try this year in the reimbursement of
farm labor. A second step to the evaluation of the formula will be to attempt to
create a more workable formula to correct any deficiencies which may be apparent
after the summer's work.*

The study's objectives were (1) the estimation of the average hourly earnings
received by Mexican Nationals picking pickles in Southern Michigan, and (2)
the evaluation of the Worker Yield Return Formula (WYRF) generally followed by the industry and accepted by the USDL in determining the rate of reimbursement for Mexican Nationals picking pickles in Michigan in the summer
of 1958. Concerning the first objective, particular attention was given to Nationals receiving a season average wage of less than the then minimum wage
of 70 cents an hour. Both the situations under which they worked and the personal characteristics of the workers receiving low wages were studied.

Concerning the second objective, particular attention was given to ways
of correcting apparent deficiencies in the operation of the formula. Possible
improvements considered included educational and research programs and
changes in the WYRF itself. It was expected that the project would generate
recommendations for solving the problem of guaranteeing that Mexican Nationals would receive the minimum wage rate without sacrificing other valuable
characteristics of the industry. Clearly, the research fell into the problem-solving
category.

Kinds of Knowledge

Because the research was problem-solving in nature, it sought *prescriptive*
knowledge. In turn, *value-free* knowledge and *knowledge of values* as well as
knowledge about decision rules used or usable in the industry were required.

The approach was twofold. An attempt was made to describe the situation existing in 1958 and to predict the consequences of various alternative actions. In addition, as a partial basis for determining a set of prescriptions to
solve the problem, much time was spent trying to clarify and make consistent
the values that motivated the interested parties. In short, both value-free and
value information were pursued.

Contracting arrangements and growing conditions for pickling cucumbers
varied in different areas of the state. Therefore, it was necessary to work with
a random sample of pickle producers if the results were to be generalized to
the universe of pickle growers. The part of the state where pickles were picked
by Mexican Nationals was divided into small areas and a random sample of

*Letter dated June 19, 1958, from L. L. Boger to W. E. Dailey, Jr., President of Daily Pickle
Company.

these areas was selected. Within each sample area, all farms employing Mexican Nationals were included as sample farms.

The sample included 81 farmers, 76 of whom furnished usable data. These 76 farmers employed over 1,100 Mexican Nationals and sold pickles to 15 companies through 25 receiving stations.

Each farmer in the sample was asked to provide positivistic information about the cultural practices used in producing pickles, certain costs of production (monetary values), his knowledge and attitude (often normative) regarding the WYRF, and his general attitude (again, often normative) and practices about the use of labor in picking pickles. In addition, the farmers were asked to keep detailed records of the hours spent by their workers in various activities.

The workers were interviewed in Spanish about their reasons, many of which involved values, for entering the pickle picking labor force, their understanding and knowledge of the WYRF, their attitude (often normative) toward picking pickles, and certain personal characteristics thought to influence their earnings.

Daily receipt and weight slips for each field were microfilmed in the offices of the pickle companies. The earnings statements of all workers were also microfilmed.

The data from all of these sources were transferred to IBM cards for tabulation and analysis. Cross-referencing permitted reconciliation of data produced by other organizations, such as the USDL, with data from the study. Where inconsistencies appeared, further investigation was done to determine which sets of data (both value-free and about values) were most reliable in terms of being consistent with other accepted propositions as well as with current experience and observations.

Investigations of nonmonetary values were less formal than those of monetary values. During the study, researchers held regular meetings with executives of the NPG and NPP Associations to ascertain the values held by these two organizations. In addition, all meetings held with growers, whether by the NPGA or by the new Michigan Pickling Cucumber Growers Association (MPCGA), were attended by at least one MSU researcher. At these meetings, the *experienced* goodness and badness of different conditions, situations, and things were often discussed.

As the work of the researchers progressed through the summer, accounts of experiences with goodness and badness were accumulated and the value picture was further clarified by fairly logical discussions of value experiences. Value and value-free positivistic propositions were interrelated, and conclusions began to emerge about what was bad (and what was wrong) with the 1958 formula and what prescriptions might solve the problem.

The decision rules and processes followed in reaching tentative decisions about what would be right to do were difficult to understand. At times, some participants tended to make decisions on the basis of what they thought was best in the long run. In doing so, they seemed to be trying to maximize the present net value of expected net returns. At other times, some people wanted to play it safe by adopting a course of action that would ensure that the worst that could happen would be good enough to guarantee certain minima. Some were unwilling to follow courses of action that would hurt themselves for the benefit of others; others with more empathy were willing to do so. This compassion for others was often encountered in interviews with farmers with first-hand experience of the plight of the Mexican Nationals.

A Major Iteration

At this point in approximating what would be "right to do," it was decided that the value and value-free propositions and tentative prescriptions should be checked with interested groups for important omissions and for such things as logical inconsistencies (lack of coherence), inconsistency with experience (lack of correspondence), and lack of clarity (ambiguity). A statement was prepared as a basis for discussions with members of interested groups.

This first iteration was not received with great enthusiasm. Interested parties were uneasy about certain positivistic value-free and value propositions assumed or presented in it. There was also dissatisfaction with some of the tentative conclusions and prescriptions. This arose in part from the decision rules being used to reach conclusions about what should be done, given the value-free and value propositions then at hand. These are some of the propositions that caused dissatisfactions:

1. Data on hourly earnings of Mexican Nationals were viewed with suspicion. At least one company president found the study data inconsistent with data he had on the earnings of Nationals working for farmers selling pickles to his plant.
2. Details about how earnings per hour were related to hours worked per season, characteristics of farms, characteristics of Mexican Nationals, when employed during the season, and so forth were not regarded as sufficient.
3. Information about the earnings of farmers producing pickles, including the relationship between farmers' earnings and the earnings of Mexican Nationals, was not regarded as sufficient.
4. Information about the influence on earnings and the industry of the WYRF, developed by the industry and put into effect by the USDL for the 1958 crop, was not regarded as sufficient.

Dissatisfaction with propositions involving nonmonetary values were also expressed:

1. Companies and farmer groups were concerned about their independence. They seemed to fear that researchers placed less value

on their independence than they themselves and would therefore make unduly strong recommendations for governmental control of the industry.

2. There were conflicting ideas about the nonmonetary values associated with higher pickle prices. Growers wanted higher prices. Processors wanted an unchanging or higher processing margin without the reduction in volume of sales that would result from higher retail prices. The USDL wanted the minimum hourly earnings of Mexican Nationals increased to reflect both the USDL's interests in negotiating with the Mexican government and the concern of labor organizations with qualitative and price competition from Mexican Nationals for Michigan jobs. As a result, the USDL was not opposed to increases in pickle prices.

3. The survival of pickle producers was important to pickle producers, processors, county agents, and local authorities. There was much concern over the fate of small producers encountering financial problems. Some interested groups feared that the researchers might not value survival of pickle producers highly enough.

4. There was strong preference for education (to teach farmers how to increase both their earnings and those of the Nationals) and voluntary adjustment as opposed to controls involving coercion. Although there was little fear that the research group undervalued education, there was some fear that they might not perceive of the badness of control through coercion.

Another target of dissatisfaction involved the decision rules then being used by researchers in analyzing value-free positivistic and value propositions to arrive at prescriptive conclusions about what ought to be done. For example:

1. At one point, a company representative complained that the researchers had been asked to carry out what he termed an "objective evaluation," by which he meant value-free as opposed to normative evaluation. To him, *evaluate* meant to determine a quantity, as when a mathematics student is asked to evaluate $y = 5 + 4x + 2x^2$ for $x = 2$. Determination of the average hourly earnings of Mexican Nationals in Michigan was an example of evaluation to him. He was uncertain about how an investigation would lead to conclusions about what action to take without considering values.

2. Among the researchers, those trained in modern welfare economics had a preference for Pareto-better solutions—i.e., solutions that make at least one person better off without making anyone worse off. The same researchers would also have accepted solutions that provided for the compensation of those made worse off by those made better

off. The difficulty, however, was that fundamental aspects of the problem involved a dissatisfaction with the status quo—making certain persons worse off in order to make others better off. This, in turn, raised questions about the interpersonal validity of welfare knowledge available to the study team.

Value-free and normative propositions found to be deficient were investigated further by the researchers. New propositions were developed from experiences recorded as data in the various survey efforts and noted while working with interested groups in the industry. Inconsistencies between propositions and experience were also reduced. Researchers focused their attention on the workability of recommendations that would follow from certain propositions.

Final Evaluations and Adoption of the Recommendations

The general conclusion was that while in the first year of operation of the WYRF, average hourly earnings were over 70 cents, certain deficiencies were noted. These included:

1. About 30 percent of the Nationals averaged less than 70 cents an hour for the season as a result of conditions over which they had little control but that were partially controllable by industry associations, individual processors, and individual growers.
2. 38 percent of the growers had net returns (including rent charges for land and risk) of less than 20 dollars per acre.
3. There was a tendency for the WYRF to encourage practices by packers and growers that were contrary to the long-run interests of the pickle industry.

To correct these deficiencies, it was recommended that:

1. Consideration be given to the possibility of placing the WYRF on a dollar yield per acre basis rather than on its then-used bushel yield per acre basis. As the dollar value of the crop per acre reflects both yield per acre and quality, it was even more closely related to average hourly earnings than bushel yield per acre. According to this study, the average price paid per bushel of pickles was 96.3 cents. Using this price per bushel, the dollar yield equivalent to 120 bushels is $115 per acre. Placing the WYRF on a dollar basis had the advantage of eliminating the inefficiency resulting from increasing per acre yields through the production and marketing of large, unusable pickles not normally classified as 4s. Where practiced, this had circumvented the intent of the WYRF, preventing that formula from increasing the

average hourly earnings of Nationals. It is important to note that pickles were not a profitable enterprise for growers with yields so low they found it necessary to engage in such activities. In addition, there were indications that a change to a value basis would significantly reduce the bookkeeping and computations for farmers and processors to determine bushel yields.

2. Consideration be given to means of reducing the proportions of both Nationals receiving less than 70 cents an hour and growers netting less than $20 an acre to cover land charges and profits. It was suggested that this reduction be brought about with some combination of educational programs and an increase in standards in the WYRF.

3. The basic materials for three educational programs were produced by the study, by other research at the Michigan Agricultural Experiment Station, and by the industry and its associations. It was recommended that:

   a. Any educational programs contemplated for growers be carried out by the industry associations operating through their representatives and cooperating with the MSU Cooperative Extension Service. Available material had to do mainly with increasing yields per acre and eliminating poor labor supervision.

   b. Any educational programs contemplated for packers be carried out largely by the NPPA. Available material was regarded as useful in screening contractees, in formulating contracts, and in guiding the operation of receiving stations.

   c. The labor associations use the materials from this study that bore on recruitment of Nationals for their own enlightenment. These materials indicated the kinds of Nationals who were likely to have unproductive low earnings regardless of the circumstances under which they work.

Educational programs appeared to be a promising partial alternative to higher standards in the WYRF whether or not that formula was converted from bushel to dollar yields per acre as recommended above. They involved less regulation of individuals, businesses, and organizations and placed the responsibility on the individuals making the decisions. Raising the standard in the WYRF to 200 bushels or about $195 per acre would have eliminated almost all 1958 season average hourly earnings below 70 cents per hour for individual Nationals. Serious side effects would accompany such actions, however. As growers producing less than $200 make very meager returns without penalties, the imposition of penalties would have imposed severe hardships on them. Raising wages by regulation also seemed less satisfactory to all concerned than treatment of the basic causes of low earnings—namely, low yields and poor labor supervision by some growers; unwise contracting, supervision, and buying practices by some packers; and unwise recruitment of Mexican Nationals.

Reliance was placed on education, in preference to regulation, to the extent that the industry and public agencies could carry it out.

4.   Because of the upward trend in wages and incomes of farmers and nonfarmers, it seemed advisable for the industry and individual packers to:

a.   Encourage the development of labor-saving technology. The industry was commended for its forward-looking support of research on the pickle-picking machine. More support (both through public appropriations and private contributions) seemed justified.

b.   Reappraise hourly earnings and net returns of growers periodically. Depending on future rates of progress in labor-saving technology in pickle production, it was anticipated that these reappraisals would have to include the price structure for the raw product for pickles to compete with alternative uses for the labor of farmers, productive resources, and the labor of Mexican Nationals.

5.   For the season then ahead, it appeared that care to avoid overcertification, prompt withdrawal of workers at the end of the season, the educational programs mentioned above, and/or higher WYRF standards were capable of decreasing the proportion of Nationals averaging below 70 cents per hour substantially below that for the 1958 season.

In addition, it was recommended that the industry investigate alternative ways of combining the incentive pay system then used with some method to create an inducement for the grower to avoid overhiring and retaining workers too late in the season. This investigation should recognize that incentive plans appear to be of great importance in pickle picking. Thus, minimum hourly rates, which might be used to protect the worker in such situations, could not be as high as the minimum acceptable season average hourly rates without endangering the benefits from incentive plans in pickle picking.

These recommendations were submitted to the National Pickle Packers and the National Pickle Growers Associations. They in turn presented the conclusions at hearings conducted by the USDL. As a result, the recommendations were adopted in toto. The industry operated according to governmental regulations based on these recommendations for three years—1959, 1960, and 1961. The educational programs recommended were carried out in 1959 by the Michigan State Cooperative Extension Service and by the NPPA. Pickle growing contracting policies followed by the processors were also changed to eliminate a high proportion of growers with low yields.

Although no specific studies were made of the effects of the regulations and educational programs, the general impression existed throughout the industry that earnings of both Mexican Nationals and pickle growers improved as a result of (1) the concentration of pickle production on better land and in the hands of farmers able to carry out practices that would increase yields per acre, and (2) the tendency of the new formula to discourage certain of the undesirable practices that had developed under the earlier WYRF. Certain growers unable to produce higher yields were eliminated. They did not object strenuously partly because the research and educational programs made it clear to them that they had little to gain from staying in pickle production. It appears that the prescriptive conclusions from the project about what was right to do met the test of workability in the sense that it solved the problem faced by the Michigan pickle-producing industry when the problem was posed to the researchers.

This problem-solving piece of research very nicely illustrates what is typically involved in (1) supporting and accounting for the support of problem-solving research, (2) administering and conducting multidisciplinary research, (3) the review and evaluation of problem-solving research, and (4) the practical importance and lack of long-run durability of this kind of research.

Support and Accountability for Support

It is often true that research organizations do not have to seek support for problem-solving research. In this case, part of the support came from agencies seeking assistance from the Michigan Agricultural Experiment Station. The NPPA and NPGA came to the Dean of Agriculture and the Experiment Station Director with a problem. They were also prepared to defray part of the cost of the desired research. Since they were part of an industry that provided political support and, through the political channel, general financial support for the Michigan Agricultural Experiment Station, they felt that the Station should bear part of the cost. In effect, budget support was split about evenly between the Michigan Agricultural Experiment Station and the two Associations. The Dean of Agriculture and the Director of the Agricultural Experiment Station saw that this was one of the practical problems the Experiment Station had been established to help solve. They also realized that the two Associations had a considerable amount of knowledge to contribute. Hence, they sought support from the Associations in the form of information and iterative/interactive consulting as well as in the form of money.

During the project, a considerable amount of information was simply transferred from knowledgeable members of the two Associations to the researchers through conferences and the provision of data and information readily

available from the offices of the Associations. In addition to support for the
project, there was also some opposition. The USDL, representing the interests
of the industrial labor unions so important in Michigan, opposed Public Law
78, which provided for the importation, supervision, and regulation of Mexican Nationals to help in U.S. crop production.

Financial support from outside agencies to work on problems does not
come without additional accountability. The two Associations that provided
financial assistance were keenly interested in the results of the research. Because
the research was done iteratively and interactively with all concerned, it was
difficult to distinguish between accountability and advantageous interaction
with concerned decision makers. Good faith on the part of both Experiment
Station researchers and officials in the two Associations resulted in a productive interaction that simultaneously provided the accountability desired by the
two supporting organizations and the information and interaction required by
the researchers. Researchers more oriented to disciplinary work might have
found the accountability requirements and the interaction offensive. The
problem-oriented researchers who participated in this project found the
simultaneous accountability and interaction a productive source of information. Even the USDL, which opposed the project and refused to supply valuable
data it had at its disposal, eventually approved the results of the research by
adopting recommendations from the project in toto.

Administration and Conduct of the Project

Like almost all problem-solving research, this project was multidisciplinary and
multidepartmental. It crossed the administrative lines that separate the
multidisciplinary "institute-like" departments in the College of Agriculture as
well as the lines that separate more disciplinary departments elsewhere in the
university. Also, the project did not fit established administrative lines among
colleges at Michigan State University. The Department of Labor and Industrial
Relations in the College of Social Science possessed important skills and
knowledge needed in conducting the project. The "soft money" provided by
the two Associations was extremely important in obtaining the skills and
knowledge from that department for use in this project.

With such soft money available, it was unnecessary to invoke university
authority above the dean and college level to obtain intercollege cooperation.
Instead, the assistance of the Department of Labor and Industrial Relations
was simply purchased. Nonetheless, the project nicely illustrates the administrative problems likely to arise when the multidepartmental and
multidisciplinary dimensions of a problem-solving project cross college lines.

Within the College of Agriculture, the Dean, Agricultural Experiment Station Director, and Director of the Cooperative Extension Service provided the
administration necessary to make resources from the Horticultural, Agronomy,

and Agricultural Engineering Departments available as needed. This was true for both the research and extension phases that followed to carry out the educational recommendations.

While the administrative structure of the College of Agriculture performed well in this instance, participants in the project were impressed with how much administration was required, and some wondered how many such projects could be successfully administered at one time with the limited administrative structure of the College of Agriculture. Clearly, the administrative requirements for this kind of problem-solving research are very great. Had it not been for the readily available flexible "soft money" that was used to obtain intercollege "cooperation," one wonders in retrospect whether there would have been enough administrative capacity at the university level to provide the administrative services for what was a relatively small project at Michigan State University.

Review and Evaluation of Project Proposals and Results

Disciplinary research is typically reviewed and evaluated by peers from a single discipline. By contrast, this project was examined and evaluated by peers from several disciplines. The project proposal was also evaluated (1) within the Agricultural Experiment Station by researchers and administrators who looked at the research proposal from a multidisciplinary, problem-solving perspective, and (2) outside the Agricultural Experiment Station by concerned agencies and people. The USDL, responding to the interests of the industrial labor unions of Michigan, evaluated the proposal negatively but evaluated the results positively. The project proposal, conduct, and final results were more or less continuously evaluated by Experiment Station personnel, personnel from concerned agencies, and concerned farmers. Evaluation was not kept separate from the "process of iterative interaction," which was a crucial source of positivistic knowledge without value content, knowledge about values, and prescriptions as to what kinds of decision rules should be used in developing ultimate prescriptions (recommendations) to solve the problem under consideration.

Practical Importance and Durability

Pickles are more important in agricultural and consumer affairs than many realize. The State of Michigan was then the leading producer of pickling cucumbers. A visit to a supermarket quickly shows that cucumber pickles occupy as much or more shelf space than any other canned vegetable. Thus the project was important to consumers, producers, the pickle-packing industry, and the Mexican Nationals who were being given the opportunity to work in the United States at much higher wages than they would have received in Mexico and under governmental supervision from both countries provided, in turn, through diplomatic negotiations between the two countries.

However important the research was, like most practical problem-solving research it was unlikely to win the award from the American Association of Agricultural Economics for "research of enduring value." Problem-solving research, as noted in the introductory chapters of this book, is specific to a decision maker and a particular problem. Once a problem is solved, research on it tends to be forgotten. In addition there is a tendency for the solution of one problem to create another problem, which then attracts the attention of decision makers and problem-solving researchers.

The labor problems of the Michigan pickle industry were not solved once and for all by this research. Labor union opposition to the use of Mexican Nationals was not eliminated by improvements in the formula for guaranteeing that Mexican Nationals would be paid the U.S. minimum wage rate. The unions were much more concerned about foreign competition in the Michigan labor market than about the plight of Mexican Nationals not making the minimum wage rate; hence, no revision of the WYRF could have eliminated union concerns. Within three years after completion of the study, Public Law 78, under which Mexican Nationals were brought to the United States under supervision of both governments, was repealed largely because of labor union opposition. Further, the industry and Agricultural Experiment Station agricultural engineers went forward with the development of a mechanical pickle picker as recommended in the research project considered here. At the same time, the cucumber plant was rebred to produce its pickles more nearly at one time and on plants structured to facilitate mechanical picking.

The result of the legislated elimination of the Mexican National labor force, the unwillingness of domestic workers to pick pickles at wage rates that would not have priced pickles out of the market, the availability of a mechanical picker, and new varieties adapted to mechanical picking created a new set of problems for pickle growers and processors. And, the problem of how to pay Mexican Nationals largely became a matter of historical interest.

CONSUMERS POWER COMPANY'S APPLICATION FOR AN INTERIM RATE INCREASE

In July 1981, Consumers Power Company filed an application with the Michigan Public Service Commission for authority to increase its rates for the sale of electricity to yield additional annual revenue of over $339 million. There was also a motion for partial and immediate rate relief to increase revenues by over $178 million. This motion is considered here.

The Michigan Public Service Commission had before it the question of whether to approve rate increases by Consumers Power Company that would cost customers $180 million per year [Michigan Public Service Commission, 1982]. The *problem* the Commission faced was whether to grant the increase.

Clearly, the Commission was involved in problem-solving activity. It had to decide "what ought to be done" in order to solve the problem posed by the motion before it. Like most problem-solving activities, several disciplines, such as economics, law, political science, and engineering, were involved.

Was the Michigan Public Commission Engaged in Research in Solving the Problem It Had Before It?

Some disciplinary oriented researchers would argue that the Michigan Public Service Commission was not engaged in research in solving this problem. Some disciplinarians regard problem-solving activities as beyond the scope of science and research, this being particularly true if the disciplinarians are so positivistic that they regard any attention to values as unscientific. The answer to the question of whether the Commission was engaged in research should not depend on whether or not the Commission was engaged in problem-solving activity. Clearly, it was.

Instead, the question is whether the activity of the Commission can be classified as problem-solving research or whether it was engaged in another kind of problem-solving activity. The Commission was clearly responsible for generating prescriptive knowledge. It had to reach a conclusion about "what ought or ought not to be done" about the applicant's application for *partial and immediate rate relief*, hereafter referred to as *interim relief*. It is also clear from reading the order in which the Commission granted the interim relief that the Commission accumulated both positivistic knowledge and knowledge about values it used in reaching a conclusion about what ought to be done. Its problem-solving procedure resulted in the accumulation of positivistic knowledge and knowledge about values, both of which were used to generate prescriptive knowledge. If the general object of research is one of accumulating and organizing knowledge, clearly the activities of the Michigan Public Service Commission can be regarded as research.

However, the process by which the knowledge was accumulated in this case was considerably different from the process in the Michigan Pickle Study. A word about the nature of a hearing before the Michigan Public Service Commission is in order here. The hearings are open in the sense that any interested party is free to petition to intervene. In the course of this particular hearing, 12 agencies and individuals so petitioned. They included the Attorney General for the State of Michigan, various public interest groups, including the Public Interest Research Group in Michigan (PIRGIM), the Michigan Citizen's Lobby, the Michigan Agricultural Conference, and the Michigan Business Utility User's Committee. Private businesses involved included the Dow Chemical Company, the Clark Equipment Company, St. Regis Paper Company, and the Apartment Owner's of Michigan via their association. One individual petitioned. In the end, briefs were filed by the Commission staff, the Attorney General, the Association of Businesses Advocating Tariff Equity, Dow Chemical Company, the Michigan Business Utility User's Committee, the Clark Equipment Company, and an individual, Lyle C. Miller.

The Commission followed a procedure that can be described as "positivistic jurisprudence." The "standards for partial and immediate rate relief" are well specified in Michigan. While the Commission itself established those standards, the Commission now regards its task to be one of determining whether or not the standards for interim relief have been met. The Commission held open hearings to permit interested parties to put knowledge before it to establish whether the standards had been met. The Commission staff that investigated the matter was a separate party in the case. It is given great weight by the Commission but it is a party nonetheless. The staff is, in effect, a resarch branch of the Commission that generates and accumulates value-free and value knowledge to determine whether standards for interim relief have been met.

The briefs of the petitioners were adversarial and frankly biased, the possible exception being the brief prepared by the staff. Petitioners openly presented value-free and value knowledge positions in support of the decision they advocated while ignoring or suppressing contrary evidence. However, the objectivity of the total process was protected by its openness, which permitted petitioners opportunities to present other "sides." This opportunity was open to opponents and supporters of the rate increase. Also, the briefs and testimonies of petitioners were subject to "reply briefs," which can test the accuracy of the information in the original brief. Commission staffers are subject to cross examination. The overall process is a dialectic, adversarial one in which participants test each other's knowledge before a Commission responsible for deciding what ought to be done about final rate relief. The general procedure followed was pragmatic and, as such, involved dialectic adversarial activity in testing prescriptive theses and antitheses.

Lest the reader think that the Commission is an entirely objective group of three people, it should be pointed out that the Commission is political (Republican versus Democratic). A consumer advocate on the Commission represents the consumer point of view. The chairman of the Commission, on the other hand, appears to have been more sympathetic to the problems of the utility as a producer of electrical services. The third member of the Commission tended to support the chairman. Thus, the three-member Commission was split, with two viewing the position of the utility and the consumers somewhat objectively and one who concentrated more on the position of consumers. Eventually, the Commission produced a "commission order" supported by the chairman and his colleague on the Commission, with a dissent from the "consumer representative." The majority report granted interim relief. The minority report objected. A distribution of power was clearly part of the decision rule used by the Commission.

Administration

As for the other case studies in this book, this section deals with financing and accountability, conduct, review and evaluation and, finally, the durability and practicality of results.

The Michigan Public Service Commission is permanently financed by the State of Michigan to handle such legal and administrative problems for the government of Michigan. As these problems occur regularly, the Public Service Commission and its staff is a permanent part of the government of the State of Michigan. The Commission and the staff are financially accountable to auditors from the State of Michigan. They are only weakly accountable to the governor and, through the governor and the government of Michigan, to Michigan voters, including the customers of the applicant—the Consumers Power Company. The Commission's staff has considerable accounting, economic, and engineering expertise to use in evaluating rate proposals. In a sense, the Commission and the staff earn their financial support through their effectiveness in handling problems of the type under consideration here.

The Commission had to first establish that the proposal for an interim rate increase satisfied the Commission's interpretation of the statutory requirements for consideration as a motion for interim relief. After establishing that the proposal met these requirements, the Commission then had to establish whether according to law and the regular procedures of the Commission the applicant was entitled to interim rate relief. The Commission order indicates that the Commission believed it had an appropriate proposal for an interim rate increase and that the conditions for granting the increase had been established. A little reflection will show that the conduct of the hearings was along the lines followed in "positivistic jurisprudence" as well as dialectically pragmatic. The Commission order does not question the rightness or wrongness of either the law or the Commission's customary regulations and procedures. Instead, in accordance with procedures advocated by students of positivistic jurisprudence, the Commission's job was to establish whether it was factually true that the applicant was entitled to interim rate relief, given the law and its own customary regulations and procedures.

The dissent by the consumer representative on the Commission did not follow the procedures of positivistic jurisprudence nearly as closely as the majority report. While not questioning the law very much, the dissent questioned the customary regulations and procedures of the Commission. In particular, the minority report argued that the Commission had consistently closed its eyes to what the minority member regarded as poor management and unwise decisions by Consumers Power Company in connection with the construction of its now "cancelled" nuclear power plant in Midland. The cost of this plant almost quadrupled over many years of construction without ever going "on line." The dissenting member of the Commission was inclined to redefine the problem and tackle it in a more pragmatic manner than the majority. This would have made the proceedings more pragmatic and eclectic and its regulations and procedures less customary.

Because an *interim* rate decision was reached, the decision is part of a broader determination. Commission orders are subject to review and reevaluation either at subsequent meetings of the Commission or in the courts. Clearly, the author of the dissenting report was recording information and points of view for use in later reviews of this and related decisions by the Commission.

PHILOSOPHICAL AND METHODOLOGICAL CONCLUSIONS ABOUT PROBLEM-SOLVING RESEARCH

The two case studies summarized in this chapter are classified as problem-solving research studies though they are markedly different. Their common characteristic is that they sought prescriptive knowledge about right actions for public agencies. Both were concerned with the regulation of prices—wage rates in the pickle study and electrical rates in the Consumers Power Company study. Though there are differences between the studies concerning philosophical orientations, administration, conduct and methods employed, there are also similarities that I use along with knowledge of other problem-solving research efforts to reach the general conclusions presented here.

Both studies based the prescriptive knowledge they attained on knowlege of values as well as value-free positivistic knowledge. Both used decision rules in converting these two kinds of information into prescriptions. Both studies were multidisciplinary.

Philosophically, the studies were very different. The pickle study, while eclectic, employed positivistic and normative methods to generate value-free and value knowledge (especially about monetary values) for the pickle industry. However, the pickle study was not confined to positivistic and normative methods as iterative interaction took place between researchers and concerned people in the industry to develop pragmatically interdependent value-free knowledge and knowledge about values in a somewhat dialectical manner.

The Consumers Power case study was less eclectic. It proceeded in a dialectic manner, with public adversarial hearings at which people with opposing interests could frankly advocate their own prescriptions while trying to discredit the prescriptions of their opponents. Positivistic and normative methods were employed in preparing materials for the hearing, but in a minor way compared with the pickle study. The hearings before the Public Service Commission were conducted according to positivistic jurisprudence. Procedures for rate hearings were well established. Rate relief is to be granted if the specified preconditions for relief can be established according to majority vote of the three-member Commission—i.e., the prescription is determined by conclusions reached by majority vote as to whether prespecified conditions have been met.

By contrast, the pickle study did not have a set of prespecified decision rules that could be used along with factual information to determine what the wage rate for Mexican pickle-picking Nationals should be. Instead, the normative and positivistic aspects of what and how Mexican Nationals were paid were examined along with possible solutions in an iterative interactive manner until an acceptable consensus was reached between researchers and concerned people.

Financial accountability in the case of the pickle study was to the administration of Michigan State University and via that administration to funding agencies. There were two sources of funds: (1) the regular sources of support for the Michigan Agricultural Experiment Station from the federal and state governments, and (2) funds provided in a special agreement by the National Pickle Packers and National Pickle Growers Association. By contrast, the public service agency that conducted the hearings in the Consumers Power Company case is an on-going established commission supported directly by the State of Michigan to solve such problems. The cost of carrying out the investigation by the staff of the Commission was borne by the State of Michigan and by utility assessment, while the cost of preparing the presentations made by private groups and individuals was borne by those parties. The Attorney General's costs are borne from state and federal appropriations.

In addition to financial accountability, there is accountability for the accuracy of information and for the procedures and methods used in reaching prescriptions to solve the problems. The researchers on the pickle study were accountable to their Michigan State University administrators, to decision makers in the U.S. Department of State, to the industrial representatives who furnished financial support for the project, and to a lesser extent their colleagues in the discipline of economics and in the subject-matter Department of Agricultural Economics. There was also accountability to the pickle producers of Michigan and their elected representatives and to the clientele of the U.S. Department of Labor. In the case of the Consumers Power study, the Commission was accountable to the governor and through him to the Michigan electorate, and to the customers of the Consumers Power Company. Because the hearings were legalistic in nature, there was a special legal accountability involved in the Consumers Power Company case. While accountability to disciplinary peers was not close for either study, it was closer for the pickle study than for the Consumers Power study.

Both studies were multidisciplinary, and any peer accountability was spread throughout many different disciplines. In the Consumers Power study, there was probably more accountability to legal peers than to any single disciplinary peer group for the pickle study. Because this is a chapter on problem-solving case studies, the many interesting contrasts in accountability under problem-solving versus disciplinary and subject-matter studies are left for Chapters 13–17.

The conduct and administration of both studies was similar in that definite administrative procedures were involved. In both cases, information was generated and processed according to specific time schedules. The pickle study involved schedules for collecting, processing, and analyzing information. The Consumers Power case study involved schedules for preparing presentations, presenting cases before the Commission, and for action and reporting by the Public Service Commission. A major difference between the two studies was the administrative problems encountered at Michigan State University because of the multidisciplinary and multidepartmental nature of the pickle problem. The problem required personnel from more than one college and more than one subject-matter department in the College of Agriculture. The availability of "soft money" to the project administrators made it possible to obtain the necessary multidisciplinary expertise. For the Consumers Power study, parties making presentations before the Commission drew on or recruited the multidisciplinary expertise they judged to be advantageous.

Like most problem-solving studies, neither case produced information of *long-term durability*. The prescriptions reached in the pickle study were in effect for two to three years. The rate relief granted in the Consumers Power study was recognized to be "interim" pending a more permanent rate adjustment. Even the new rate prevailed only until a further rate adjustment was needed. One of the most durable consequence of cases such as the Consumers Power Company's rate case involves the precedents that are established as cases are settled over time. Both case studies were extremely practical, and participants had the satisfaction of knowing that what they did was of immediate *practical usefulness* even though they contributed little to the long-run development of academic disciplines and our store of subject-matter knowledge.

ADDITIONAL REFERENCES

Johnson, Glenn L. and L. K. Zerby. 1973. Some Problems of Michigan's Pickle Producing Industy, in *What Economists Do About Values*, East Lansing: Department of Agricultural Economics, Michigan State University, Ch. 6.

Stuckman, Noel W. 1959. Michigan Pickling Cucumbers: The Grower, the Picker and the WYRF, *Quarterly Bulletin*, East Lansing: Michigan Agricultural Experiment Station, Michigan State University, **42**(1):2–23

——— 1959. Some Economic Aspects of Increasing Pickling Cucumber Yields in Michigan, Unpublished M.S. Thesis, East Lansing: Department of Agricultural Economics, Michigan State University.

Michigan Public Service Commission. 1982. Case No. U-6923. Proceedings in the matter of the application of Consumers Power Company for authority to increase its rates for the sale of electricity, Lansing, Michigan, 13 May.

Part III

Implications of the Study of Philosophic Underpinnings and Methodologies and Case Studies

Chapter 13 deals with differences in maintaining research support and being accountable for resources used in disciplinary, subject-matter, and problem-solving research. Chapter 14 deals with differences in the administration and conduct of these kinds of research. Chapter 15 deals with the review and evaluation of research, with particular attention to differences between the three classes of research vis-à-vis proposals, results, and relevant peers. Chapter 16 deals with the implications of the durability and practical impact of the research. Chapter 17 deals (1) with the implications of the three kinds of research for support and accountability, conduct and administration, review and evaluation, and durability and practicality; (2) with the implications of studying philosophical underpinnings, research methodology, and the case studies for teaching research methodology and one's individual philosophy toward economic research; and (3) with a number of research and methodological issues not covered in Chapters 1–16.

Chapter 13

Research Support
and Accountability
For Economic Research

This chapter considers the implications of Part I (on undergirding philosophies and methods) and Part II (on case studies) for the mobilization of research support and demands for accountability for research resources used. It is a practical chapter for research administrators, researchers, and their supporters in state legislatures, the U.S. Congress, contracting and granting agencies of the U.S. government, international agencies, and the foundations that support economic research. The chapter also has practical importance for administrators of agencies making research grants and contracts. There are important general differences in the preparation of project proposals, the funding of such proposals, the writing of grants and research contracts and the rendering of final accounts and preparation of final reports on research projects for the three broad kinds of research—disciplinary, subject-matter and problem-solving—considered in Chapter 2 and illustrated in the case study chapters of Part II.

MOBILIZATION OF RESEARCH SUPPORT IN GENERAL

First, a few generalizations about mobilization of research and support. Economists need support for their research—whether it is research done in their spare time on a disciplinary topic of interest or it is subject-matter and problem-solving research running into millions of dollars involving many years of work from many disciplines. Some kinds of economic research have become "big business." Research contractors now actively seek government contracts ranging into the millions of dollars. Many economists have found it advantageous to abandon prestigious academic and governmental positions to join firms doing economic research on a "for profit basis." Others remain in academic or research institutes where research is on a "not for profit basis." Even not for profit research, however, seems to involve substantial amounts of what would be regarded by an economic theoretician as profit. Overhead charges, for instance, often run in the neighborhood of 65–70% of research contracts with universities.

Expensive economic resarch is also done by economists as "in house" employees of national, state, or provincial governments. Departments and ministries in such governments often have major research branches with large numbers of economic researchers regularly doing research relevant to their activities. In the land grant universities, many agricultural economists are employed in agricultural experimental stations on research with substantial budgets.

Individual researchers interested in a particular project often find themselves devoting much of their time to mobilizing support for their proposals and accounting for the support they have received. Administrators and project leaders may devote full time to acquiring, administering, and accounting for research funds.

DEMANDS FOR ACCOUNTABILITY IN GENERAL

There is *direct* accountability for money, time, and the services of key individuals committed in grant and contract proposals. There is also direct accountability for accomplishing objectives and producing specific results by specific dates. Results are often required at certain stages in a project before further funds will become available or even considered.

There is also *indirect* accountability for resources used. Taxpayers, philanthropists, and legislators have objectives that must be met if granting and contracting agencies are to maintain the flow of research money. Administrators of funding agencies may be able to avoid such demands for indirect accountability for a while even if their grantees and contractees are not accomplishing the objectives of those who supply their funds. But eventually supporters know whether or not their objectives are being met and they adjust their support accordingly.

Two factors now motivate funding agencies to increase their demands for accountability. First, research budgets in the 1970s and 1980s are major expense items of funding agencies. Second, the demands placed on public and philanthropic funds for nonresearch activities are continuously increasing. So research funds must be well spent and evidence of productivity must be forthcoming.

DISCIPLINARY RESEARCH (OF KNOWN AND UNKNOWN RELEVANCE)

Disciplinary research was defined in Chapter 2 as research on the questions of a discipline. As illustrated by the Leontief and Schultz case studies in Chapter 10, disciplinary economic research deals with questions about economic theory, quantitative techniques, and the basic measurement of phenomena of concern to economists. Sometimes, disciplinary economic research is done to provide a theoretical component, a quantitative technique, or a basic measurement needed to solve a practical problem. This is disciplinary research of known relevance. Though sometimes a missing piece of knowledge is all that is needed to solve a particular practical problem, solving most problems also requires knowledge from disciplines other than economics. More likely, a particular piece of disciplinary knowledge is but one input in the problem-solving process. Though disciplinary research of known relevance is also often labeled applied, it is specialized on economics and is regarded here as disciplinary not problem-solving or subject-matter research.

Support for Disciplinary Research

Disciplinary knowledge and the research required to produce it are often sub-dividable. This facilitates specialization among economic researchers. Therefore, support for disciplinary research projects may be small in terms of both money and personnel. A professor may moonlight a piece of disciplinary research for years, working on it when time is available. Similarly, a research professor and one or two graduate students can work on a piece of disciplinary research with a relatively small budget but with a tighter time constraint because of the need of the students to complete their dissertations and find jobs. Graduate students and professors commonly meet the students' time constraint by specializing on a small enough subject to get the degree completed on schedule. Some disciplinary research projects, however, are major and may require a lifetime's financing for a competent economist and associated colleagues and graduate students. This is well illustrated by the case studies for Wassily Leontief and T. W. Schultz. Such support sometimes goes with the endowment of chairs in major universities and the granting of tenure to professors or researchers.

It is difficult to mobilize support for disciplinary research of *unknown relevance*. The major funding agencies have difficulty financing programs for research on basic disciplinary questions in economics unless the relevance of those questions for practical decision-making can be established. Realistically, the major source of support for disciplinary research of unknown relevance is a tenured appointment in a university or institute. Earning support to do disciplinary work of unknown relevance in economics is ordinarily a long, arduous, time-consuming task which leads, eventually, to an appointment to such a well-financed, tenured disciplinary position.

Many tenured professors and institute employees, however, elect not to use their positions to support disciplinary research of unknown relevance, preferring instead to devote their efforts either to disciplinary research of *known relevance* and of direct applicability or to subject-matter and problem-solving research. Many work in a gray never-never land on research of fundamental signifcance to economics but no less relevant to the solution of specific problems or sets of problems. Relatively well-endowed professors at a university with small industrial and agrarian departments may find it advantageous to specialize on disciplinary research of known direct or indirect relevance rather than getting involved in multidisciplinary problem-solving and subject-matter research that would require contributions from disciplinarians and practical subject-matter specialists unavailable at their university.

For example, the small group of agricultural economists at the University of Chicago has tended to concentrate its efforts on disciplinary work of known relevance for agriculture. Such work has not required the ready availability of personnel from such multidisciplinary subject-matter departments as animal husbandry, soils and crops, and horticulture commonly available in the major land grant universities where the typical agricultural economist works.

This strategy has paid off extremely well at Chicago, where much disciplinary research relevant for agriclture has been done on such subjects as the economics of agricultural research (induced technological change), the economics of agricultural education and extension (induced human change or human capital formation), and the modification of agricultural institutions, programs, and policies (induced institutional change). As indicated in the Schultz case study of Chapter 10, such research at the University of Chicago has attracted substantial research funding from Rockefeller Foundation and the National Institutes of Health. On the other hand, agricultural economists at Chicago have not drawn heavy financial support from such funding agencies as the Agency for International Development, the Department of Energy, and the Department of Agriculture when those agencies want research done on specific multidepartmental and multidisciplinary problems and subjects requiring direct cooperation with technical agricultural scientists—as in the pickle case study of Chapter 12.

Accountability for Disciplinary Research

Disciplinary researchers are always professionally accountable to their disciplinary peers, who are generally their most important evaluators (see Chapter 15). As illustrated in Chapter 10, disciplinary peers are highly qualified for evaluating disciplinary research. For this reason, administrators often rely on disciplinary peers to hold disciplinarians accountable for their time and resources. When research is of known relevance and is financed by some agency aware of its relevance, the users of the research are also relevant peers whose evaluations are important in accounting for resources used. Even in such instances, though, the highly specialized nature of relevant disciplinary economics research may make disciplinary peers from economics better able than practitioners to judge how well resources have been used. When disciplinary research is financed out of our own time, we are only accountable to ourselves for the resources used.

It is difficult to make disciplinary advances in economics because economists have been working at it for several centuries. Truly new disciplinary questions in economics are difficult to pose, and the attainability of results is difficult to predict. Thus, both the financing agencies and the recipients have to be careful about contracts that guarantee output.

SUBJECT-MATTER RESEARCH

In Chapter 2, subject-matter research was defined as research on a multidisciplinary subject important in solving a *set* of problems faced by a *set* of decision makers. Both research support and accountability can be accomplished more effectively when the two sets are well defined. Subject-matter research is multidisciplinary in nature. If it is not, it should be classified as relevant disciplinary research (which was considered in the last section).

By definition, subject-matter research is relevant for solving practical problems. It may seek value-free positivistic knowledge or knowledge about values, though it can be specialized on either and involve both. As illustrated by the two case studies in Chapter 11, subject-matter research does not generate prescriptions to solve particular problems. Instead, it produces knowledge about a subject relevant to the set of problems faced by the set of decision makers, the subject itself being multidisciplinary in nature. Mobilizing support for such research generally involves the development of research proposals capable of attracting efforts from members of other disciplines as well as of producing support from funding agencies and administrators interested in contributing to the solution of the set of problems for the set of involved decision makers.

Support for Subject-Matter Research

Examples of subject-matter research on which economists work and for which support is provided include food and nutrition, technical change, institutional change, energy, development, the exhaustion of nonrenewable resources, labor and industrial relations, poverty, agricultural economics, marketing, business administration, regional economics, and environmental quality. Each is important for solving significant sets of problems for substantial sets of decision makers. The relevant sets of problems are those that require each of these kinds of information for their solution. The subjects mentioned are important and societies make substantial amounts of money available to research them.

Obtaining this support first involves establishing a reputation for being able to do multidisciplinary research and deliver results. Once this reputation is established, obtaining support entails the active selling of projects. Competition is keen and not always purely academic—vested interests and politics play a part. For instance, public universities and institutes sometimes exploit their position as parts of governments to obtain public funds, while private universities sometimes compete with great emphasis on public relations, "old boy" systems in philanthropic organizations, and institutional representations in Washington. As research is big business, there is a politics of research, some of which lacks objectivity. Feyerabend [1978] stresses the use of "subterfuge, rhetoric, and propaganda" by scientists in obtaining support for research by "huckstering" their capabilities and results.

Preparing subject-matter project proposals involves ascertaining where and how the necessary multidisciplinary expertise can be obtained, developing appropriate procedures for administering the projects, then carefully budgeting the money, time, and personnel to produce results.

Disciplinary chauvinism is incompatible with subject-matter research. As agencies that fund subject-matter research have practical objectives, project proposals are best designed to attain those objectives instead of promoting the disciplinary interests and careers of the proposer. Thus, it is necessary to be eclectic philosophically and academically in obtaining support for subject-matter research. Tolerance of philosophic orientations permitting normative as well as positivistic research and pragmatic as well as nonpragmatic research is often an important asset so that consideration can be given to knowledge of values as well as to the value-free positivistic knowledge required to address the relevant issues and sets of problems. Positivistically oriented researchers are often unable to conceive of doing the objective research on values required to address such issues. Further, conditionally normative researchers may leave answers to value questions up to arbitrary assumption rather than recognizing that they may be legitimate subjects for empirical research and even unavoidably dependent in a pragmatic manner on the results of positivistic research.

Accountability for Subject-Matter Research

Generally, accountability requirements are more stringent for subject-matter than for disciplinary research. Administrators of the agencies funding such research often have sets of practical problems in mind and desire improvement in rather well-defined bodies of knowledge to help solve those problems. Further, the multidisciplinary nature of those problems and their practical significance often result in large commitments of funds and resources to producing the essential knowledge. Such large commitments engender demands for careful accountability from the granting agencies. This is clearly discernible for the Karl Fox and WFNS case studies of subject-matter research in Chapter 11.

The demands for accountability start with project preparation and design. Major grants and contracts are not awarded to sloppy project proposals and designs, the main exceptions arising when prior favorable experience has created faith in the proposer and his agency. A proposal is more likely to be accepted if it indicates an awareness of the knowledge needed, demands for accountability, and the ability to meet deadlines. Disciplinarians often find the demand for accountability in subject-matter research distasteful, feeling that they know more about what is needed than the granting agency. While this may be true of disciplinary research in the proposer's discipline, it is less likely to be true for subject-matter research. It should not be forgotten that the granting agency wants results. It pays the bills and can legitimately insist that the conflicting, often chauvinistic, interests of the different disciplines be reconciled to its requirements. Disciplinarians have notoriously poor judgment about the practical importance of the knowledge they produce. They often oversell their discipline in practical situations, while unwisely denigrating the contributions needed from other disciplines. Proposals of this kind are properly rejected.

Progress reports and final reports are part of accountability. One breach of contract procedure or demand to refund grants quickly teaches research administrators and project leaders to keep project commitments in mind and to see that they are fulfilled completely and on time. Such legal actions destroy the reputations of grantees and contractees and make it difficult for them to obtain support for new proposals. Research administrators and project leaders soon learn to minimize the chances of such actions occurring.

There is also an *indirect* form of accountability required of research administrators and project leaders. Administrators of funding agencies get their funds from legislators, foundations, and private companies. Funding agency administrators are generally required to deliver documentation to legislators and governing boards concerning the effectiveness of the research grants and contracts they make. Thus, research administrators and project leaders often receive requests from funding agencies to document their past accomplishments with earlier grants and contracts. The preparation of such documents for successful projects not only furthers the capacity of funding agencies to finance research but enhances the reputations of individual research administrators, project leaders, and their universities and research institutes. Even for unsuccessful projects, complete honest documentation often preserves reputations and the ability to finance, as neither scientists nor knowledgeable research administrators expect success from every project.

may be concerned about too much attention to "crass mundane" value-free facts. Disciplinarians are likely to ignore other essential disciplinary dimensions of the problem the research is supposed to solve.

CONFUSIONS ABOUT KINDS OF RESEARCH DETRACTS FROM RESEARCH SUPPORT AND CONFOUNDS ACCOUNTABILITY

Researchers, research administrators, and even funding agencies often confuse the three kinds of research considered in this book. Disciplinarians working on a question in their discipline often refer to the question as a problem. In a sense they are correct, because answering the question is a problem for disciplinarians. However, answering such a question in a discipline is far different from solving a practical problem for a decision maker in government or industry—and the two should not be confused.

A related difficulty arises when disciplinarians and others overstate the practical importance of answering disciplinary questions in their desire to obtain research support for their pet disciplinary puzzles. This does not imply that disciplinary research is unimportant, rather that people who claim practical significance for disciplinary research of unknown relevance or of only indirect relevance are likely to detract from long-term financing of disciplinary as well as subject-matter and problem-solving research. Funding agencies will be disappointed by the results of disciplinary research falsely presented as problem-solving or subject-matter research and become distrustful of disciplinarians and even of research in general.

An econometrician interested in a new method for estimating a parameter is well advised to seek support for doing precisely that rather than implying that the proposed disciplinary research will be of great practical significance to decision makers interested in short-term solutions to practical problems. This is particularly true when the econometrician knows that the practical significance of the new methods will only become evident over the long run.

It is easy to confuse subject-matter research with problem-solving research. For example, those seeking financial support for subject-matter research on food or energy often refer to *the* food problem or *the* energy problem. The use of the definite article is generally misleading and inappropriate as there are literally millions of problems faced by millions of decision makers involving food and energy. There is not *one* energy or *one* food problem. When people want research done or want to do research on food and energy, they are generally considering subject-matter research, not problem-solving research. What they really propose is mobilization of a multidisciplinary body of information about food or energy they believe a group of decision makers will find useful in solving a set of problems about food and energy.

It detracts from support for both subject-matter and problem-solving research in the long run and confounds accountability when researchers unconsciously or deliberately confuse subject-matter with problem-solving research. While it is true that subject-matter research has practical significance, it is also typically true, for example, that a subject-matter project on energy will not solve any one problem involving energy faced by any one decision maker. If we imply that we are going to produce a body of information about energy that *will actually solve* specific problems for specific decision makers when in fact we propose to do subject-matter research that *will only help solve* problems, we will produce false expectations in the decision makers and funders.

DIFFICULTIES IN REALLOCATING SUPPORT FROM PROBLEM-SOLVING AND SUBJECT-MATTER RESEARCH TO DISCIPLINARY RESEARCH

Disciplinarians often believe that their research is basic and more important, especially in the long run, than subject-matter and problem-solving research. Further, disciplinary research is more appealing to disciplinarians as it produces more approval from their peers and their discipline-oriented academic administrators. Consequently, one often sees pressure exerted by disciplinarians to reallocate research resources from problem-solving and subject-matter research to disciplinary research. As we saw in the WFNS case study of Chapter 11, there has been considerable pressure to reallocate resources from problem-solving and subject-matter research efforts of the USDA/Agricultural Experiment Station system to fundamental disciplinary research. This pressure has come particularly from the biological and physical sciences, but also from economics, sociology, political science, and anthropology [Johnson, 1984].

The difficulty with such reallocative efforts is that subject-matter and problem-solving research funds are made available because of the concerns of decision makers and funders over particular problems. When disciplinarians get control of money furnished by decision makers with problems or originating in broad political support based on the conviction that problem-solving or subject-matter research can help solve a problem, they often use it to produce disciplinary research results of little known relevance. Further, as we have noted, disciplinary research results are relatively unpredictable and hard to attain. Consequently, even relevant disciplinary research does not look very productive to the funders and to those providing broad-based political support for subject-matter and problem-solving research.

Disciplinary research of unknown relevance looks even less productive and is likely to receive a "Golden Fleece Award" from Senator Proxmire if financed with Federal funds intended for problem-solving or subject-matter research. Diversion of money actually appropriated for problem-solving and subject-matter research to disciplinary research of unknown relevance looks like (and often is) misappropriation of funds.

When the immediate objectives of those providing financial aid and political support for problem-solving research are not met, the result is likely to be withdrawal of financial political support and an attempt by those providing the support to find a different way of getting the research done. Basically, problem-solving and subject-matter research funds are not easily reallocatable to disciplinary research. Disciplinarians would do well to make their case for disciplinary research as an addition to the case for problem-solving and subject-matter research rather than as a replacement. Attempts to reallocate funds from problem-solving and subject-matter to disciplinary research are almost sure to erode the total research base. It is much more effective in the long run (and more honest) to encourage problem-solving and subject-matter research while making a separate "true case" for disciplinary research than it is to try to reallocate problem-solving and subject-matter research support to disciplinary research.

Economists who want to do disciplinary research, for example, on the effect of technological change on employment in abstract two-sector models are better off to ask directly for support for such research than they are to try to co-opt research resources originally supplied to make recommendations to develop a particular sector of the economy of an underdeveloped country. Similarly, cell microbiologists are better advised to make the case directly for research on photorespiration than they are to try to divert money obtained with the political support of wheat growers needing new rust-resistant varieties of wheat. When problem-solving plant breeders produce the needed varieties of wheat, the productivity of research in general is demonstrated. Wheat growers can see the long-run connection between fundamental disciplinary research in cell microbiology on the one hand and the solution of practical problems on the other hand, and therefore support funds for both problem-solving and disciplinary research. Disappointing wheat growers expecting the development of a replacement rust-resistant variety destroys their support for problem-solving research and may create opposition to disciplinary research.

IMPROVING POLICY FOR SUPPORT
OF ECONOMIC RESEARCH

A correct or optimal policy for economic research should provide support for the optimum amounts of research in each of the three areas considered in this book. To determine the optimum amounts to provide, it is necessary to know about costs and returns to each kind of research and their interrelationships. Costs and returns are more predictable for subject-matter and problem-solving research than for disciplinary research. Each kind of research can be shown to be supportive of the other two.

Returns for research occur in the form of both monetary and nonmonetary values. To know and measure returns is to have knowledge of values. Similarly, costs are incurred in both monetary and nonmonetary terms; hence, to know costs is to have knowledge of values. Allocating funds between the three types of research to maximize the difference between costs and returns is to become involved in decision making—in a form of science ethics or economics concerned with prescribing what ought to be done.

Economists can be expected to know a great deal about primary costs and the nature of expected results from economic research. Improving economic research policy requires great attention to the direct, secondary, and more remote monetary and nonmonetary costs and returns to economic research. There seems to be no alternative but to become eclectic in setting economic research policy. Policy makers need to be normative as well as positivistic because they are making decisions and therefore are deeply involved in the ethics or economics of setting economic research policy. Objectivity is required with respect to their positivistic and value knowledge and, especially, their prescriptive conclusions.

ADDITIONAL REFERENCES

Agricultural Network Fights Unwelcome Gift. 1979. *Science,* **205:**1108–1109.

Accountability: Restoring the Quality of the Partnership. 1980. Washington, DC: National Commission on Research, March.

Carey, W. D. 1979. Concerning the Technology Base, *Science,* 203(4379)

Denny, B. C. 1978. Renegotiating the Society-Academy Contract, *Science,* 201(4357).

Eliot, Marshall. 1979. White House Seeks to Reform USDA Research, *Science,* **206:**307.

Funding Mechanisms: Balancing Objectives and Resources in University Research. 1980. Washington, DC: National Commission on Research.

Fusfeld, H. I. 1980. The Bridge Between University and Industry, *Science,* **209**(4453).

Johnson, Glenn L. 1984. Academia Needs a New Covenant for Serving Agriculture, Mississippi State, MS: Mississippi Agricultural & Forestry Experiment Station, Mississippi State University, Special Publication, July.

Morgan, M. G. 1978. Bad Science and Good Policy Analysis, *Science,* 201(4360).

Prager, D. J. and G. S. Omenn. 1980. Research, Innovation, and University-Industry Linkages, *Science,* **207:**379–384.

Schmandt, J. 1978. Scientific Research and Policy Analysis, *Science,* **201**(4359).

Schultz, T. W. 1977. What Are We Doing to Research Entrepreneurship? No. 77-11, presented at seminar sponsored jointly by the American Academy of Arts and Sciences and the University of Minnesota on *Transforming Knowledge into Food in a World-Wide Context,* April 21–22, Minneapolis, MN.

Testimony by Dr. Frank Press, Director, Office of Science and Technology Policy before
the Subcommittee on Science, Technology and Space Committee on Commerce,
Science and Transportation, U.S. Senate, March 21, 1979.
The Academy of Sciences, 1980. *Herald-Tribune*, June 18.

Chapter 14

Administration and Conduct of Economic Research

Effective administration and conduct of economic research is necessary because of the enormous resources devoted to such research annually. Though a relatively small proportion of the total research budget of the United States is devoted to economic research, the absolute amount is large. Further, as much of the research done by economists is done as members of multidisciplinary teams, the total budget involving economists is still larger, while the administrative problems involved in coordinating the research are magnified.

The importance of good administration and effective conduct of economic research is seen to be even greater when attention is paid to the nonmonetary costs and benefits of research done by economists and to the committed economists who dedicate their lives to research in the conviction that they have a unique opportunity to serve the human race. Not all costs can be monetized, as the clients of experimental economic and social programs well know. On the returns side, many benefits are received that escape the dollar as a unit for measuring value. We need only mention the value of the research behind the decision to make more public recreation facilities available to Michigan citizens than are provided in most states to see the importance of nonmonetary values.

Further, the lives and careers of economic researchers have values that escape the dollar as a measuring stick. Some economists place a high value on being directly useful and on participating in problem-solving research. Other economists value disciplinary contributions more highly and believe such results to have great long-run usefulness. Both groups of researchers often sacrifice monetary returns for opportunities to do the kinds of research to which they attach high nonmonetary value. Between these two are the subject-matter researchers who partake of both worlds. All three groups mentioned need and are entitled to good administration and administrators capable of knowing and understanding the different motivations and each kind of research.

Though individual economic researchers have a great stake in adequate administration of research, they often denigrate administration and verbally abuse research administrators. Though such behavior is sometimes justified by the inadequacies of research administration, even greater inefficiency in research administration follows when individual researchers reject administration and exercise institutional power to reject administrative efforts. Administration is particularly important for conducting problem-solving and subject-matter research. Some of the inappropriate attitudes of researchers toward research administration grows out of failure to see how the amount and kind of administration needed varies among the three kinds of research considered here.

DISCIPLINARY RESEARCH

Of the three kinds of research, disciplinary research requires the least administration. Because disciplinary research is confined to one discipline and is typically under a single administrator in a university or research institute, it is seldom necessary to set up an administrative superstructure capable of crossing departmental and disciplinary lines. This reduces the need for administrators with enough power to bring departmental administrators and their personnel into special structures for administering and conducting multidisciplinary research as in the pickle case study of Chapter 12.

Some administrative difficulties arise even when administrators attempt to get disciplinarians to do disciplinary research of known relevance—when it becomes clear that a practical problem cannot be solved without an improvement in the discipline of economics. Both disciplinary case studies in Chapter 10 were of known relevance. An example of needed disciplinary research is the acquisition of interpersonally valid welfare measurements for solving problems of the redistribution of the ownership of rights and privileges among people.

Disciplinary researchers may sometimes resent attempts to guide their research into areas of known relevance by their direct administrators and those in the agencies that finance their work. Fundamentally, many disciplinary researchers would like to have a grant of money or a research contract to do what they find interesting and likely to further their careers, hence the conflict with their funding agencies and research administrators.

Administrators of many universities and research institutes often proceed in the faith that disciplinary research of unknown relevance will be relevant later on. These bodies are maintained by the public in the faith that this is true. Some are also maintained in the faith that disciplinary research is worthwhile if for no other reason than to improve a discipline and that the test of practical relevance is, itself, irrelevant.

Well-developed disciplines provide a "discipline" for their members that is itself a form of administration. The two disciplinary case studies of Chapter 10 indicated that this greatly reduces the need for "live" administration of disciplinary economic research. The theoretical structure of a discipline reveals its inadequacies to its own practitioners. Discipline-wide awareness of these inadequacies guides disciplinary researchers; similarly, they are guided by their knowledge of the inadequacies of ancillary disciplines such as mathematics and statistics.

Disciplinary economists are often highly motivated to remedy these inadequacies. Much disciplinary research is published in journals, where it is subjected to peer review. This ensures that respected members of the discipline get an opportunity to review and, in effect, administer disciplinary research. Thus, peer review and "peer administration" ensure that even disciplinary research of unknown relevance will meet the needs of a discipline for data, techniques, and improved theories.

Peer review and administration also play an important role in disciplinary research of known relevance. There are, however, good reasons to expand the peer group for administering disciplinary research of known relevance to include those who will use the research results to solve practical problems. The Leontief case study indicates how review by both disciplinarians and users improves the administration of disciplinary research of known relevance.

It is simpler to administer disciplinary research than problem-solving and subject-matter research because it is more easily subdivided into topics for investigation by individual researchers or by small groups. Again, the disciplinary case studies of Chapter 10 illustrate that this ability to subdivide combines with the administrative effectiveness of the discipline itself to make it easy to provide effective administration of disciplinary research. Universities and research institutes structured along traditional disciplinary lines can handle disciplinary research well, particularly that of unknown relevance.

Another consideration that simplifies administration of disciplinary research is the tendency for there to be less difficulty with conflicting philosophic orientations. Universities and institutes doing disciplinary research are generally structured so that individual researchers report to department heads and intermediate level administrators who understand the philosophic positions and implied methods of those disciplines under their administrative control.

However, economic research probably suffers more from philosophic dif-

ferences than research in the hard sciences and humanities. This is because of
the concern of economics with decision making in both public and private
spheres. A concern with decision making implies an interest in both value-free
and value knowledge and in using them to produce prescriptive knowledge (see
Figure 2, Chapter 2). The peculiar difficulty for economists is that some of
them have become highly specialized or committed to positivistic philosophies
whereas others are committed to normative and pragmatic philosophies. This
results in disagreement as to legitimate methods of inquiry. Other decision
disciplines such as engineering, architecture, medicine, dentistry, and law share
this difficulty with economics.

On the other hand, chemistry, botany, geology, astronomy, physics, etc.
have not suffered from disagreement to the same extent as economics and the
decision disciplines. In psychology, positivism has become so dominant that
conflicts between normativistic and positivistic psychologists are probably less
important than in economics. The normativists among psychologists apparently
tend to become clinicians rather than researchers. In philosophy, students concerned with ethics (and, hence, decision making) seem to suffer less from this
bifurcation than economists perhaps because philosophy has to contend with
its own differing points of view.

SUBJECT-MATTER RESEARCH

By definition, subject matter research is multidisciplinary. When the emerging
issues and changing problems of society bring a new subject to the forefront
and to the attention of research administrators, there is a need for researchers
from different relevant disciplines to work together. Each new subject presents
an opportunity to serve society and each such opportunity creates the administrative difficulties involved in restructuring the administration of research.
This was nicely illustrated in the World Food and Nutrition Study examined
in Chapter 11.

A new subject typically requires that research specialists from different
disciplines start working together in an often unfamiliar configuration. Some
disciplinarians who value individual freedom do not like to submit to the administrative control necessary to bring many disciplinary specialists together
to concentrate on a subject important at a particular time. The responsibility
for exercising this control over disciplinary specialists lies with administrators
of universities and research institutes organized along disciplinary and
multidisciplinary, subject-matter department lines. In many of the older universities and institutes, tenured personnel and recurrent expenditures take up almost
all of the budget, leaving little administrative control over operating budgets
to steer research into currently important subject-matter areas. Further, even
when administrators have such control, there is the danger of demotivating

highly productive disciplinary and subject-matter researchers and disorganizing their programs. Some administrators refer to tenured personnel as people without steering wheels, brakes, or accelerators as far as administrative control is concerned.

"For profit" research firms often do better administratively in researching new subject-matter areas than universities and well-established research institutes. Their personnel realize that their livelihood depends upon the firm's ability to earn income from clients, therefore, they may be more flexible. Also, the administrators of "for profit" research firms are often more successful than their university counterparts in avoiding tenure commitments to disciplinarians and those specializing in old multidisciplinary subjects. Research firms can pay high fees for short-term, nontenured disciplinarians on leave from tenured positions. These short-termers are hired on the specific condition that they work on a particular subject-matter team.

Concerning subject-matter research, the "discipline of disciplines" may be more of an adminstrative impediment that an asset. Disciplinary interest in the theories, quantitative techniques, and basic facts of economics interfere with one's ability "to join" a subject-matter research team. This is particularly true when the subject under consideration requires a disciplinary advance not regarded as interesting and important by one's peers in economics however important it may be for researching the subject under consideration. Then, too, economists like other disciplinarians, may suffer from forms of disciplinary chauvinism that overemphasize the importance of economics [Johnson, 1984]. Such chauvinism sometimes causes economists on a subject-matter research team to press hard for tangential research in economics at the expense of balance for other disciplines important for the subject at hand.

A particularly obvious example of undue disciplinary dominance was seen in the case study of the WFNS (Chapter 11). The positivism and egocentrism of the biological and physical scientists caused them to overstate the importance of advances in biological and physical knowledge and fail to recommend adequate budgets for research (1) to improve the poor policies that keep new biophysical technologies from being used, and (2) to adjust the distribution of the ownership of the means of producing income that condemns so many people to starvation and malnutrition despite improvements in technology or agricultural policies.

There are also examples when the chauvinism of disciplinary economists has had equally adverse effects—for example, the research on central economic planning which, for many years, neglected the importance of technological advances, particularly in agriculture. The point is that *overemphasis* on any discipline is an impediment to subject-matter research.

Typically, administrative structures in research organizations are not large despite the complaints to the contrary by disciplinary researchers. The demands of subject-matter (and problem-solving) research for administration are large relative to the size and capacity of most administrative structures. This makes it difficult for research administrators to keep up-to-date on subject-matter research. Often, subject-matter and problem-solving researchers in an organization will be better informed than their administrators as to the important problems and subject-matter areas that need researching. In such instances, the need is to get this knowledge from the researcher to the administrator or to give administrative responsibility to the researcher.

Philosophic biases are also important in the administration of subject-matter research [Johnson, 1984]. For example, a positivistic administrator trained in the biological and physical sciences may believe all knowledge of values to be arbitrary and unscientific. Even when such an administrator leans over backward to allow concerns over values to influence his decisions, the fact that he feels the need to lean is evidence of the constraints of positivism. When the subject matter involves real values, it is difficult for positivistic administrators to administer objective research on a relevant value as they are likely to be suspicious of the objectivity of any research on values. Even when the administrator is an economist who should be expected to be able to work with nonmonetary as well as monetary values, positivistic biases may be encountered because, as previously noted, there are committed positivists among economists.

A particular difficulty for economists who are administrators has been created by the many mistakes made in the past by quantitatively oriented economists. It has been common for quantitatively oriented disciplinary economists to oversell and misuse econometric models, linear programming models, input/output models, and models based on other special techniques and, hence, to produce inappropriate subject-matter data for decision makers. Administrative economists and other administrators who have been burned by such unduly specialized research in the past tend to have antiquantitative biases.

Similar antiquantitative biases by pragmatic economists in research administration may also be damaging to administration of subject-matter research. While pragmatic administrators may be sympathetic to researching value questions (albeit interdependently with value-free ones), antiquantitative biases may deprive them of results obtainable with quantitative methods, particularly those obtainable through systems science simulation analyses which, as we saw in Chapter 9, are often pragmatic, holistic, multidisciplinary, and unspecialized.

Evaluation of research designs, project proposals, work plans, and results is an important part of research administration. Although evaluation will be covered in more detail in the next chapter, it is important to note that peers from many different disciplines are appropriate *partial* evaluators of subject-matter research. It must also be recognized that subject-matter research is done to provide a kind of information to *sets of decision makers* facing *sets of problems*. This means that the decision makers and those affected by their decisions are also relevant peers. Disciplinary peers are likely to look askance at research results that serve the need of problem solvers better than they serve to remedy the deficiencies of economics as a discipline.

What is needed is to have subject-matter research proposals, work plans, and results evaluated by an appropriate combination of disciplinary peers, decision makers, and affected people. This requires an administrator able to work with disciplinary peers from the positivistic sciences, the humanities, and the decision disciplines, while drawing on evaluations from the appropriate decision makers and affected people. Advisory groups are often used to obtain this kind of evaluation.

PROBLEM-SOLVING RESEARCH

Multidisciplinarity is even more essential for problem-solving research than for subject-matter research because a specific problem of a specific decision maker involves a multidisciplinary mix unique to that problem. The unique mixes involved in doing problem-solving research are more specific than for subject-matter research, which involves sets of problems for sets of decision makers. Also, subject-matter research can be defined and redefined to exclude or include different disciplines. By contrast, problem-solving research *must* deal with the different disciplinary dimensions of the specific problem under consideration. This was nicely illustrated in the pickle case study examined in Chapter 12.

When Ernest Nesius was director of the Cooperative Agricultural Extension Service at the University of Kentucky, he observed that his administrative problem was that the farm people of Kentucky had problems whereas the University of Kentucky had departments. Nesius recognized the need to cross disciplinary and subject-matter departmental and college lines in doing problem-solving extension and, by implication, problem-solving research.

Another difficulty that complicates the administration of problem-solving research is that such research always involves decision making and prescriptive as well as value-free and value dimensions. The positivistic research methods advocated by Lionel Robbins in his "The Nature and Significance of Economic Science" are simply not adequate for problem-solving research. If problem-solving research is to be complete, it must produce knowledge of values as well as value-free knowledge. And if it is to be objective it must deal with values in an objective manner. In many instances, value propositions are needed about values that conditions, situations, and things really have rather than just about who attaches what value to what.

Administrators of problem-solving research often need to command resources from the positivistic physical and biological sciences, from the normativistic humanities, and from the decision-making disciplines. The proportions in which different disciplinary resources are needed are dictated by the domain of the *unique* problem under consideration. Few universities and few research institutes have the administrative structures required for adequate mobilization and administration of multidisciplinary, problem-solving research teams. Even administrators of institutes and other research organizations doing problem-solving research are tempted to let organizations set up to solve an ephemeral problem become permanent even after the problem is solved.

The March of Dimes organization, with its original emphasis on poliomyelitis research, is a case in point. Once poliomyelitis was brought under control, that organization either had to go out of business or change its structure to one able to mobilize resources to research birth defects. It took the latter course.

In many ways, "for profit" research firms do better than universities and institutes in regrouping after successful research. Again, this is because they have been able to avoid rigidities in their personnel structures by employing highly paid disciplinarians on a short-term basis and in the combinations needed to tackle problems under consideration in their current research contracts. By contrast, universities and research institutes have found it difficult to maintain the administrative resources, capacity, and flexibility to identify current problems and then to mobilize financial and political support from the relevant decision makers. Even when substantial resources are available for administering problem-solving research, administrators often find they are hampered by having granted so many rights and privileges to researchers that they have no power left to reallocate researchers from one problem to the next. A great deal of operating money is needed to refocus research efforts on new problems, to hire graduate students and other assistants, to pay for data collection and processing, and to provide the administrative services required to tackle new problem-solving research projects.

Administration of problem-solving research also requires enough freedom from disciplinary biases and chauvinism to recognize the appropriate multidisciplinary dimensions of the problem at hand and enough freedom from philosophic biases to develop both the value-free and value knowledge needed to feed the decision rules and processes that produce prescriptions to solve problems. I have observed administrators with years of experience who have not been able to free themselves enough from the disciplinary and philosophic orientations they acquired in a few years of graduate work and disciplinary research to be good administrators of problem-solving research projects. It is essential that problem-solving administrators as well as their researchers be free enough from philosophic bias to entertain the possibility of doing objective research on value questions.

It is also important that administrators be free enough of antiquantitative biases to entertain research procedures that permit the quantitative consequences of alternative courses of action to be envisioned in terms of several performance or criterion variables relevant for solving the problem at hand. It is also important that administrators be flexible enough to realize that their view of the domain of a problem will probably have to be revised repeatedly and interactively with decision makers and affected people. These are tough requirements for problem-solving research administrators. Given the tendency to convert successful disciplinary researchers into administrators of research, it is not surprising that many research administrators fail to meet them.

The difficulties of research administrators are increased by anti-administrative biases of individual researchers, disciplinary chauvinism, and undue philosophic specialization. Researchers who join problem-solving research teams should be expected to bring disciplinary excellence to their team *along with a tolerance* for (1) having their work directed to the domain of the problem under consideration, and for (2) the contributions of researchers in other disciplines. This has to include tolerance for research on value as well as value-free questions, decision processes, and prescriptions. It also has to recognize the need to iterate interactively with decision makers and affected people. Researchers and administrators should recognize that decision makers and affected people are relevant peers for problem-solving research and important sources of value-free and value knowledge. Knowledge from decision makers and affected people is highly useful in designing research proposals, developing work plans for the research, and in evaluating the results of problem-solving.

The relevant peers for evaluating research proposals, project designs, and results are, in effect, part of the administration of problem-solving research. These peers include the disciplinary peers of the different disciplinarians working on the project. The decision maker or group facing the problem and the people affected by decisions on the problem may be more relevant than the disciplinary peers.

"SOFT MONEY" AND THE PROCUREMENT OF ADEQUATE ADMINISTRATION FOR PROBLEM-SOLVING AND SUBJECT-MATTER RESEARCH

We have considered the administrative inadequacies of many universities and institutes. They involve (1) the disciplinary and multidisciplinary departmental structures of such organizations, (2) the privileged positions of tenured personnel, and (3) the tying up of budgets in tenured salaries with little operating money left over.

In such administrative environments, the pickle study examined in Chapter 12 illustrated the critical role played by the soft money available on a short-time basis through grants and contracts. Much of this money is available from agencies to get subject-matter and problem-solving research accomplished. In a very real sense, the soft money that flows to universities and institutes from these agencies tends to keep the research of these organizations relevant to the problems of society, while crusty academic barnacles grow on hard money.

A researcher who acquires a substantial grant or contract for problem-solving and subject-matter research also acquires the ability to command personnel resources from different disciplinary departments in proportions dictated by the domain of the subject or problem he or she is obligated to research. These researchers often command a high proportion of the operating budgets of their departments and institutes. As long as such researchers have control over the money, it is impossible for department heads and intermediate-level administrators to get it without supplying the needed personnel. This has the effect of *augmenting the supply of administrators.*

While such administrators are better than the voids they fill, there are often difficulties. For one thing, this administrative responsibility often disrupts worthy disciplinary research and teaching programs. Also, administrative conflicts can develop with established line administrators. These conflicts sometimes result in efforts by regular line administrators to convert soft money for problem-solving and subject-matter research into hard money for disciplinary research under the control of an established line administrator already stretched to supply the large amount of administrative services required by problem-solving and subject-matter research. In turn, success in these attempts tends to dry up the source of the soft money and the salutary effect of that money on the practical relevance of universities. This happens because administrators of the funding agency are interested in subject-matter and problem-solving research results and recognize that the conversion of soft money to hard money results in the money being used instead to support disciplinary research of questionable relevance for its original intended use.

In trying to improve the administration of problem-solving and subject-matter research, it should be recognized that there is an administrative need to keep in touch with evolving issues. After this is met, it is easier to know which problem-solving and subject-matter research needs to be done. We have noted that administrative structures are often stretched too thin to keep in touch with emerging issues (subjects) and problems. Often, the soft money available to a nonadministrative grantee or contractee becomes available because that person is sensitive to a subject-matter area or problem unknown to his administrators. When the administrative establishment succeeds in converting this soft money to hard money, it squeezes out this kind of research entrepreneurship. A way is needed to make such research entrepreneurship an integral part of research administration, thus encouraging (1) a much-needed continued flow of soft money into research organizations, and (2) the development of a much-needed increase in administrative capacity for problem-solving and subject-matter research.

One solution is to encourage individual researchers who are not part of the regular administrative structure to become research entrepreneurs. In selecting and encouraging individuals, particular attention should be given to the following qualifications. They should be free enough of disciplinary chauvinism to permit them to see the "true" multidisciplinary dimensions of subjects and problems and to seek active participation from the relevant disciplines. At the same time, they should be people who recognize, seek out, and accept excellence in many disciplines.

For instance, when a sociologist is required on a subject-matter or problem-solving project, excellence as a sociologist is required. There are people who call themselves interdisciplinarians, implying that they can serve as sources of many different kinds of disciplinary excellence. By and large, interdisciplinarians fail to furnish hard-core excellence from all the disciplines they purport to represent. Sometimes they lack such excellence in even one discipline. An additional requirement is that the individual researchers selected as research entrepreneurs have to be philosophically flexible, especially for problem-solving research, which involves research on both value-free and value questions.

Much subject-matter research also involves research on values. As problem-solving research always involves decision processes and the need to interact iteratively with decision makers and affected people, problem-solving project leaders should recognize the nature of that process. A subject-matter research leader has to recognize that the research results produced will be used by a set of decision makers in solving a set of problems and that she or he must also be aware of decision processes and of the need to interact, probably iteratively, with decision makers and affected people.

There is always the danger that a problem-solving or subject-matter research leader will not want to disband the structure and the administrative position he has established once the research is complete. The need here is to ensure the termination of the project, the disbandment of its organization, and the elimination of the temporary administrative responsibilities given to the project leader. This can be done by making it absolutely clear that these research projects are temporary and that there is no tenure in them. This will be more acceptable to the research entrepreneur who has a permanent disciplinary home and the disciplinary excellence needed to return to it as well as the administrative qualifications outlined above. The research entrepreneur so equipped has less of a vested interest in the projects he temporarily administers.

To make the disciplinary home attractive, there should be rank and salary rewards for effective research administration, and, if possible, public approval for successful problem-solving and subject-matter research to offset the lack of disciplinary peer-group approval. At the same time, it should be made clear that such research entrepreneurs must maintain disciplinary excellence if a disciplinary home is to be kept open to them. If some such problem-solving and subject-matter researchers are unable to attain or maintain disciplinary excellence, they should be placed in the permanent administrative structure; however, as the number of permanent administration slots is limited, it is advisable to use persons of demonstrated disciplinary excellence as short-term leaders of subject-matter and problem-solving projects.

REQUIRED READINGS

Handler, P. 1976. The American University Today, *American Scientist*, **64**:254–257.
Johnson, Glenn L. 1984. "Academia Needs a New Covenant for Serving Agriculture,"
    MAFES Special Publication, Mississippi State: Mississippi Agricultural and Forestry
    Experiment Station, Mississippi State University.
Wolfle, D. 1971. The Supernatural Department, *Science,* **173**(3992).

ADDITIONAL REFERENCES

Johnson, Glenn. L. 1971. The Quest for Relevance in Agricultural Economics, *American Journal of Agricultural Economics*, **53**(5):728–739.

Chapter 15

Review and Evaluation
of Economic Research

The processes whereby project proposals, project statements, work plans, and results are reviewed or evaluated are essentially prescriptive, the objective being to produce conclusions about what "ought" or "ought not" to be done or to have been done.

When problem-solving processes were diagrammed in Figure 1 of Chapter 2, it was seen that prescriptions depend on both value-free knowledge and knowledge of values processed via some decision rule into conclusions about what ought and ought not to be done. Review and evaluation exercises are evaluative in two senses: (1) actual or anticipated results are evaluated as to their goodness and badness, and (2) the project is evaluated prescriptively as right or wrong. The first form of evaluation is a prerequisite for the second. If the review and evaluation process is ex ante, the "oughts" and "ought nots" have to be expressed in the future tense. If it is ex post, they are expressed in the past tense.

Recognition of the prescriptive nature of review and evaluation creates some difficulty for logically positivistic reviewers and evaluators. Their undergirding emotivism often indicates to them that there can be no objective knowledge of goodness and badness as characteristics of an objective real world on which to base objective statements about what ought or ought not to be done. Such positivists are, in effect, trapped by their own emotivism. Nonetheless, positivists prescriptively review and evaluate research. Some of their prescriptive reviews and evaluations even condemn research designed to generate prescriptions as unobjective because it deals with values.

Project reviewers and evaluators should be expected to examine research proposals and results for objectivity—both of the results produced and the process used. The tests of objectivity—coherence, clarity and workability—should be applied to the value, value-free positivistic, and prescriptive content of the research. The test of correspondence should be applied to the value-free and value content if not the prescriptive results of reviews and evaluations. Further, part of project review and evaluation involves ascertaining whether the researchers are willing to apply those tests and to abide by the results.

Thus, evaluation and review processes also encounter questions about the *objectivity of the reviewers and evaluators themselves and of the prescriptive conclusions* they reach about the research under consideration. They have to deal with value and value-free questions about the proposals and results they review and evaluate. Questions arise in the process about what value-free knowledge should be considered in appraising the research. A parallel question is what value knowledge should be considered. If different people hold conflicting value-free judgements, the reviewers and evaluators have to find an objective way of reconciling them. Similarly, if there are conflicting value judgements, the reviewers and evaluators must find an objective basis for reconciling those conflicts among themselves.

As in all prescriptive efforts, research reviewers and evaluators find perfect value-free positivistic knowledge and perfect knowledge of values infinitely expensive to acquire and, hence, may need to substitute distributions of power for some kinds of knowledge in order to reach prescriptions. Some holders of power may support a given interpretation of positive reality concerning the research, while others deny it. Similarly, on the value side, some holders of power may accept a certain value proposition, while others deny it.

The prescriptions that are reached are found by processing value-free knowledge and knowledge about values through a decision rule. The decision rule will reflect distributions of power such as those just referred to as well as to the power of those who pay for the research, the administrative power that has been granted to research directors, and the power of evaluators and reviewers. Distributions of power count in reaching prescriptions. In the absence of perfect knowledge, covenants regarding power distribution or, in the absence of such covenants, tests of power (among administrators, schools of thought, and between researchers and administrators) are necessary in order to resolve disagreements concerning prescriptions. There seems to be no alternative to covenants or tests of power in decision making other than the impractical one of paying the near infinite cost of perfect knowledge, including perfect knowledge of interpersonally valid measures of values.

From the above, each of the specialized philosophies we have examined can be inconsistent with objective evaluation. Positivists are likely to feel that the required knowledge of the real values of conditions, situations, and things cannot be provided to use in research review and evaluation. Conversely, some normativists may downgrade or ignore value-free knowledge. Pragmatists may become involved in unduly expensive project review and evaluation procedures as it is not always necessary to regard value-free and value knowledge as interdependent. Objective review and evaluation requires a philosophic willingness to tolerate the different philosophic viewpoints necessary to evaluate projects in the prescriptive sense summarized above.

It is chauvinistic for academicians to believe that knowledge itself is all powerful and that they can attain knowledge so perfect—so accurate and complete—that all existing holders of political, market, military, police, social, and administrative power will accept it fully and be willing to act on it. Such chauvinism on the part of academicians reduces their capacity to make *workable* evaluations and reviews of problem-solving and subject-matter research project proposals, work plans, and results. The costs (in the broadest sense) of using existing distributions of power as substitutes for knowledge should be compared with the cost of producing more knowledge before deciding that more knowledge should have been or should be acquired.

We now turn to the special problems encountered in evaluating and reviewing research proposals and results for the three kinds of research considered throughout this book.

EVALUATION AND REVIEW OF
THE THREE KINDS OF RESEARCH

This section deals with the unique aspects of reviewing and evaluating disciplinary, subject-matter, and problem-solving project research and results. Again, it is stressed that evaluations and reviews are prescriptive, and it is presumed that the evaluators and reviewers will produce objective prescriptions through objective procedures.

Evaluating and Reviewing Disciplinary Research

Disciplinary research is the easiest of the three classes of research to evaluate. By definition, disciplines are well organized and their members are well disciplined by the continual exchange of information in their journals, meetings, and other professional activities. Some disciplines concentrate on generating, organizing, storing, and teaching positivistic information. Other disciplines concentrate on information about values. Decision disciplines such as economics deal, generally speaking, with both value-free positivistic and value information and the decision processes that use this information to generate prescriptions.

Because disciplinary peers should know their own discipline well, they are usually the most important source of competent reviewers and evaluators for disciplinary research. If the research under investigation is positivistic, it can be evaluated and reviewed from that standpoint without becoming involved in questions about how to produce knowledge of values and prescriptions. Positivistic disciplinary peers should be capable of doing this; however, their positivism cannot be carried so far over into the review and evaluation procedure that it prevents them from reaching prescriptive reviews and evaluations. Generally speaking, even positivistic reviewers and evaluators from positivistic sciences know enough from their experience in their discipline to be relatively sure about what possesses value within it—what "really has value"—so that they can proceed objectively with their reviews and evaluations. The same is likely to be true when disciplinary research on values and prescriptions is reviewed and evaluated by normativistically oriented disciplinary peers. However, there is a danger that some economists may become so positivistically inclined as to be unobjective in reviewing disciplinary economic research on values and the improvement of theories and quantitative techniques for generating prescriptive knowledge.

Disciplinary Research of Known Relevance

The question of relevance for disciplinary research introduces a need for review by more than disciplinary peers. When disciplinary research is of known relevance, evaluation and review require that its practical usefulness be considered. This requires knowlege of values. In many instances, testing for practical relevancy involves the need for review by (1) the decision makers who face the problems the research would allegedly help solve, and (2) those affected by the decisions of the decision makers. The review and evaluation of such research, then, should include input from the relevant decision makers and probably from people affected by their decisions.

While the research may not involve iterative interaction, the evaluation and review process likely does. In some cases, reaching prescriptions about the research being evaluated may involve pragmatic interdependence between value-free and value concepts, with their truth being determined substantially by consequences best foreseen and assessed in iterative interaction with decision makers and affected people.

Review and evaluation of disciplinary research should question whether or not there are clear-cut procedures for applying the tests of coherence, correspondence, and clarity. When the disciplinary research is alleged to be relvant or of practical significance, the test of workability is also applicable, and reviewers and evaluators should check to see if that test is indeed being used by the researchers. In addition, the test of correspondence should be applied to the value-free and value knowledge used in reaching prescriptive evaluations.

It should be remembered that positivism, normativism, or pragmatism do not regard the knowledge generated by researchers as perfect or absolutely true in a descriptive sense. All descriptive synthetic knowledge is to be regarded as fallible. Review and evaluation, therefore, is not against the standard of perfect knowledge. Instead, the general standard is the self correcting, objective pursuit of knowledge—value free, about values, and/or prescriptive. The objective use of the tests of coherence, correspondence, clarity, and workability is more important than whether or not mistakes are made. Objective evaluators expect to make mistakes, which the "self healing" nature of the objective pursuit of knowledge will correct. The objective pursuit of knowlege is a great source of freedom as it provides reviewers and evaluators forgiveness for making mistakes. This permits them to accept responsibility for reviewing and evaluating even though reviews and evaluation are inevitably imperfect.

Evaluation and Review of Subject-Matter Research

By definition, subject-matter research is relevant to a set of practical problems. It generates a body of multidisciplinary knowledge usable by a set of decision makers facing a set of problems. The composition of the multidisciplinary body of knowledge is relevant to the set of problems. Thus, subject-matter research should always be relevant. The relevance and multidisciplinary nature of subject-matter research complicate its review and evaluation. They make it appropriate—even necessary—to include among the relevant peers (1) members of more than one discipline, often with very different undergirding philosophies; (2) representatives from the set of decision makers dealing with the set of problems involved in defining the subject-matter area; and (3) representatives of those affected by the resulting decisions.

The dangers of disciplinary and philosophic chauvinism are more important for subject-matter research than disciplinary research but not as important as for problem-solving research [Johnson, 1984]. When subject-matter research is dominated by disciplinary interests or philosophic orientations, important dimensions of the subject-matter domain are likely to be neglected and others overemphasized.

Chauvinism by positivists may focus attention on minor positivistic questions to the neglect of value questions crucial to solving the set of problems under consideration. Subject-matter research on energy, for instance, often concentrates on the value-free questions asked by geologists, engineers, and technologists to the neglect of basic questions concerning the value of consuming energy now versus consuming it ten, twenty, or fifty years later. Certainly in the case of research on energy, answers to questions about the value of conserving fossil energy supplies are as crucial as questions about the badness of various forms of pollution produced by nuclear power, oil shale, high-sulfur petroleum, and coal. Conversely, preoccupation with environmental values may override important positivistic questions that must be answered in order to solve the many energy problems faced by decision makers.

Philosophic chauvinism can be damaging to subject-matter research, which can be almost all positive, almost all normative, and often both. Though subject-matter research is seldom prescriptive, it is relevant enough for decision making that decision processes must be kept in mind. In some cases, the decision processes are pragmatic enough to make independent research on value and value-free questions infeasible. The evaluation and review of subject-matter research can also be seriously damaged by disciplinary chauvinism.

Academic chauvinism is also dangerous in reviewing and evaluating subject-matter research. The danger is one of precluding decision makers and affected people as important sources of information and relevant peers. Conversely, there is a dangerous form of anti-academic chauvinism by business and governmental decision makers who sometimes denigrate the contribution of disciplinarians and prevent research project and review and evaluation teams from exploiting the intellectual resources of the academic community.

Reviewing and evaluating subject-matter research requires that the reviewers and evaluators inquire into whether the researchers apply the tests of coherence, correspondence, clarity, and workability in evaluating their research results. Research results can be evaluated as objective or unobjective according to whether these tests were adequately applied in generating the information to solve the set of problems at hand. The researchers themselves can be judged objective or unobjective according to whether they apply the same tests to the knowledge they generate and abide by the test results. In turn, the reviewers and evaluators themselves must use the same tests in generating the value-free and value knowledge on which they base their prescriptions for the research they are reviewing and evaluating. Because they are reaching prescriptions, the objectivity of evaluators is often severely challenged.

Evaluation and Review of Problem-Solving Research

The output of problem-solving research is a prescription—a goal statement about what ought to be done. Goal statements are in the future tense and therefore not testable in the present according to the correspondence criterion, though eminently testable by the coherence criteria. When tested after the act is performed, the value-free and value consequences of an act may be subjected to testing as to correspondence. However, the prescription that led to the act is a definitional consequence of using a decision rule and is not testable as to correspondence.

Problem-solving research proposals are more difficult to review and evaluate than their disciplinary and subject-matter counterparts. The same is true of the results. The greater difficulty arises from the prescriptive nature of problem-solving research. Subject-matter research only feeds decision-making processes, while problem-solving research *includes* those processes. Often, problem-solving research includes iterative interaction with decision makers and/or affected people. The need to evaluate decision-making rules, decision-making processes, and the results of using those rules and processes is unavoidable in evaluating prescriptive research results and proposals. Disciplinary research tends to be more highly regarded than problem-solving research, which is often looked down upon as brush fire research of little enduring value. Because of this, much more academic effort is devoted to reviewing and evaluating disciplinary than problem-solving and subject-matter research despite its relative simplicity.

In evaluating proposals, project statements and work plans for problem-solving research, it is necessary to examine (1) how both value-free and value knowledge will be generated and tested, (2) how the decision rules to be employed will be selected with attention to the realities of various power distributions as necessary parts of those rules, and (3) the procedures whereby those rules will become part of the research effort. It is necessary to know if the processes of and knowledge used in selecting the decision rules will be subjected to the tests of coherence, correspondence, clarity, and workability (as appropriate) and whether the results of using those rules—the prescription itself—will be adequately tested. It is necessary to ask whether researchers will consider the possibility of pragmatic interdependence between value-free and value knowledge in reaching the prescription.

Because problem-solving research is necessarily multidisciplinary, it is necessary to use disciplinary peers from a number of disciplines, both positivistic and normativistic, to evaluate the basic information being fed into the decision process. It is also necessary to use disciplinary peers from the decision disciplines involved—ethics, economics, engineering and the like.

The decision maker facing a problem is also a relevant peer who deserves a say in evaluating research proposals, projects and work plans. This is especially true if the decision maker is also paying the bill. But this is not the end of the relevant peers. Many decision-making units reach decisions that affect others, in which case the affected people are also relevant peers. I remember a situation in South Korea when I was participating in a seminar with top decision makers of the Ministry of Agriculture. Midway through the seminar, the President of South Korea detected allegedly illegal activities by the Minister of Agriculture and immediately relieved him and his top decision makers of their assignments, thereby eliminating several of the seminar participants. At that point, it was clear that interaction was needed with the Koreans affected by the decisions of the decision makers as they played a more stable fundamental role than the decision makers in government.

The reality of distributions of power must be an important consideration in selecting decision rules to use in reaching prescriptions. The power of knowledge is limited by the relationship between its marginal cost and marginal value. It is difficult and uneconomic to extend the power of knowledge beyond that point. The void of knowledge—the domain of the unknown—is filled within the decision process by distributions of market, administrative, legal, military, police, and other kinds of power relative to the decisions being made.

REQUIRED READINGS

(Read in Order Indicated)

Among New Studies, *News Report*, National Academy of Sciences/National Academy of Engineering/Institute of Medicine/National Research Council, **XXV**(6), Autumn 1975. (Fourth)

Gibson, J. E. 1979. Performance Evaluation of Academic Research, *Science*, **206**(4417) editorial. (First)

Information for Reviewers of Proposals, and NSF Criteria for the Selection of Research Projects, National Science Foundation, undated. (Second)

Johnson, G. L. 1976. Who is a Peer? *American Scientist*, Letters to the Editor, **64**:124. (Fifth)

——— 1979. Point of View: Quality Assessment in Graduate Dissertations, *The Graduate School Newsletter*, Michigan State University, **3**(5);3-A. (Sixth)

——— 1984. Academia Needs a New Covenant for Serving Agriculture, Special Publication, Mississippi State; MS: Mississippi Agricultural & Forestry Experiment Station, Mississippi State University. (Seventh)

Review Processes: Assessing the Quality of Research Proposals, Washington, DC: National Commission on Research, May 1980, pp. ix-x, 1-2. (Third)

Chapter 16

Durability, Practical Importance, Opportunities, and Complementarities, by Research Classes

Practical problem-solving research is often downgraded by disciplinary researchers who refer to it as "putting out brush fires" while extolling their own disciplinary research as fundamental and of enduring quality. Practical researchers reciprocate by referring to the results of disciplinary research as the output of ivory tower residents unacquainted with the practical problems of the real world while extolling their own research results as relevant, realistic, and useful and referring to disciplinary work as abstract, esoteric, and of questionable value. Overall, it appears that scientific advance and the worth of research are hampered by competition and self-aggrandizement by too many problem-solving and disciplinary researchers. Disciplinarians often seek a form of intellectual immortality through the production of disciplinary research results with enduring value, while problem-solving researchers seek current fame, approval, and active participation in the affairs of their time. Such exchanges between disciplinarians and problem-solving researchers tend to ignore the fact that both practical and disciplinary research have value and that it may be possible to exploit important complementarities between them and even accomplish both in the same effort.

Subject-matter researchers tend to fall between the extremes of disciplinary and problem-solving research. Results of subject-matter research can be expected to have a longer life than problem-solving research because subject-matter research is designed to produce information useful to a set of decision makers facing a set of problems. Sets of decision makers and problems are fairly stable and spread out enough in time to give a longer useful life for subject-matter research results than for research to solve one particular problem for one particular decision maker at one point in time. The exception to this is a solution to a problem that reoccurs in the same form. Such a solution, like the recipe for Aunt Min's spice cake, has enduring value.

In addition to avoiding the elevation of any of the three kinds of research to preeminence over the other two, we note that there are important complementarities among them. Practical problem-solving and subject-matter research sometimes reveal disciplinary shortcomings that must be remedied to solve a problem. Remedying shortcomings in a discipline's theoretical structure, its quantitative techniques, and its basic measurements complements and gives purpose and direction to disciplinary research.

Kuhn [1970] in his book, *The Structure of Scientific Revolutions*, has pointed out the importance of such complementarities by stressing that a discipline will go along routinely until challenged in a major way by problems and questions it cannot handle. At that time, its established way of looking at its phenomena—its paradigm—is challenged and it has to make a major revolutionary change. In Chapter 10 we saw, for example, that Schultz was challenged by the inability of changes in the use of conventional inputs to explain changes in the output of U.S. agriculture. Thus, practical and subject-matter research complement disciplinary research to motivate advances in the latter. Disciplinarians who cut themselves off from the practical tend, therefore, to condemn themselves to be disciplinary hewers of wood rather than disciplinary innovators [Johnson, in Press[a]].

Disciplinary economic research also complements the other two classes of research. A theoretical advance in a discipline (as seen in the Leontief and Schultz case studies of Chapter 10) often introduces a new way of looking at practical problems and experiences, so that practical problem solvers and subject-matter researchers can make new observations to be interpreted more meaningfully in finding solutions to practical problems. Problem-solving and subject-matter researchers who isolate themselves from disciplinary research deprive themselves of increased ability to observe and analyze and, hence, to prescribe solutions to the practical problems of concern to them.

DISCIPLINARY RESEARCH

Proper design and execution should assure the durability of disciplinary research. Those doing such research should know enough about the discipline to select research that will contribute to the discipline and thus be of enduring value. Disciplines have demonstrated their durability by establishing a place for themselves in the great universities of the world over long periods of time. As our knowledge base increases, the number of established disciplines also increases. The justification for having basic disciplines such as economics in universities is that these disciplines produce, organize, store, and make available knowledge of enduring value to succeeding generations of students. Some of the students, in turn, become disciplinarians to continue the process. Some become problem-solving and subject-matter researchers who use the knowledge of their discipline for practical purposes. Other students trained in a discipline do not do practical or subject-matter research. Instead, they use the knowledge generated by the discipline in private practice, in adminstrative positions of government, and in professional consulting practices—all in manners sometimes difficult to differentiate from problem-solving research.

The practicality of disciplinary research of *known* relevance is assured. People designing and evaluating disciplinary research of known relevance do so because the research will have practical importance, at least in the short run.

Disciplinary research of *unknown relevance* often has long-run practicality, though this is a matter of chance since it is the absence of reliable evidence of long-run practicality that causes it to be classified as of unknown relevance. However, because disciplinary research corrects deficiencies in a discipline that has maintained a place for itself in universities and research institutes by being useful over long periods of time, there is some presumption in favor of expecting improvements in a discipline to have long-run practical significance.

It is relatively difficult to develop disciplinary research projects in economics. Economics is a highly developed discipline with vast, well-developed theoretical structures, some of which have been in place for decades. For instance, it is difficult to find deficiencies in static microeconomics as opposed to dynamic microeconomic theory, which can be tackled with reasonable hope of success as too many economists have looked for such opportunities too long for many to be left.

There are many important deficiencies in dynamic theory, particularly in the never-never land interfaces with political science, psychology, sociology, and the physical and biological sciences, whose members research and develop new institutions and technologies and create human capital to change the structural characteristics of an economy. Progress at these interfaces awaits the development of improved theories of institutional, human, and technological change in disciplines where theory is often less complete and less advanced than in economics.

Recently developed economic theories of induced technological and institutional change and human capital formation are important but are not really capable of dealing with the nonmarket origins of these changes.

With respect to research on quantitative techniques, opportunities are abundant but difficult. In some instances, progress in econometrics awaits progress in theoretical statistics. In others, the basic difficulties are in economics but are so great as to offer little hope for success. Included are difficulties of attaining interpersonally valid welfare measures and non-price weighted indexes of production and consumption [Johnson, in Press[b]].

To summarize, successful completion of a well-designed disciplinary research effort almost assures the enduring value of its results. The practicality of disciplinary research is assured mainly for disciplinary research of known relevance. However, even disciplinary research of unknown relevance is likely to later prove to have long-run practical importance.

SUBJECT-MATTER RESEARCH

The short-run practical relevance of subject-matter research should be assured because such research is by definition designed to produce knowledge useful in solving problems for sets of decision makers facing sets of problems. Subject-matter research falls between disciplinary and problem-solving research as to its practical relevance.

Concerning durability, subject-matter research also falls between disciplinary and problem-solving research. The information it produces is designed to be useful to sets of decision makers solving sets of problems. These sets almost always have time dimensions, some of which are long enough to give the results of subject-matter research more durability than those of problem-solving research. Research results of considerable durability have been produced by multidisciplinary teams including economists. Examples include the multidisciplinary bodies of knowledge now available on food and nutrition, environmental quality, minority rights, energy, agricultural economics, labor and industrial relations, and marketing.

There are many more opportunities to do subject matter research than disciplinary research. Also, the chances of success in subject-matter research are higher than in disciplinary research. One impediment to success is the shortage of administrative capacity to provide cross-disciplinary administrative structures flexible enough to create projects to address new subjects and to terminate obsolete subjects (see Chapter 14). Another impediment is the restraints different philosophies impose on research to produce the three different kinds of knowledge.

The following generalizations about subject-matter research seem justified. Subject-matter research can be expected to have short-run and some intermediate-run practicality, with moderate durability. In some instances, subject-matter research will also have long-run disciplinary significance. There are generally more opportunities to do subject-matter research with a high probability of success than there are for disciplinary research.

PROBLEM-SOLVING RESEARCH

Problem-solving research differs greatly from subject-matter and disciplinary research with respect to opportunities, durability, and practicality. It is the most practical of the three, and with good research design and execution, its practical impact is assured. On the other hand, problem-solving research results are the most ephemeral. Economists serving as problem-solving researchers, administrators, and decision makers often work for years with great success but without producing enough knowledge of enduring value for economics to justify a single article in a disciplinary economic journal. While it is often difficult to ascribe long-run importance to problem-solving research, it is easy to see that it has great short-run practical significance.

Some aspects of problem-solving research, however, may also have disciplinary significance in the short-run; some may have it in the long term. This is particularly true for the work economists do on multidisciplinary problem-solving teams for which the dynamic theories of economics are inadequate. Economic theory deals with optimization and decision making. So does practical problem-solving research. It follows that the experience of doing problem-solving research produces insights into dynamic decision-making theory that may have long-run disciplinary significance for economics.

Almost all problem-solving research experiences can be treated as case studies of some importance for disciplinarians trying to conceptualize and understand dynamic decision-making processes [Mintzberg, et al., 1976]. To the extent that problem-solving researchers study the question of which decision-making rule to use and how to incorporate important distributions of power into these rules, they are conducting case studies that should be useful to economists trying to conceptualize these important decision-making processes.

Other fortuitous sources of complementarity between problem-solving and disciplinary economic research include (1) the multidisciplinary nature of problem-solving research, (2) the fact that much problem-solving research involves finding solutions "outside the market," and (3) the normative aspects of problem solving. These three sources of complementarity discussed above are important to both pragmatists and nonpragmatists. For pragmatists, explanation of these complementarities is an important way to make disciplinary progress.

Difficult disciplinary deficiencies in economics are found at its interfaces with the disciplines concerned with institutional, human, and technological changes. Multidisciplinary problem-solving research provides experience at these interfaces.

Neoclassical economic theory is at its strongest in understanding how markets work but weakest in understanding the economics of adjusting the institutional structures and technological and human constraints affecting market operations. Again, much problem-solving research deals with phenomena poorly understood by economists, even by the pragmatic institutionalists who understand change better than many of their colleagues.

Quantitative techniques for measuring nonmonetary values are weak in economics as are its basic data and other knowledge of these values. Again, problem-solving research provides experiences in dealing with nonmonetary values useful for improving the quantitative measures and techniques of economics as a discipline.

SUMMARY

Our discussion of the three classes of research vis-à-vis, durability, practicality, opportunities, and complementarity has shown that it is not simply a matter of disciplinary work being impractical and durable, problem-solving work being practical and ephemereal, with subject-matter research falling in between. Instead, we see that there are tendencies for complementarities to exist among problem-solving, subject-matter, and disciplinary work. It does not behoove the disciplinarians to denigrate the problem-solving and subject-matter research. Similarly, problem-solving and subject-matter researchers can be grateful to the disciplinarians for providing them with theories, quantitative techniques and basic measurements instead of downgrading disciplinary work as the abstract, impractical activity of ivory tower residents [Johnson, in Press[b]].

ADDITIONAL REFERENCES

Kuhn, Thomas S. 1970. *The Structure of Scientific Revolutions*, Chicago: University of Chicago Press, Vol. II, No. 2, 2nd ed., enlarged.

Johnson, Glenn L. In Press. a. "Agricultural Economics: Dwindling Support and Expanding Opportunities." Brinkman Lecture, University of Bonn, Oct. 9, 1985.

———. In Press. b. "Technological Innovation with Implications for Agricultural Economics," Paper presented at post conference seminar, Aug. 7–9, 1985, Ames, Iowa. Proceedings to be published by Iowa State University Press.

Mintzberg, Henry, Durn Raisinghani, and Andre Theoret. 1976. The Structure of "Unstructured Decision Processes," *Administrative Science Quarterly* 21: 246–75.

Chapter 17

Appropriate Philosophic Underpinnings and Research Methodologies for Economists

The first 16 chapters have dealt systematically with methodological issues growing out of three philosophic orientations important in producing value-free knowledge, knowledge about values, and prescriptive knowledge necessary in doing disciplinary, subject-matter, and problem-solving research. The uniqueness of the book relative to other books on research methodology is the attention it gives to subject-matter and problem-solving research so important in the applied work of economists. It does this without neglecting basic disciplinary research. The task of covering specific techniques from such fields as econometrics, statistics, systems science, linear programming, input-output analyses, and industrial organization was left to other books.

This chapter first summarizes what Chapters 10–16 have revealed about financing, conducting, and evaluating the three kinds of research. This is followed by a section on philosophic underpinnings. The last section considers additional methodological issues and topics including the scope of economics that escaped the systematic net of the first 16 chapters but are often encountered in the classroom.

GENERALIZATIONS ABOUT PROBLEM-SOLVING, SUBJECT-MATTER AND DISCIPLINARY MATTER

The case studies in Part II demonstrate that economists can work on the three kinds of research with substantial objectivity. Even economists who do not do research use the results of all three in their work.

The three kinds of research were seen in Part II to be important and highly respectable. Disciplinary research in economics is highly respected among disciplinarians, and is important not only because it contributes to economics but also because it undergirds and facilitates subject-matter and problem-solving research, both of which *must* be part of serious studies of research methodology for economists. Applied economics work in schools of business administration, departments of labor relations, in parastatal agencies, in government agencies, departments of agricultural economics, and other practically oriented institutions is simply too important to be ignored.

Mixtures of Problem-Solving, Subject-Matter, and Disciplinary Research

The case studies in Part II involve research that falls neatly into the three categories. Much research done by economists, however, mixes problem-solving, subject-matter, and disciplinary research in various combinations. The prevalence of these mixtures further underscores the conclusion that studies of research methodology for economists should not focus exclusively on disciplinary research.

Fortunately, the usefulness of the distinctions between the three kinds of research does not depend upon being able to find clear-cut examples falling exclusively into each of the categories. Ability to distinguish which parts of a research project are disciplinary, problem-solving, or subject-matter is extremely useful. Once the different components are identified with each of the three types it is easier to understand whether or not philosophic orientations are varied appropriately between parts of the project and between people working on different parts. It becomes clear that some parts of a research project have to be more concerned with knowledge about values than, say, parts that are more concerned with positivistic knowledge. Such classification makes clear which parts of a project have to be concerned with prescriptive knowledge. Further, knowing which parts fall into each of the three research categories facilitates the mobilization of support for, administration and conduct, and the evaluation of the different parts.

**Differences in Obtaining and Accounting for Support,
Administering, Conducting, and Evaluating the Three
Kinds of Research, with Attention to Durability
and Practicality**

When the case studies of Part II were examined in Chapters 13–16, great differences were found between the three kinds of research concerning financing and accountability, conduct and administration, review of project proposals and evaluation of completed projects, and the durability and practical importance of the results. These are briefly summarized here.

Disciplinary research tends to be financed in universities and institutes having responsibility for (1) transmitting disciplinary economic information from one generation to another, and (2) advancing the discipline of economics. Subject-matter research tends to be financed by institutions able to draw on public or private funds to generate knowledge on multidisciplinary subjects important to significant sets of decision makers in society. Problem-solving research tends to be financed by both private and public agencies facing specific problems. Some of this research is also financed by the public sector to assist important groups such as farmers, small entrepreneurs, municipalities with waste disposal problems, consumers, and the aged. Accounting for research resources varies between the three kinds of research. Accountability is generally closer for subject-matter research than for disciplinary research but not as close as for problem-solving research.

There are systematic differences in the conduct and administration of the three kinds of research. Much disciplinary research can be advantageously administered by the "discipline of the discipline." Hence, it tends to be simpler to administer than problem-solving and subject-matter research, both of which are more complicated to administer because they are multidisciplinary. Conduct and administration of research is also much more complex at the problem-solving end of the spectrum than at the disciplinary end because of the many administrative layers often found in research agencies above the disciplinary level.

Though it is difficult to administer problem-solving projects that cross disciplinary lines under the control of a single dean, it is still more difficult when the problem crosses the administrative domains of several deans. There are corresponding administrative problems in research institutes. Similarly, it is more difficult to conduct problem-solving research than disciplinary research because project administrators and personnel continually have to adjust their work and efforts to the interests of the other disciplines involved, particularly to the interests of the decision-maker whose problem is being researched. The conduct and administration of subject-matter research tends to fall between the relative simplicity of disciplinary research and the great complexity of problem-solving research.

The review of research proposals and the evaluation of results varies substantially between the three kinds of research. A discipline provides peer review of disciplinary research proposals and the results of completed disciplinary research projects. Economists as disciplinarians know what needs to be done to improve their discipline. This permits them to evaluate disciplinary research in terms of contributions made to the discipline. However, disciplinary economists are often uninformed about many of the other multidisciplinary dimensions of practical problems. Disciplinary peer reviews and evaluations are relatively less important but more numerous for subject-matter research than for disciplinary research. However, they are relatively less important for subject-matter research because the set of decision makers interested in the output of a subject-matter research project is also an important group of reviewers. At the problem-solving extreme of our research spectrum, relevant disciplinary peer reviewers often come from still more disciplines but are together relatively less important than (1) the decision maker facing the problem being researched, and (2) those affected by that person's decisions.

Of the three kinds of research, problem-solving research is obviously of greatest practicality and disciplinary research the least. It should not be concluded, however, that disciplinary research is impractical. Much of it is known to be relevant and of practical importance because practical problems can't be solved without it. Even disciplinary research of presently unknown relevance is likely to have long-run relevance and practical importance for subject-matter and problem-solving research. We should remember that most long-sustained disciplines have maintained support by being useful and that anything that improves a discipline is likely to be of practical significance later on.

Among the three kinds of research, disciplinary research results are the most durable and problem solving the least. An exception to this generalization is problem-solving results that prescribe solutions to repetitive problems; such prescriptions can become standing durable "recipes" for solving these repetitive problems.

PHILOSOPHIES AND METHODOLOGICAL GENERALIZATIONS ABOUT THE RESEARCH OF ECONOMISTS

In Part I we examined three broad philosophies—positivism, various forms of normativism, and pragmatism—concerned with the acquisition of value-free, value, and prescriptive knowledge. We also examined the methods associated with each of these philosophies. We have seen that solving problems requires research on values as well as positivistic research. In Part II, six research case histories demonstrate that economists do, indeed, successfully research value and value-free questions in order to help develop prescriptions for problems, and to help predict the behavioral responses of producers, consumers, resource owners, entrepreneurs, and public administrators to changes in demand, supply, technology, institutions, people, and the biophysical capital of society.

This section interrelates contributions from the different philosophies and associated methods considered in Part I in view of the research experiences examined in Part II, to indicate appropriate philosophic orientations for economists doing the three kinds of research. The conclusions presented here on philosophic orientations relate to the work of both *practicing* economists and disciplinary economists.

These conclusions may even serve the needs of disciplinary economic researchers better than conclusions focused on the needs of disciplinary research because of (1) their own substantial emphasis on the disciplinary, and (2) the opportunities to exploit the complementarity between disciplinary and applied research revealed by more equal attention to the three kinds of research. Serving the needs of applied research economists should also serve the needs of nonresearch economists who use the results of practical research in their work in much the same way as problem-solving research economists.

As this section uses the terminology developed in Chapter 2, someone reading it before Chapter 2 may not understand it well.

Economists doing problem-solving, subject-matter, and disciplinary research probably think less about philosophic orientations and research methodology than professors of economic research methodology, who often focus on disciplinary research to the neglect of subject-matter and problem-solving research. Because of this, research economists are often less aware than they should be of the problems resulting from a commitment to a single philosophy.

Research economists doing subject-matter and problem-solving research require more flexibility in their philosophic orientations than granted by any single philosophy examined in Part I. None of the three stock philosophic positions examined in Chapters 2–9 turns out to be individually adequate for problem-solving and subject-matter research. Even disciplinary economic research may be seriously constrained by each of the three philosophies. Part II indicates that various mixes of these philosophies and their associated methods are used by economists. Using these mixtures will be seen to be consistent and rational after we summarize the strengths of logical positivism, normativism, and pragmatism and the constraints they place on each other in the following sections.

Positivism

In philosophy, the movement known as logical positivism is now increasingly being questioned. Its peak influence probably occurred at about the beginning of World War II. Though logical positivism began its decline with the dispersal of the members of the Vienna Circle when Hitler persecuted many of its members, the decline was not primarily due to the dispersal. Serious questions had begun to arise among philosophers about the sharp distinctions in logical positivism between the analytic and synthetic, theory and observation, and discovery and validation. Also, philosphers were becoming increasingly concerned about (1) the positivistic rejection of the possibility of knowledge of values as characteristics of an objective real world, and (2) the idea of a value-neutral science.

Arguments among philosphers on these issues indicate that it may be reasonable to assume no a priori synthetic knowledge at some early point in history, but that it is also reasonable at any point in current time to assume ex ante synthetic knowledge in a good "Bayesian manner." Questioning of the a priori/a posteriori distinction regarding value-free positivistic knowledge opens up the question as to whether there might also be ex ante synthetic knowledge of values at given points in time. Philosophers, in appraising the legacy of positivism, have stressed problems with the analytic/synthetic distinction more than with the emotivist presupposition that there is no normative reality to experience to provide the basis for "good" and "bad" as primitive undefined experiential terms to use to translate analytical into descriptive, synthetic statements about values. In *The Legacy of Positivism*, which contains contributions from logical positivists, Scriven [pp. 199–201] rejects that emotivist presupposition as unwarranted. Discussions in Chapters 4, 7 and 8 of this book tend both to draw on and support Scriven's position, as do the case studies in Chapters 10–12.

Despite the fact that positivism is on the wane among philosophers, it has left a legacy economists cannot neglect. We have to note that regardless of the changing opinions of philosophers, positivism is still a very real force in science in general and that its methods have proven extremely effective in the verification and validation of value-free positivistic knowledge by economists as well as by biological and physical scientists. We are fortunate to have the legacy of positivism to draw on in doing research in economics. We cannot ignore the continuing contribution of positivism to the acquisition of value-free positivistic knowledge.

The methods of positivism include the combination of logic and empirical work so important in econometric research that bridges the gap J. N. Keynes noted between the "abstract deductive" nature of English classical and neoclassical economics and the "realistic inductive" nature of the German school of historical economics. The use of logic by neoclassical economists makes the test of coherence important, while the stress of econometricians on observations and experience makes the test of correspondence important. The test of clarity is important—almost a prerequisite for application of the tests of coherence and correspondence. Ambiguous statements, as Popper emphasizes, are difficult to test.

However, there are crucial weaknesses in logical positivism for economists. The constraints positivism places on the use of pragmatic and normativistic methods need to be avoided. The dissatisfaction of philosophers with the analytic/synthetic and the a priori/a posteriori distinctions need not bother us too much. In a less precise view these distinctions are useful to economists but are increasingly being modified with the techniques of Bayesian statistics. On the other hand, the positivistic, untested, emotivist assumption of many positivists about the lack of a normative reality to experience must be regarded as metaphysical. It seems empirically false to assert that one does not experience in a nonemotivist manner at least some goodnesses and badnesses as real world characteristics of conditions, situations, and things. For instance, we do experience the badnesses of lingering deaths from cancer, starvation, burns, and nuclear exposure as well as the goodnesses of Salk vaccine, healthy bodies, and recreation in ways that seem more than merely emotive.

For the most part, practicing economists (consultants, advisors and administrators, both public and private) reject the metaphysical presupposition that the values we attach to such conditions, situations and things are merely emotivist and that therefore we can have no descriptive knowledge of their reality. Practical economic researchers, particularly, commonly disregard this emotivist stricture despite the strong admonitions of such authoritarian figures in economics as J. N. Keynes [1963], Robbins [1949], and Friedman [1953], who have tried to impose the emotivism of some logical positivists on economists. We do do objective descriptive research on monetary and nonmonetary values (both of which are normative) when, for example, we do price analyses, work empirically with the expected utility hypothesis and estimate consumer and producer surpluses.

If the analytic/synthetic and a priori/a posteriori distinctions of positivism are taken as less than always binding and reliable, and if the emotivist positivistic rejection of objective research on values as real characteristics of the world is dropped, economists have at their disposal a modification of the strong philosophy of logical positivism and its associated methods to use in accumulating, validating, verifying and analyzing not only value-free positivistic knowledge but knowledge of values as well. This is important as both are needed by problem-solving, subject-matter, and disciplinary economic researchers and by practicing economists.

To show that this is a fairly modest claim, it is worth stressing again in this summary that value-free positivistic knowledge in economics, like the value-free knowledge of the physical and biological sciences, is culture- and time-dependent and based on interpretations of sensory stimuli involving insight, inspiration, intuition, originality, and empathy. It should also be stressed that positivistic knowledge is not regarded as absolutely true even by logical positivists. Instead, the most that can be claimed for it is that it has been adequately tested for purposes at hand and that it may be subsequently rejected. Realization of these shortcomings of value-free positivistic knowledge make it easier to accept the possibility of objective descriptive knowledge of "real" world values.

Normativism

Historically, economists have placed great emphasis on various philosophies concerned with normative knowledge, including both knowlege of values (goodness and badness) and prescriptive knowledge (about what ought to be). Indeed, such economists as Jeremy Bentham were important developers of utilitarianism, while David Ricardo, J. S. Mill, and Karl Marx contributed to the labor theory of value. Knowledge of values is crucial in reaching prescriptions for solving problems and predicting the behavior of resource owners, producers, consumers, and even government officials in administering public agencies and private firms. Though the positivists readily admit behavioristic statements about who values what into their realm of objective descriptive knowledge, they reject statements regarded as descriptive of what values are real whether or not anyone holds that they are. Value statements of this type are needed if prescriptions are to be regarded as anything more than the consequences of emotivist and arbitrary value judgments. In order to have objective prescriptive knowledge, one needs descriptive knowledge of what values are real and that is as independent of the knower as positivistic knowledge.

Having found sufficient reasons in our summary of positivism for rejecting the emotivist stricture of some logical positivists on research on real values in the above section on positivism we are now free to consider the possibilities of an objective normativism. Part of the argument for such an objective normativism was provided by G. E. Moore in his book *Principia Ethica*. Moore argues that goodness and badness are synthetic, never analytical, and likens knowledge of good to knowledge of yellow; however, he does not assert that goodness is experienced. In the case of positivistic experience, we learn as members of communities—and especially as members of disciplined communities of scientists—to interpret our sense impressions as perceptions of what is "really out there." To do this requires "a leap of faith" that there is something in reality that corresponds with our interpreted sense impressions. This leap of faith is needed because value-free positivistic concepts can never be proven to correspond with reality. Moore's argument that "good" is a primitive undefined synthetic term makes it possible to extend his position in a way that puts knowledge of real values on a similar basis to that of our unprovable positivistic knowledge. For both kinds of knowledge, logic and theory guide (and perhaps misguide) our interpretation of our sense impressions into perceptions of what we regard as real.

A "leap of faith" is also required concerning the existence of real values to correspond with our value judgments. Further, inspiration, intuition, insight, originality, and empathy are probably no more important for knowledge of real values than for value-free positivistic knowledge, as we try to perceive what experiences tell us about the real world. In both cases, descriptive conclusions are never proven because (1) we can never experience all possible events, and (2) because of the difficulties we have in interpreting our experiences. Both value-free and value "facts" can be regarded as "facts" only in the sense of being adequately tested for the purposes at hand and until disproven later.

Moore's position that primitive value terms as well as primitive value-free terms are possible can be viewed as implying that the answering of descriptive value-free positivistic and value questions is essentially similar if we also reject the emotivist presupposition that there are no normative experiences of values as characteristics of a real world. The analytic, synthetic, and a priori/a posteriori distinctions, while questionable on both sides, remain potentially important for descriptive research on values as well as on value-free positivistic phenomena. For both, coherence, correspondence, and clarity remain the main criteria for disproving synthetic descriptive statements, there being no way of conclusively proving either descriptive value-free or value statements.

While this argument is followed here, it should be stressed in this summary that Moore did not go this far because, it can be hypothesized, he feared that to do so would come dangerously close to committing the naturalistic fallacy for which he had a great aversion. We stress here that the naturalistic fallacy is one of concluding that something possessing the characteristic of goodness is goodness itself. To assert, as done here, that something really has the characteristic of goodness is not to assert that that thing is goodness any more than to say that an apple is red is to say that redness is an apple. This position does not make it a naturalistic fallacy to assert that life really possesses the characteristic of goodness unless we also say that goodness is life.

There are monetary and nonmonetary values but both are values and both are normative. Knowledge of prices and other monetary values is acceptable to many positivists because they regard prices and monetary values as behavioristic in the sense that they describe the behavior of an economy. Emotivists, logical positivists, and some economists object if prices are interpreted as measuring real exchange values. There are also nonmonetary exchange values as well as intrinsic nonmonetary values. The objectivity with which we test the results of price analyses for coherence, correspondence, and clarity attests to the possibility of objectively researching behavioral values. Though nonmonetary values are clearly more difficult to research, the above argument indicates that attempts to do so should not be proscribed by the presuppositions of positivists and emotivists.

The distinction followed in this book and borrowed from C. I. Lewis between knowledge of values—about goodness and badness—and prescriptive knowledge—about rightness and wrongness—makes it much easier to conceive of objective knowlege of values as characteristics of a real world. Prescriptions, as we saw in earlier chapters result from processing value-free positivistic knowledge and knowledge about values through decision rules. Decision rules define prescriptions. As definitions, prescriptions are not observable phenomena.

When knowledge is imperfect, conflict resolution ordinarily requires that decision rules include distributions of power among "interested people." Those with vested interests in prescriptions exercise power to generate prescriptions acceptable to them—for example, majority rule in democratic voting, with each voter having equal power. Holders of power may attempt to introduce false unobjective *value-free or value concepts* into decision processes. However, if they really hold power, and if that power is part of the decision rules, they have little need to falsify either value-free knowledge or knowledge about values. They need merely exercise their power within the decision rule to reach prescriptions that reflect their "interests" without misleading either themselves or others.

When power is uncertain, it is easily threatened by the results of objective positivistic research and objective research on values. Such threats motivate holders of questionable power to falsify and to fear the results of objective research—either positivistic or about values. Thus, there is more danger of unobjectivity with respect to both value-free positivistic and value knowledge by those holding *uncertain* power than by those who are *certain* of their power. Strong power holders can simply see to it that their power is part of the decision rule.

Positivists such as Gunnar Myrdal, who regard value premises as unobjective, advocate the explicit statement of values. When we seriously entertain the possibility of objective (but, of course, imperfect) knowledge of values, the corresponding need is to state explicitly the distributions of power that are built into the decision rules used to convert reliable descriptive, value-free, and value knowledge into prescriptions.

Pragmatism

Pragmatism has been important in institutional economics. It tends to focus on problem-solving, therefore to be less precisely focused on any discipline, including economics.

For pragmatists, the truth of concepts is determined by their consequences including, particularly, consequences for solving problems. This view makes the test of workability (as a test for truth and objectivity) important in pragmatism. Another important characteristic of pragmatism is the interdependence of value-free positivistic and value propositions, which arises when the truth of these propositions is tested against their consequences in solving problems.

A strength of pragmatism is its orientation to practical problems and its ability to deal with values. When independence between value and value-free propositions is important and the focus is on problem solving, pragmatism has substantial advantages over an independent positivism and an independent normativism. When interdependence is lacking or is relatively unimportant, the complexity of a pragmatic orientation may involve costs that exceed its benefits.

Pragmatism has had its impacts on economics via the German historical school, American institutionalism and in the dialectical materialism of Marxist economics. Currently, resource economists draw heavily on the pragmatism of American institutionalism, which is alive and apparently in better health than before the unrest of the 1960s and 1970s.

Prescriptions (Including Pragmatic Ones)

The problem-solving research of economists and the problem-solving activities of economists in administrative positions make it necessary for the philosophic undergirding and methods of economists to deal with prescriptive knowledge. Further, the prescriptive is close to the heart of economics as a discipline. Economists use the calculus to define optima, which are used for both prescriptive and predictive purposes. The supply and demand functions used by economists in predicting production, consumption, and prices all posit optimizing behavior by consumers, resource owners, and even government officials, whose behavior is successfully predicted on the assumption that they do what the economic calculus prescribes as best for them and their agencies. An economics without prescription would hardly be economics. One can state that when an economist is "out of prescription, he is out of economics" to paraphrase the advertisement that says, "When you're out of [a brand name for beer], you're out of beer."

Economists deal with prescriptions pragmatically and nonpragmatically. The institutional and resource economists are particularly inclined to use pragmatic methods, especially when working on problems solvable only with market interventions.

Nonpragmatic prescription proceeds under the assumption that value-free knowledge and knowledge of values used in reaching a prescription to solve a problem are independent of each other. If applicable, nonpragmatic techniques for reaching prescriptions have substantial advantages. Most of the neoclassical theory of market behavior views the world nonpragmatically—i.e., the underlying wants and preferences of producers, consumers, and resource owners are assumed to be independent of value-free facts about technology, institutions, resource control, and people. Nonpragmatic prescriptive methods are relatively simple and lead directly to prescriptions and predictions of behavior. The main disadvantage of nonpragmatic methods of researching prescriptions and behavior is that knowledge of values and value-free knowledge do not always appear to be independent [Johnson and Zerby, 1973, Chapter 11].

The advantage of pragmatic methods arises when the pragmatic presupposition appears to be so true that value-free and value truths must be regarded as interdependent in their consequences for solving a problem. While this leads to complicated methods in which value and value-free knowledge are treated as interdependent in complex ways, those prescriptions that are obtained are more realistic and users are not misled by erroneous analyses that presume independence in the face of interdependence. Basing predictions on pragmatic prescriptions is also complex for the pragmatic analyst, but either can or cannot be done. If pragmatic methods are required but are too complex to be carried out, those facing the problem are so warned rather than being misled into accepting unduly simplistic results. The disadvantage of reaching prescriptions pragmatically, of course, is the cumbersomeness and complexity of pragmatic methods, especially when making predictions. Thus the analyst is well advised to be quite sure that value-free and value knowledge are interdependent before engaging in a complex pragmatic exercise to reach a prescription.

C. I. Lewis' distinction in Chapter 2 and elsewhere in this book between knowledge of values and prescriptive knowledge is extremely helpful. Failure to make this distinction may mislead one into employing unnecessary cumbersome pragmatic methods when values could have been investigated independently of value-free knowledge and both processed into prescriptions via simpler, more efficient nonpragmatic decision rules. Another advantage of the distinction between knowledge of values and prescriptions is that the role of "vested interests" in decision making is clarified by seeing the need to incorporate distributions of power in decision rules for use in converting value knowledge and value-free knowledge into prescriptive knowledge.

In earlier chapters we noted that perfect knowledge is infinitely expensive. We have to accept knowledge that has only been adequately tested for the purposes at hand but is still unproven. Because of the expense of perfecting both value-free positivistic knowledge and knowledge of values, almost all decision rules contain distributions of power. Though often quite arbitrary, these distributions assist in conflict resolution. The kinds of power distribution include the ownership of rights and privileges that generate income; military and police power; and various forms of political, religious, and social power. The distribution of the power of knowledge is also important; however, the power of knowledge is limited by the great expense of obtaining near-perfect knowledge.

Power is power. If it is really power, it is not redistributable. Political, bureaucratic, intellectual, and military battles are fought over failures to assess correctly the true distributions of power. Generally speaking people do not start battles they expect to lose, yet battles generally involve one side that has correctly assessed its power and another side that has incorrectly assessed its power.

Once it is recognized that prescriptive knowledge is essentially different from knowledge of values and depends upon value-free and value knowledge as well as decision rules involving distributions of power, it can be seen that it is important in prescriptive research to take explicit account of existing or assumed distributions of power. Except in the utopian case of perfect knowledge, prescriptions always depend in some degree on a distribution of power. Myrdal stresses the need to state what he regards as arbitrary value premises clearly and explicitly in doing prescriptive problem-solving research. This need is greatly reduced when values are regarded as objectively researchable. However, there is a corresponding different need—to state clearly and explicitly the distributions of power built into the decision rule used to produce prescriptive knowledge for use in either solving problems or predicting behavior. Fortunately, there is no absolute need to make arbitrary assumptions about the distribution of power as the distribution of power is a researchable topic.

Abstractly, objectivity seems attainable with respect to knowledge of values with essentially the same methods as value free knowledge [Boulding, 1956]. Objectivity about prescriptive knowledge, however, does not appear to be as easily attainable. We can observe the value-free and value characteristics of reality before and after an action is taken to solve a problem, but the prescription that led to the action was deduced from value-free and value propositions through the use of a decision rule and is not observable.

An Overall Approach to Research Methodology for Economists

We have reviewed the strengths and shortcomings for research by economists of logical positivism, various forms of normativism, and pragmatism. These strengths and shortcomings differ for purposes of doing disciplinary, subject-matter, and problem-solving research. It was seen that all three of the main undergirding philosophies for economics have essential contributions to make to the economist's tool kit. Further, all three place constraints on the ability of economists to benefit from the strengths of the other two. Our need is for justification to reject some of these constraints in order to develop an eclecticism—possibly a synthesis—that will enable us as economists to benefit from the strengths of the different philosophies without being hampered by the constraints they place on each other.

In what follows we draw on the different philosophies in an opportunistic way. In doing so, we put aside some of the constraints particular philosophies impose on using the strengths of other philosophies. The position developed in this section is disorderly from the standpoint of an academic philosopher. No apology will be made for this disorder as our objectives have been to summarize what economists do and to relate their activities to existing philosophies. One important task of philosophers is to establish order by explaining and clarifying what researchers do and how they produce, verify and validate knowledge. Philosophers working with the simpler biological and physical sciences have made considerable progress. However, they have not yet completed their work on research being done in the more complex social sciences dealing with the behavior of people and organizations. Perhaps philosophers and students of research methodology for economists may be able to work together in developing a coherent, more complete synthesis from the somewhat ad hoc eclectic view that follows.

Concerning positivism, we reject the emotivist presupposition that there are no experiences of real values to use in doing objective, descriptive research on "real" values. Rejecting this constraint has two advantages: (1) it does not interfere with using the powerful methods of positivism to attain value-free knowledge and behavioral knowledge about who values what, and (2) it frees us to use the same methods in the pursuit of descriptive knowledge of real values.

We noted earlier that there are many forms of normativism. We have dubbed the form we find most useful "objective normativism" and have partially identified it with the works of G. E. Moore and C. I. Lewis. Lewis has demonstrated how propositions about goodness and badness can be used to derive prescriptions as to what it is right to do in order to solve problems. When forms of normativism reject the possibility of there being objective, value-free knowledge, their constraints on such possibilities, like the corresponding emotivist constraints of positivism on value research, are rejected. Still other forms of normativism commit what Moore calls metaphysical and naturalistic fallacies. These forms of normativism are also rejected as they constrain the ability to do objective research on values by ignoring or in other ways misusing concepts of the goodnesses and badnesses of conditions, situations, and things.

Turning now to pragmatism, we find a philosophy and associated methods that have been highly productive in the hands of institutionalists and resource economists for reaching solutions to practical problems under the presupposition that the truth of propositions is determined by their consequences. When value-free and value propositions are used to solve problems, the prescriptions they warrant have consequences for action and the bearing of responsibility. Pragmatism treats value-free positivistic knowledge and knowledge of values as interdependent. While this presumption is justified by considerable observed interdependence between value-free and value truths, it does not always appear to be empirically true [Johnson and Zerby, 1973]. When value-free positivistic and value truths are not interdependent, the presupposition that they are is a constraint that imposes unnecessary complexity on the work of economic researchers and interferes with their ability to use the effective methods of independent normativistic and positivistic methods. It seems essential that economic researchers entertain the possibility that value-free positivistic and value knowledge may sometimes be interdependent, sometimes independent.

The above outlines some steps toward either a synthesis or an operational eclecticism that permits economic researchers to continue to do what different schools and groups of economists have done successfully in the past. This eclecticism rejects some of the constraints of (1) positivism on the possibility of objective knowledge of values as characteristics of the "real world," (2) normativism on objective value-free knowledge, and (3) pragmatism on both normativistic and positivistic methods. The rejection of the constraints of these philosophies on each other does not interfere with utilization by economists of their respective strengths in doing problem-solving, subject-matter, and disciplinary research. This provides an outline of a modus operandi for economists while students of research methodology for economists and their colleagues in philosophy work out a more complete synthesis to justify and formalize more rigorously what different groups and schools of economists are already doing with varying degrees of success.

ADDITIONAL SELECTED METHODOLOGICAL TOPICS FOR ECONOMISTS

The topics discussed in this section more or less escaped the systematic net of the first sixteen chapters and can be better discussed now that the sixteen chapters have been summarized. Some of these topics deal with the scope of economic research that is itself a reflection of philosophic orientations and the kinds of knowledge that economists believe they can successfully research.

Are Realistic Assumptions Important or Is Prediction Sufficient?

The importance of realistic assumptions depends, in part, on the "economics of classification" and the question of causality. Frank Knight [1946-orig. 1921] discussed the problem of classification in very succinct terms. Before presenting Knight's argument, it should be noted that the variables we identify and name in a science are themselves classes or categories of classifications [Georgescu-Roegen, 1971]. For some purposes, the labor variable can include skilled and unskilled, female and male, and adult and child labor; for other purposes, however, labor must be disaggregated according to skills possessed, sex, and age.

Knight pointed out, pragmatically, that all items falling into a useful class are similar with respect to characteristics important for purposes at hand, though dissimilar with respect to characteristics unimportant for the same purposes. He also pointed out that because our minds are finite and the complexity of the world approaches infinity, it is necessary that our classifications be unrealistic with respect to unimportant characteristics if they are to be useful. The important "kicker" in his argument is that unrealism with respect to variables *unimportant* for the purposes at hand is necessary in order to obtain realism with respect to characteristics *important* for purposes at hand.

This is not to endorse unrealistic assumptions about important characteristics. Friedman argues that assumptions can be unrealistic as long as they result in a "class" or kind of theory that accurately predicts. Knight argued that unrealism about unimportant characteristics is needed in order to economize on the utilization of the finite resources of our minds. However, he did not argue that classifications should be unrealistic with respect to important variables. Friedman is often interpreted, perhaps unfairly, as not seeing the difference.

Knight's arguments also seem to be related to causality [Keeton, 1961]. If a characteristic of an event is causally related to or is a necessary precondition for a later outcome, that characteristic is important in prediction. Unrealistic assumptions about these causal characteristics result in inaccurate predictions. Reliance on prediction in the evaluation of theories and analyses reveals the consequences of unrealistic assumptions about important causal characteristics in a manner that reconciles Friedman with Knight. Viewed in this way, the question "is prediction enough?" is not very different from "are unrealistic assumptions important?"

The concept of causality has been a difficult one for philosophers [Joad, 1957, Ch. 13]. A positivistic orientation makes it difficult to address the question of causality, particularly when causality involves the wills, purposes, and values of human beings. Economics, which is concerned with optimization in solving problems and as a basis for predicting the behavior of individuals and groups, deals with the causal roles of will, purpose and values. The statement that "water *wants* to run downhill" contains no more information than the statement that "water runs downhill," because water has no mind in which to will and to conceive of purpose or value or to make decisions about what it is best to do.

Human beings, however, do have minds capable of ascertaining values and making decisions to purposefully and willfully seek the good and avoid the bad. There is an inherent causality involving purpose, will, and decision making in the behavior of individuals and groups of human beings. The behavior of humans can be predicted more effectively with analyses that realistically account for purpose and value than with analyses that ignore or make unrealistic assumptions about such matters. When I reflect back to the days when my son was in his teens and early twenties, it is clear that predicting the behavior of that young man at that time on any one evening could be better done when

I knew the relative value he attached to the young women in his community than if I did not.

Axiomatization and Empirical Work

In logically positivistic science, it is often prescribed that one should first develop a rigorous (preferably axiomatic) logical statement of a particular theory. Next, one should do empirical work to (1) estimate the important parameters of the theory, (2) test the "hypothetico-inductive" parameters against data not used in estimating those parameters, and (3) test the truth of contingent statements of the theory. I have no argument against this technique, which can often be prescribed as an ideal to which economists "should" strive.

The difficulty, however, is that this ideal must often be seriously compromised in doing research work. Compromises are particularly important in problem-solving and subject-matter research, which are multidisciplinary and more holistic and complex than disciplinary research. Nonpragmatic disciplinary research makes it easy to subdivide one's discipline into small, easily axiomatized, simple components. Holistic, multidisciplinary, and possibly optimizing domains of human activity are much more difficult to axiomatize and become even more difficult when pragmatic interdependence is apparent.

While the argument in favor of logic and axiomatization as part of an empirical research program is strong, full axiomatization of the logical structures of the complex domains of practical problems or of multidisciplinary subjects is not always feasible. Some research domains involve long periods of structural change or are broad in other dimensions over which changes occur in numerous variables. For such domains, complete, carefully developed axiomatic systems often become prohibitively expensive to design and analyze relative to their limited usefulness. In many instances, a historian or an industrial organization analyst can work his way through time or over the broad domains of such large complex systems to develop "a descriptive understanding" of what goes on in the domain and of the causality in it without rigorously axiomatizing many of its details at different points in time and in other dimensions.

The story telling by institutionalists to which Blaug [1980, p. 127, 267] objects can often be used effectively and far more economically to research such domains than large complex axiomatized models with much seldom-used detail. As McCloskey [1983] argues, a nonquantitative rhetoric may be more efficient that an axiomatized quantitative rhetoric in developing an understanding of such domains and of the causality in them.

There also seems to be a danger that people well versed in the axiomatization of logical systems will fail to go beyond logical to empirical work [Mini, 1974; Leontief, 1982]. When axiomatic systems are developed but not used in empirical work, unrealism and oversimplifications go undetected. Axiomatic researchers can investigate the logical consequences of unrealistic assumptions from now to eternity without discovering their irrelevance if not disturbed with empirical observations that reveal the inability of their systems to produce predictions corresponding with experience.

Modernism and Rhetoric

McCloskey [1983] has made a special case for different rhetorics in discussing modernism in economics. The modernism that concerns McCloskey is the positivistic tendency toward axiomatization and highly quantitative procedures in economics. McCloskey argues that this general approach to research is un-workable and is not used in many important instances and by many important researchers. I find McCloskey's argument partially convincing, especially concerning problem-solving and subject-matter research case studies such as those in Part II.

McCloskey seems to be arguing that some systems are so complex that stable axiomatic systems representing them cannot be developed. If models of these systems are to handle their complexity, they have to involve many variables that change through time and in the other multidisciplinary dimensions of problematic and subject-matter domains. As noted in the section on axiomatization and empirical work, an understanding and an explanation of phenomena can often be developed without axiomatic models. The truth of this assertion is often demonstrated when economic historians develop a descriptive picture of the variables, causality, and time sequences involved in a system that is extremely helpful to decision makers, while more "rigorous" theorists and quantitative people fail because their models are either grossly oversimplified or too complex to be handled by their minds and computers and too complex to be quantified with available and obtainable data.

Economics: Is Its Opposite Uneconomic or Noneconomic?

In a sense, this is a boundary question for economics—a question about the scope of economics. It is important to remember that the scope of economics as a discipline is different from the scope of the work of economists. Though some say that economics is what economists do, it is clear that the many economists doing subject-matter and problem-solving research do much more than economics. If we can distinguish the domain of economics from that of other disciplines, we can better understand what an economic researcher can contribute to multidisciplinary subject-matter and problem-solving efforts.

Welfare economics, consumption economics and production economics are concerned with attaining nonmonetary as well as monetary values and with avoiding both nonmonetary and monetary costs. These three subdisciplines of economics deal with optimization—finding the best (most economic) amounts and combination of values (goods) to attain or finding the best way of avoiding the various bads (also values). In this sense, the opposite of economic is "uneconomic," not noneconomic.

As Lionel Robbins and others have noted, there are economic (more efficient) and uneconomic (less efficient) ways of attaining any good or avoiding any bad, both of which are values. Efficiency is always an instrumental value whose meaning depends on attaining more ultimate goods and avoiding more ultimate bads [Knight, 1933; Boulding, 1981]. Thus, it is also extremely difficult to separate economic values from noneconomic values and to separate economics from other disciplines according to the nature of values being sought and avoided. Whenever we seek to attain any good or avoid any bad (monetary or nonmonetary), there are always more or less costly ways of doing so, regardless of what values are involved.

Sometimes lay people and even people purporting to be economists attempt to confine economics to the attainment of monetary returns and the avoidance of monetary costs. Such attempts leave consumption economics unattended, with its stress on the attainment of nonmonetary satisfactions. The same would be true for welfare economics, with its emphasis on welfare. Much dynamic production economics, with its attention to the nonmonetary objectives of dynamic firms operating under imperfect knowledge, would also be seriously neglected. Similarly, attempts to classify nonmonetary values into economic and noneconomic ones (social, political, religious, humanitarian) also run into difficulties because economics deals with questions of efficiency in the attainment of any value.

I cannot conceive of a single so-called social or noneconomic value whose attainment or avoidance does not involve questions of efficiency or economy. Again, the opposite of economic is not noneconomic; it is simply uneconomic. This makes economics (or ethics) an inherent part of many multidisciplinary subject-matter studies and an essential part of all problem-solving studies. In turn, this justifies the necessity of giving extensive attention to subject-matter and problem-solving research in a book on research methodology for economists. As the scope of economists' work includes potential contributions to all problem-solving research and much subject-matter research, their research methodology must be attuned to all kinds of research.

Interfaces of Economics with Structural Changes in Technology, Institutions, and People

Neoclassical market economics typically answers optimization questions and predicts consequences of changes in input and product prices in terms of what optimizing actors find it advantageous to do in a market constrained by existing technologies, institutional arrangements, and a population possessing given amounts of human capital and given stocks and distributions of land and biophysical capital. Clearly, investigation of such market phenomena is a responsibility of neoclassical market economists within the broader domain claimed by the classical and other neoclassical economists.

Recently, some neoclassical market economists have staked out a broader claim under the rubrics of induced technological and institutional change and human capital formation. In this connection we associate the names of Schumpter with technological change; Georgescu-Roegen with entropy; Commons, Veblen, and others with institutional change; and Marshall and T. W. Schultz with changes in human capital. In the works of these economists, the "givens" of much neoclassical market economics are at least partially endogenized in broader but equally neoclassical theories of human capital formation and induced technological and institutional change. Similarly, the magnitudes of resource stocks have long been at least partially endogenized with theories of capital formation and investment and disinvestment.

Here again is an issue involving the scope or boundary of economics. Economists are concerned with the growth, stagnation, and/or declines in the productivity of economies and of such subsectors as manufacturing, trade, and agriculture. This concern generates an interest in the origins of technological, institutional, and human change and in the investments that determine the growth of economies. In modern societies, technological change results increasingly from the basic disciplinary research of biological and physical sciences as well as from expenditure on subject-matter and problem-solving research. Similarly, institutional changes result from the basic disciplinary activities of political scientists and economists, the works of Marx, Bentham, Adam Smith, and John R. Commons being cases in point. Futher, one desiring to understand more fully the origins of human change needs increasingly to understand the basic disciplinary research of psychology, sociology, human nutrition, and physiology.

These tendencies of basic disciplinary research to become relatively more important relate to the feasibility of making output-increasing investments through time in human and biophysical capital and in institutional infrastructure. Thus, the question of where economics leaves off and other disciplines take over is difficult to answer, especially as we approach the practical end of the research spectrum. As demarcation between disciplines becomes more difficult, cooperation, tolerance, and understanding between them become more important.

As implied in the section above, there are economic and uneconomic ways of generating these technical, institutional, and human changes. Decisions about how the changes should be generated make it inevitable that the maximizing calculus be used in practical research on these changes. It seems to me that all practical activities by biophysical scientists generating technical change, social scientists generating institutional change, and basic human behavioral scientists generating human change are subject to economic (ethical and moral) analysis. The practical question is always one of whether changes are economic or uneconomic, not whether they are economic or noneconomic. This requires that such practical activities be subjected to economic analysis and that the boundary of economics ends when it is no longer possible or important to distinguish between activities that generate a net advantage and those that generate a net disadvantage for human beings. In this sense, economics and ethics and morality are as similar and as essential today as they were in the day of the common classical forebearers of economics and ethics.

Ordinality, Cardinality, and Interpersonal Validity of Utility Measurements

This old topic in research methodology for economics has been dealt with repeatedly both directly and indirectly in this book. The arguments and experiences examined have tended toward the conclusion that the utility of some goods and services can legitimately be viewed as cardinally measurable with interpersonal validity. The large amount of recent work involving the expected utility hypothesis provides substantial evidence that utility is cardinally as well as ordinally measurable. At the same time, the continued redistributive decisions of executive and legislative branches of government indicates widespread acceptance of the interpersonal validity of our welfare or utility knowledge and a rejection of the constraints of Pareto optimality and of the compensation principle. This is because many of these redistributions do not involve compensation or even consideration of the possibility of compensation.

A recent interesting article [Cooter and Rappoport, 1984] raises the question as to whether the introduction of ordinality into welfare economics by Hicks in 1939 was a mistake. In answering the question they pose, Cooter and Rappoport argue that an important ability to make interpersonally valid cardinal measurements of utilty was lost and disregarded when economists went to the Hicksian treatment of ordinal utility functions and Parcto optimality from what Marshall and Pigou regarded as interpersonally valid cardinal utility functions.

Cooter and Rappoport argue that interpersonally valid cardinal knowledge of the utility of the basic needs for life was part of Marshall's and Pigou's neoclassical economics. They argue that it was then accepted that the marginal utility for additional income was clearly higher in a cardinal sense for people deprived of basic material needs than for people so well off they can easily meet their basic needs and are more concerned about allocating income between alternative expensive theater tickets. The argument in their article is that restricting the concept of utility to an ordinal, interpersonally invalid status resulted in an unjustified loss or disregard of available knowledge about utility.

The reason for bringing up the Cooter and Rappoport discussion of utility is that if cardinal and interpersonally valid knowledge of the value of materials satisfying basic needs is possible, then research to acquire more interpersonally valid cardinal measurements of utility and welfare is likely to be justified. The first 16 chapters of this book have tended toward this conclusion. Importantly, this tentative conclusion supports the possibility of doing objective, inductive, empirical research as well as the deductive, rational research on restructuring societies done by Nosick, Rawls, Sen, and Harsanyi referred to in Chapter 8. The argument here is for at least entertaining the possibility of doing such research. Some cardinal interpersonally valid measures of changes in welfare resulting from satisfying basic needs is possible and the four tests for the objectivity of this knowledge—coherence, correspondence, clarity, and workability—are applicable. This establishes the point that some objective research on real values is possible, including research on values associated with satisfaction of somewhat less basic needs. I believe that the possibility of doing objective research on less basic values is so promising that such research should not be preemptorally precluded from the work of economists.

Ideology and Economics

Neoclassical market economics has often been regarded as ideological by Joan Robinson and others as supportive of capitalism [Harry Johnson, 1975] and the status quo. While neoclassical, Pareto optimal market economists often assume a given set of technologies and a given set of institutions with a given distribution of the ownership of rights and privileges among the people in the economy, the theory itself does not specify how these rights and privileges ought to be distributed among individuals and between individuals and the state. The theory can be as logically regarded as defensive of an existing given socialist system as of an existing given capitalistic one. Because no particular distribution is prespecified in the theory other than that producers, consumers, and resource owners have some significant freedom of choice, the avowed socialist Aba Lerner and the practicing economists of many socialist states employ the maximizing calculus of neoclassical economics to solve allocative problems.

   Neoclassical market economics would have virtually no role in an abstract system so authoritarian that it permits no freedom of choice by entrepreneurs (if any), resource owners (if any), owners of rights and privileges (if any), consumers, and governmental officials. While it is true that the distribution of the ownership of rights and privileges among these groups of actors is consistently different (but often no less concentrated) in socialist countries than in capitalist countries, I have not observed any country so authoritarian (left or right) that the optimizing calculus was entirely inapplicable in describing, analyzing, and predicting the decisions of consumers, government officials, owners of rights and privileges, and producers. I doubt whether either Marxists or fascists would accept the proposition that the kinds of societies and economic institutions they advocate restrict freedom of choice so much that one can predict variables important in economics without taking freedom of choice into account.

Ideologies have to do (among other things) with the structure of societies. When the boundaries of economics are extended to optimizing decisions about technical, institutional, and human change, and the possibility of objective descriptive research on real values is accepted, an economics of choosing among ideologies advocating different institutional, human, and technical structures is conceivable. In a sense, such an economics would be an economics of ideologies. The previously discussed existence or possibility of interpersonally valid cardinal measures of utility or welfare is important for optimizing decisions about alternative ideologies. Even without this view of its boundaries, neoclassical economics contributes to an understanding of the operation of economics involving free choice— whether those economies are predominantly capitalistic or socialistic.

Equality and Equity

At the risk of going beyond methodology for economists into the substance of economics and other social sciences, it is worth noting that the words equality and equity are often used interchangeably in dealing with proposed non-Pareto optimal solutions to problems involving distributive justice and the structure of societies. Also, the literature of economics contains ambiguous discussions of trade-offs between equity (alternatively equality) and production. According to the dictionary, the word equity has to do with justified or justifiable distributions of rights and privileges. An equitable distribution is justified but not necessarily equal. By contrast, the word equality has to do with how equally rights and privileges are distributed [Johnson, 1983]. Keeping this distinction in mind helps make our discussions and writing less ambiguous.

Economic theory indicates that redistributions of the ownership of income-producing resources change the relative equilibrium prices in an economy. Such changes, in turn, create an "index number" difficulty when production is measured with indexes weighted by the relative prices generated in markets. Consequently, figures displaying indifference curves and possibilities or opportunities lines between equality and such production indexes lose precision and meaning.

Justice and equity are the subjects of an increasing body of literature by such people as Daniels [1975] and Ackerman [1980] who draw on Rawls, Nozick and others. The contents of Chapters 4–9 and the two subsections above on "Ordinality, Cardinality, and Interpersonal Validity of Utility Measurements" and "Ideology and Economics" open the way methodologically for the participation of economists in research on the values of justice, equality, equity, and related conditions and research designed to generate prescriptive conclusions on restructuring society.

The Design Mode and Creativity

As long as economics is conceived to be purely descriptive and predictive but not prescriptive, the design mode and the question of creativity are less important then when economics is conceived to help with problem-solving activities and subject-matter research. Prescription is an objective for both of these kinds of research, the latter being oriented to helping solve sets of problems if not to the solution of specific problems. As prescriptions to solve problems often involve the creation of something that has not previously existed, creativity becomes more essential and description and prediction less adequate than for disciplinary research.

Similarly, subject-matter research often leads less directly to prescriptions that require creation of new technologies, new institutional arrangements, and the development of new human skills. The creativity required in these instances seems to be a broader, more important form of creativity than that involved in descriptive work. This seems to be true even when a descriptive investigator conceives of a new way of interpreting observed phenomena that he did not help create. This kind of creativity is also important for problem solvers as they attempt to perceive new technologies, institutional arrangements, and human skills and abilities to use in solving practical problems.

Communication Difficulties and Chauvinism

In Chapters 4–9, three philosophic orientations of economists were examined. In the second main section of this chapter we concluded that problem-solving, subject-matter, and disciplinary research advantageously involves the eclectic use of various philosophic orientations. If this is true, chauvinistic adherence to any of these philosophic orientations can create communication difficulties with adherents to other orientations as well as between adherents to those orientations and decision makers facing practical problems.

Closely related to these philosophic chauvinisms are the chauvinisms of those economists who advocate pursuit of some kinds of knowledge to the exclusion of other kinds [Johnson, 1984]. Problem-solving researchers need knowlege of values and value-free positivistic knowledge to generate prescriptive knowledge. Adherence to any one of the three kinds of knowledge to the exclusion of the others generates difficulties between economists, and especially between economists and the decision makers who are served by economists. These difficulties are likely to involve communications. Most damaging to effective communication of disciplinary economists is the chauvinism of economists who are so committed to their own discipline as to virtually exclude the other disciplines whose contributions are required in doing subject-matter and problem-solving research.

There are important communication difficulties between these groups—difficulties so important that disciplinarians from different disciplines sometimes fail even to try to communicate with each other and simply talk past each other when they do try. Perhaps this book does something to smooth out these difficulties.

ADDITIONAL REFERENCES

Ackerman, Bruce A. 1980. *Social Justice in the Liberal State*, New Haven: Yale University Press.

Blaug, Mark. 1980. *The Methodology of Economics or How Economists Explain*, Cambridge, UK: Cambridge University Press.

Boulding, Kenneth. 1981. *Evolutionary Economics*, Beverly Hills, CA: Sage Publications.

—— 1956. *The Image*, Ann Arbor: University of Michigan Press.

Cooter, Robert and Peter Rappoport. 1984. Were the Ordinalists Wrong About Welfare Economics? *The Journal of Economic Literature* **XXII**(2):507–530.

Daniels, Norman (ed.) 1975. *Reading Rawls: Critical Studies of a Theory of Justice*, New York: Basic Books.

Friedman, M. 1953. *Essays in Positive Economics*, Chicago: University of Chicago Press, pp. 3–16, 39–43.

Gerogescu-Roegen, N. 1971. *The Entropy Law and the Economic Process*, Cambridge: Harvard University Press.

Joad, C. E. M. 1957. *Guide to Philosophy*, New York: Dover.

Johnson, Glenn L. 1983. Synoptic View, *Growth and Equity in Agricultural Development*, Proceedings, Eighteenth International Conference of Agricultural Economists, Oxford, England: Gower Publishing Co.

—— 1984. Academia Needs a New Covenant for Serving Agriculture, Mississippi State, MS: Mississippi Agriculture and Forestry Experiment Station, Mississippi State University Special Publication. July.

—— In Press. "Technological Innovation with Implications for Agricultural Economics," Paper presented at post-conference seminar, Aug. 7–9, 1985, Ames, Iowa, Proceedings to be published by Iowa State University Press.

—— and L. K. Zerby. 1973. *What Economists Do About Values—Case Studies of Their Answers to Questions They Don't Dare Ask*, East Lansing: Michigan State University, Department of Agricultural Economics.

Johnson, H. G. 1975. *On Economics and Society*, Chicago: University of Chicago Press.

Keeton, Morris T. 1961. Causality, *Dictionary of Philosophy*, D. Runes, ed., Paterson, NJ: Littlefield, Adams, pp. 47–48

Keynes, J. N. 1963. *The Scope and Method of Political Economy*, 4th ed., New York: Augustus M. Kelley, Bookseller.

Knight, F. H. 1946. *Risk, Uncertainty and Profit*, New York: Houghton Mifflin (originally published in 1921).

—— 1933. *The Economic Organization*, Chicago: University of Chicago Press.

Leontief, Wassily. 1982. Academic Economics, *Science*, **217**:104–107.

Machlup, F. 1969. Positive and Normative Economics, *Economic Means and Social Ends*, R. Heilbroner, ed., Englewood Cliffs, NJ: Prentice-Hall.

McCloskey, Donald N. 1983. The Rhetoric of Economics, *Journal of Economic Literature* **XXI**(2):481–517.

Mini, Piero V. 1974. *Philosophy and Economics*, Gainesville: University Presses of Florida.

Robbins, L. 1949. *An Essay on the Nature and Significance of Economic Science*, 2nd ed., London: Macmillan.

Scriven, Michael. 1969. Logical Positivism and the Behavioral Sciences, in *The Legacy of Logical Positivism*, Achinstein, P. and S. F. Barker, eds., Baltimore: Johns Hopkins Press, 1969, pp. 195–209.

Index